D1521136

THE
TRINITY GUIDE
TO TRINITY
THE

William J. La Due

TRINITY PRESS INTERNATIONAL
Harrisburg, Pennsylvania

References to the Old and New Testaments are taken from *The Catholic Study Bible.* New York: Oxford University Press, 1990. New Testament Scripture quotations are my translations from the *Novum Testamentum, Graece et Latine.* 5th ed. Edited by Augustinus Merk. Rome: The Biblical Institute, 1944.

Trinity Press International, P.O. Box 1321, Harrisburg, PA 17105
Trinity Press International is a division of The Morehouse Group.

Cover art: *The Trinity and Saints*, Pietro Perugino.
Scala/Art Resource, NY.

Cover design: Corey Kent

A catalog record for this book is available from the Library of Congress.

Printed in the United States of America

03 04 05 06 07 08   10 9 8 7 6 5 4 3 2 1

God can be *thought about*

more truly than he can be *talked about*,

and he *is*,

more truly than he can be *thought about*.

St. Augustine, *The Trinity*,
Book 7, Chapter 3, #7

CONTENTS

INTRODUCTORY NOTE

For Christians, fixing our eyes and hearts on Jesus is relatively easy. It happens almost daily for many. His generous life and engaging personality spontaneously attract our attention and generate an abiding loyalty in believers. The mystery of the Trinity, however, does not arouse the same kind of unrehearsed attraction and allegiance. From early on we were told that the Trinity is a mystery, and indeed, the loftiest and most impenetrable of mysteries. We were not expected to understand it, but simply to believe it. God, we were told, is triune. There are three distinct persons in the one Deity. These three are coequal, and we are to adore and reverence each of them. The Father is identified as the Creator, and the Son, Jesus, is proclaimed as the Savior of humankind. The third divine figure is worshiped as the one who even now touches us with the graciousness of Christ.

Over the past one hundred years, the Trinity has generated a good deal of attention from theologians, Catholic, Protestant, and Orthodox. Most of them have tried to clarify the mystery to make it more comprehensible and meaningful for Christians. The scriptural basis of the Trinity and the historical development of the doctrine from apostolic times to the present have been more thoroughly explored by such scholars as Raymond Brown, James D. G. Dunn, Karl Rahner, and Jürgen Moltmann. Furthermore, a number of scholars have attempted to create a theological portrait of the triune Deity that would render the divine identities more lifelike and approachable, for our God must be accessible, and to some extent recognizable, to be loved and adored. The theologians summarized in this book are some of the most successful in this effort to bring the divine persons down to earth to dwell among us. I hope you will agree.

At this point let me extend my appreciation to Henry Carrigan and Laura Hudson of Trinity Press International for their invaluable suggestions regarding the structure and editing of this book. Especially, I wish to express my gratitude to my wife, Margaret, who has contributed in a thousand ways to the preparation and completion of this study.

1

OLD TESTAMENT TRACES OF TRINITY

The God of the Old Testament

To tell the story of the self-revelation of the Judeo-Christian God, it is important to begin at the very beginning. The gods of the Semites, Israel's neighbors, were either the personifications of the forces of nature or the personalized embodiments of the ideals of a particular people. The God of the Hebrews, however, was neither of these. Their God was a living personality who became deeply engaged in the life and struggles of the Hebrew people and was far superior to the gods of their neighbors. For centuries after Moses (ca. 1250 B.C.), the Israelites held to the existence and the influence of the gods of their neighbors in addition to their God. It was the northern prophet Amos (ca. 750 B.C.) who affirmed that the Israelite Deity exercised power even over nearby states such as Aram, Tyre, and Edom (Amos 1:3–12). Through the efforts of the prophets Isaiah (ca. 742–700 B.C.) and Jeremiah (ca. 626–587 B.C.), the growing seventh-century Hebrew practice of including foreign gods in their worship was gradually curbed. This made way for more convincing expressions of exclusive devotion to their Hebrew God, so evident, for example, in one of the most memorable passages of Deuteronomy (6:4–6).

The Jewish people were convinced that their God had spoken to them through Moses and the prophets, and that long before Moses, "the Almighty" had revealed Godself to Abraham (ca. 1800–1700 B.C.), Isaac, and Jacob, as El Shaddai (Gen 17:1). The Canaanite priest Melchizedek spoke of God to Abraham (then Abram) as El Elyon, the Most High God (Gen 14:19), while Abraham at Beer-sheba called upon the Lord as El Olam, the Eternal God (Gen 21:33). To Moses, God was revealed for the first time as Yahweh (Exod 3:14), which identifies the Jewish God as the one who is always present and active—

a being who is ever in their midst. The northern tradition preferred to refer to God as Elohim, a plural noun that seems to insinuate that the Deity embodies a plurality of forces.

The Jewish God is described by 2 Isaiah (ca. 540 B.C.) as an active, abiding presence who never grows weary and is ever vigilant (Isa 40:28), a holy God who swears by the divine holiness. From the outset Yahweh would not tolerate the worship of other gods (Exod 20:3). During the exile (ca. 587–538 B.C.) Yahweh wanted the Hebrews to see him as a shepherd who nourishes his flock and carries his sheep in his arms, leading them with great care (Isa 40:11). Nonetheless, Yahweh frequently proclaimed Godself as a jealous God who was disposed to punish his people if they violated his laws and failed to reverence his Sabbath (Ezek 20:23–24). Yahweh let them know that he was "Spirit" and they were perishable like the grass of the field (Isa 40:7–8). Yet Yahweh treated them with the gentleness of a father (Hos 11:1–3) or a mother (Isa 49:15) and regarded them with the affection of a lover (Hos 2:9–16). Although God promised them that he would always be near at hand (Deut 4:7), he often made his utter transcendence strikingly obvious to them (e.g., Isa 6). However, from the time of the exile, God was inclined to reveal Godself through the agency of angels, and the people were not even to use the name of Yahweh. When the Lord spoke to Moses from the burning bush (Exod 3:6), he identified himself as "the God of Abraham, Isaac, and Jacob," the God of the highly revered patriarchal ancestors of the Jews. Yahweh called himself the Father of Israel (Exod 4:22–23), and later the term "father" was expressly extended to his relationships with individuals, especially the just (Wis 2:16).

Walther Eichrodt

For many years the professor of Old Testament theology and the history of religion at the University of Basel in Switzerland, Walther Eichrodt (1890–1978), tied the designation "Yahweh" to the Sinai covenant and interpreted that critical divine encounter as culminating in the revelation of the new divine name. It is this name that separates Israel from all the other nations and peoples. The name Yahweh proclaims not only his existence but his presence, his ready availability to assist and to act.[1] He is the God of the patriarchal fathers but is still near at hand as a mighty force for Israel. Second Isaiah revived the title of "king" for Yahweh and associated that designation with the Lord's anticipated final saving acts on behalf of the Jews.

In the forging of the covenant, the Hebrew Deity was given an explicitly personal character.[2] God is identified as a distinctive individual, by no means an impersonal power, but rather a being who thinks and wills and acts as a human person. From the time of Moses to Ezekiel (593–571 B.C.), there is a clear and consistent revelation of the nearness of God to the Hebrews. And during the final centuries before Christ, the undisputed assumption—even in the Book of Job (postexilic) and Ecclesiastes (ca. 300 B.C.)—is that God truly exists. Prophets like Hosea and Isaiah spoke of Yahweh in human terms, attributing to him emotions such as anger and joy. However, Yahweh's uniqueness was consistently affirmed as well his clear superiority over the "dead gods" of the pagans. Eager to portray God as warm and personal, the prophets frequently referred to his love and his sorrow, his fear and his jealousy, although they were always ready to stress his otherness. On the other hand, the writers of the priestly tradition emphasized the unapproachable majesty of the Lord, thereby establishing the foundation for a monotheism that could be defined in abstract terms. After the exile a mentality of rigid adherence to the letter of the law prevailed, and this created an atmosphere that rendered God more distant and remote. It became difficult for the Jews to comprehend the prophets' portrayal of a God who was near to them. The divine name became so unapproachable that it could no longer be uttered by believers, and Yahweh came to be referred to simply as "the Name."

Monotheism developed only gradually in Israel, according to Eichrodt. For a considerable period during the reign of the kings, it was assumed that every nation had its own gods and that in foreign lands one must pay homage to the gods of the territory (1 Sam 26:19). As mentioned above, it was in the seventh century that the monotheistic declarations clearly surfaced, identifying Yahweh as the only God (Deut 4:35). During the reign of King Solomon (961–922 B.C.), there was a considerable expansion of cult among the Hebrews. At this time the Yahwist writers appear, portraying Yahweh as the Lord of the earth and the Judge of all humankind. Two centuries later, Isaiah (ca. 740–700 B.C.) spoke about the nothingness of all the other gods (Isa 2:18). During the reign of King Josiah in Judah (ca. 640–609 B.C.), the Shema (Deut 6:4–9) set out once and for all the classic statement of Jewish monotheism. In some of the later apocryphal writings (e.g., Enoch, ca. first century A.D.), the heathen gods are even portrayed as demons.

Although God's power and control of history are especially emphasized during Israel's settlement in Canaan (Judg 5:4–5), his lovingkindness and fidelity to the covenant are what constitute the recurring theme. Eichrodt affirms again and again that God's loyalty and devotion to Israel are grounded in the covenant. Yahweh's portrayal as father and shepherd flow out of his love and his steadfastness. But because of the sins and infidelity of the people, Yahweh warned that he would withdraw his friendship and even cancel the covenant (Jer 16:5). In the age of prophecy, Yahweh's righteousness was directed not so much toward the reestablishment of Israel to its former place among the nations, but rather toward the development of certain desired virtues among the chosen people and the punishment of those ignoring the covenant. In 2 Isaiah the righteousness of Yahweh is even extended to all the nations so that he can be said to protect and save all the just who take refuge in him (Ps 34:9–11).

God's love for his people is perhaps most richly revealed in Hosea, the northern prophet (ca. 745 B.C.), who likened the relationship between Yahweh and the Jews as a marital union, describing the bond of love as the true foundation of the covenant between Israel and the Lord. Although the people had been shamelessly disloyal, Yahweh would not abandon them. In the spirit of Hosea, Jeremiah (ca. 625–587 B.C.) promised those in captivity that they would rise up again and return to their homeland (31:1–6). God would forge with them a new covenant that would replace the covenant made with their fathers in the desert. This new covenant will be written in their hearts, and Yahweh will indeed be their God and they shall be his people (Jer 31:31–33).

In the postexilic period the ultimate pledge of God's love was the Torah, the prescriptions of Yahweh handed down by the priests. After the resettlement in Judea, the judgment of God against the nation had largely run its course, but the divine wrath continued to fall upon those individuals who violated the divine will. The holiness of Yahweh came to be seen as reflected in the Law, which was venerated more and more as the ideal pattern of living for the postexilic Israelites. God's presence among them was thus perceived to be verified in the Law. Over the centuries God had revealed Godself in rather different ways to the people, according to the needs of the period. After the exile it was Yahweh's preferential, abiding love that communicated the deepest meaning of God's election, and also his fatherhood, which was then seen to extend to the whole of creation.

In volume 2 of his work,[3] Walther Eichrodt addresses the significance of "the spirit" *(ruah)* and its place in the faith of Israel. The ancients saw in the wind and in human breath a mystery, a symbol of the activity and the nearness of the divine. Every creature is dependent on God's breath of life. The Israelites believed that the breath of

God enlivens all of creation. They associated this spirit of life with the Lord's word, and these two agents—spirit and word—were responsible for establishing Yahweh's sovereignty over the whole of creation (Ps 33:6). The spirit in some contexts seems to acquire personal traits and appears as a divine phenomenon. Several religious leaders during the period of the judges (ca. 1200–1025 B.C.), as well as the early prophets, felt themselves animated by God's spirit to speak the word of God. In 2 Isaiah and in the psalms we find a more thorough description of the operations of the spirit (2 Isa 40:13–14; Ps 139:7). The Servant of God in 2 Isaiah is described as a privileged bearer of the spirit (2 Isa 42:1–5). The prophet Ezekiel (ca. 593–571 B.C.) declares that the spirit of God will be intimately related to all who share in the messianic kingdom (Ezek 11:19). Eichrodt observes that the individual's relationship with God, given by the spirit, is the central miracle of the messianic age.[4]

The spirit of Yahweh after the exile is often described as a separate entity that acts as a mediator between God and humankind, mediating God's presence to his people. The exiles upon their return brought this spirit with them as a pledge that they were entering a whole new era. One of the last of the prophets, Haggai (ca. 520 B.C.), assured the returnees that God's spirit abided among them, and hence they should not be afraid (Hag 2:4). The community as well as the individuals were to receive comfort and assurance from the spirit that dwelled in their midst (Ps 143:10–12). The wisdom writers gave further assurance that the spirit's guidance remained with the Israelites and that a personalized Wisdom (Sophia) sheds her light on all who listen to her (Prov 1:23). The close association of spirit and word came to the fore after the exile. Although the prophetic word had died out after 450 B.C. or thereabouts, the written witness of the earlier wondrous acts of God was given new force and importance through the agency of the spirit of God that enabled Yahweh to speak to the Israelites once again.

The translators of the Septuagint claimed that the spirit of God animated and directed their work so that spirit and word became linked together even more intimately. In Eichrodt's judgment, the Jews did not attest to a hypostatized spirit until the Hellenistic period (ca. 300–100 B.C.).[5] The ancients gave much more importance to the spoken word than we do presently. A spoken blessing or curse, for example, acquired a life all its own, remaining as effective as it was the day it was uttered until it visited the individual who was cursed or blessed. The Decalogue was referred to as "the ten words" (Exod 34:27). Isaiah declared that the Lord sent his word against the

Northern Kingdom like a weapon to beat down the wicked and the faithless (Isa 9:7–8). In the opening verses of Jeremiah, Yahweh is described as placing in the prophet's mouth his words that have the power to "root up and tear down . . . to build and to plant" (1:9–10). Second Isaiah asserts that God's word goes forth from him and does not return until the desired effects have been achieved, much like rain waters the earth and makes it fertile (55:10–11).

In later Judaism there can be seen a linking of the word with the spirit of God, and like the spirit, the word becomes hypostatized as it assumes the role of a divine cosmic force. Eichrodt maintains that this line was crossed when independent effectiveness was assigned to the word or to wisdom, which becomes an independently operative agent (Wis 6:12). In Jewish thought declarations concerning the word often merge with their notions of the spirit, and they never seem to be able to distinguish the two realities. The spirit is best understood as a vitalizing force, and the word as the living expression of Yahweh's thought and will.

According to Eichrodt, the word becomes the actual instrument by which the divine will is disclosed, and then in its identification with Jesus, the Word becomes an independent person. In chapter 1 of John's gospel, the Logos is no longer identified with the Hellenistic concept of the cosmic mind but is clearly related to and springs out of the Old Testament notion of the word. Eichrodt sees the full realization of the concept of the word of God verified and brought to completion in the New Testament. The intimate relationship of word and spirit in the New Testament can be observed in the guidance and direction given to Jesus by the Spirit and in the continuing efforts of the Spirit in the Christian communities after Christ's death and resurrection. In the words of Walther Eichrodt: "Word and Spirit are now given an internal rationale in the relationship of Logos and Pneuma as Persons of the Trinity, in whom, emerging from the transcendent divine glory, the One God condescends to men and becomes conceivable to them, without in any way surrendering his absolute otherness."[6]

Gerhard von Rad

Another Christian Old Testament scholar, Gerhard von Rad (1901–1971), must be ranked along with Eichrodt as perhaps the two most important contributors to the development of Old Testament theology in the twentieth century. Von Rad's two-volume *Old Testament*

Theology was produced between 1957 and 1960, with the English editions being published in 1962 and 1965. Professor von Rad, who taught Old Testament studies at Jena, Göttingen, and Heidelberg, completed his Old Testament effort with the publication of *Wisdom in Israel* in 1970. While Eichrodt constructed his presentation around the focal notion of the covenant and the interaction between Yahweh and the Hebrews as covenant partners, von Rad used as his leitmotif the story of the exodus from Egypt to the settlement in the Promised Land under Joshua (Deut 26:5–9). He contends that this narrative exercised a defining influence on the rest of Israel's life. Each successive generation retold the story with the addition of new elements to contemporize its significance.

In chapter 3 of the Book of Exodus, God revealed the divine name to Moses and identified Godself as the same God who interacted with the patriarchs of old. The statement "I AM WHO I AM" is not a philosophical observation concerning the Divine Being, but rather a declaration that God will always be available to the chosen people. It implies his "being present," his "being there" for them.[7] This rendering given by the Elohist writers bears a unique ring and is hardly similar to any other Old Testament passage. This makes it elusive and problematic, but the idea of God's "being there" for the chosen people seems to be the controlling notion and the ultimate source of their consolation. Later in Exodus the Lord describes himself to Moses as "merciful and gracious, slow to anger and rich in kindness and fidelity . . . for a thousand generations" (Exod 34:6–7). But it was Israel's possession of the divine name that assured them of God's abiding presence in their midst and gave them privileged access to him in their worship and prayer.

Because Yahweh's name participated in the divine holiness, it could not be used lightly, nor could it be profaned by the worship of any other god. The Lord's name and its disclosure to the Israelites were intimately connected. After the exile the name of Yahweh all but disappeared from the daily life of the Jews. It was never used at all, according to von Rad, in Job, Esther, Ecclesiastes, or the Song of Solomon.[8] The Lord's zealous insistence on the avoiding of all foreign cults is a sign of the divine holiness, for God does not want his people to be tainted and led astray by such exposure. In the Book of Deuteronomy, which is made up of a collection of sermons gathered together toward the end of the period of the monarchy (seventh century B.C.), the Jews are warned again and again that they must follow the Lord's call. Their faith and allegiance must not weaken. They have been selected as God's chosen not because of their size or prestige, but because they are especially loved by the Lord (Deut 7:7–8). And this love is portrayed as the love of a father for his offspring (Deut 14:1). All of Yahweh's commands are really an expression of his desire to be loved by his people because they have been set apart for him (Deut 7:6).

After the return from the exile in Babylon, wisdom became the mediator of God's revelation.[9] It came to be widely held that certain individuals were granted a privileged share in God's knowledge. Joseph in Egypt (Gen 41:39), Joshua, Moses' anointed successor (Deut 34:9), and King Solomon's good judgment (1 Kings 3:28), revealed various gifts of wisdom that served in some way as the ground for the wisdom spoken of in the first nine chapters of the Book of Proverbs (postexilic). Wisdom's injunctions are directed to Israel as a community and especially to the individual Israelites who are thereby given a special offer of salvation. Wisdom (Sophia) is to be received as a sister and a dear friend (Prov 7:4). In the Book of Ecclesiasticus (ca. 180 B.C.), wisdom is identified with the Torah and is the form in which God makes himself present and desires to be sought after by humankind.[10] However, von Rad affirms that wisdom is not an impersonal force but rather takes on the appearance of a living personality who summons followers to herself. He insists, though, that Sophia is separate from Yahweh: "It once designates itself as Yahweh's creature, albeit the firstborn of all creatures (Prov 8:22), and identifies itself with the thoughts which God cherished in creating the world (Prov 3:19)."[11]

In the Book of Sirach (Ecclesiasticus), Sophia was created before the rest of creation, having come forth from the mouth of God (1:4; 24:3). After failing to find a lasting abode among humans, God assigned wisdom a privileged resting place in the Torah. As a matter of fact, wisdom or Sophia is designated as the creator of the world in the Book of Wisdom 7:22 (ca. first century B.C.). Sophia appears at times as a person and at other times as some sort of principle emanating from God. Whether this development of the notion of wisdom was adopted from Hellenistic philosophy or originated in the thought of Israel is not at all clear.[12] Von Rad affirms that the latter development of wisdom is indeed extremely complex. He observes that the decisive encounter with God does not occur in the practice of cult or prayer, but rather in the world of the secular. This encounter is grounded not in Israel's saving history but in the events of creation.[13] The shift prompted the rise of a certain skepticism, not concerning the existence of Yahweh, but rather the divine readiness to intervene in the life of Israel and in the affairs of individuals. In the Book of

Ecclesiastes, or Qoheleth (ca. 300 B.C.), this skepticism comes dramatically to the fore. There is no reference in the work to saving history. Rather, the main issue under discussion is the significance or direction of human life. The writer is not an agnostic, but the God who created the universe seems unapproachable and withdrawn. Von Rad attests that Ecclesiastes is the farthest frontier of Yahwism. All one can do is to be resigned to this tragic existence. The readers are encouraged to eat, drink, and be merry during their limited sojourn on earth, for that is their lot, pure and simple (Eccl 5:17).

In his final work, *Wisdom in Israel,* Gerhard von Rad asks how we are to interpret the didactic poems in Proverbs 8, Job 28, Sirach 24, and Wisdom 7:22-8:1 that speak of wisdom as a personal reality somehow immanent in creation.[14] His response is that we are not dealing here with a hypostasized Wisdom, an entity who shares in the being of God, who then acts in the world in and through that entity. He is certain that we are not dealing with the personification of a divine quality in Job 28, Proverbs 8:22ff, or Sirach 24.[15] We do not have here a divine attribute that has achieved independent existence. This is not a personification, but seems rather to be a significance or intentionality implanted in the mystery of creation.[16] In Job 28 wisdom is characterized as the order implanted by God in the universe, whereas in Proverbs 8:22–31 wisdom is occasionally portrayed as a person who resides somehow in the fabric of creation. Von Rad speculates that there could be some dependence here on the Egyptian goddess of order because the Jews at times borrowed religious concepts from their neighbors to expand their own religious language.[17] He insists, however, that in Proverbs 8, wisdom does not possess a divine status. Wisdom is in fact a creature, although it is above all the rest of creation.

In von Rad's judgment, these later Old Testament passages refer to an ordering power that was experienced in Israel from its earliest history and seems to have originated under the influence of Egyptian ideas. The world order referred to in Job 28 and described in Proverbs 8 as a person who addresses humankind is understood by von Rad as a quality not of God, but of the world that is attempting to invite men and women to bring more order into their lives.[18] This wisdom is seen as immanent in the universe, existing before the works of creation, and the special favorite of God. Humankind must listen to her and learn from her, for she desires to teach the truth to humankind (Prov 8:4–7). Sirach 24 adds very little to the portrayal of Proverbs 8 but does stress that this divine wisdom lives in the Torah.

The late Old Testament writers understood wisdom as a created reality, according to von Rad. It is a bearer of revelation that interposes itself between God and Israel. This "someone" is the voice, the expression of primeval order residing in the universe.[19] This voice bears the quality of revelation that proceeds from creation itself. Wisdom presents itself as a woman (Sophia) who not only calls to man but loves him and expects love in return (Wis 8:2, 16). The divine order existing in the universe became the object of a detailed theological study for these later writers. This wisdom residing in the world is differentiated from the tangible works of creation and described in the three formidable didactic poems—Job 28, Proverbs 8, and Sirach 24.[20] Sophia is portrayed as the highest good (Prov 16:16), providing individuals with all that they might need, including knowledge of God and repose for the soul (Prov 2:6–11). It must be said that the Book of Wisdom, which reflects first-century B.C. Palestinian traditions, did move clearly toward the deification of Wisdom, for she is portrayed as God's consort (7:8–9). She is spirit (1:6) and the aura of the power of God (7:25). Although Egyptian ideas and phraseology can be discerned in these writers, the notion of a divine revelation proceeding from creation is attested to only in the sacred literature of Israel. For von Rad this Sophia proceeds from God and is close to God but does not share in the nature of the Godhead.

Walter Brueggemann

The third witness to be called upon to testify to the revelation of the identity of Yahweh in the literature of the Old Testament is Walter Brueggemann (b. 1933), the highly regarded professor of Old Testament theology at Columbia Theological Seminary in Decatur, Georgia. Hailed as one of the most creative of American students of the Old Testament, Brueggemann published his *Theology of the Old Testament* in 1997.[21] After having referred to Eichrodt and von Rad as the two major synthesizers of Old Testament theology in the twentieth century, the American scholar attests that he found it impossible to take either of the German masters as a model for his own work. Eichrodt's consistent emphasis on the covenant theme throughout his study creates a "singular consistency" of approach that has lost favor among contemporary scholars, while von Rad's focus on "the mighty acts of God" especially in tribal Israel seems to have run its course.[22] Brueggemann situates his study within the rather novel context of a trial scene wherein a plurality of voices or witnesses provides the give and take of the development of Old Testament revelation.

Although the Old Testament does not offer the reader a comprehensive picture of God, it does provide a great deal of speech about Yahweh, who is described first and foremost as incomparable. The Lord's awesome power and his abiding presence make the Deity utterly unique (Exod 15:11–13). It is Yahweh who creates simply by means of his word (Gen 1:3) and makes Israel his special inheritance (2 Isa 43:1–8). Brueggemann points out that inasmuch as God creates by word, by wisdom (Jer 10:12), and by spirit (Gen 1:12), there is a faint insinuation of a trinitarian dimension in the process of creation. He points out that the Old Testament is honeycombed with Yahweh's promises to the Israelites, beginning perhaps with the promise of a son to the aged Sarah (Gen 18:1–15). The core of the promise made to the patriarchs reflects a blessing, prosperity, and the prospect of well-being. There are promises to David (2 Sam 7:15–16) and promises communicated through the prophets, but those made during the Babylonian exile are the most sweeping, for God's words spoken through Jeremiah and Ezekiel ordain that Yahweh will be their God and they shall be his people (Jer 31:33; Ezek 37:23).

Time and time again God not only promises to do and to save, but Brueggemann observes that the Lord consistently delivers on his promises. The commitment that Yahweh made to deliver the Jews from bondage (Exod 6:6–8) was marvelously fulfilled through the Exodus and the settlement of the Israelites in Canaan. God showed again and again that he has the power to overcome the forces of the world as he responded to the needs of the poor and the helpless. Brueggemann insists that the most radical revelation concerning Godself is that he is "the relentless opponent of human oppression."[23] His first command at Sinai, however, is the requirement to worship Yahweh alone (Exod 20:1–3). None of the gods of their neighbors was to be placed before Yahweh, nor were they to carve idols in the shape of any earthly creatures and bow down before them.

The Jews never attempted to provide a complete description of Yahweh, whom they saw as "merciful, gracious, slow to anger, and rich in fidelity," but at the same time, as "refusing to consider the guilty guiltless and punishing children for the wickedness of their parents" (Exod 34:6–7). Brueggemann attests that Yahweh, frequently portrayed as a judge, has a severe side. As a matter of fact, Israel was keenly aware of the "potential disproportion in the actions of Yahweh as judge."[24] The Lord is identified also as king (Ps 96:10) and as warrior in the service of the Jews (Exod 15:4–10). Furthermore, he is pictured as a father (Hos 11:1) who is tender and kind to his chosen people yet perfectly capable of fierceness and revenge. Israel is made keenly aware of the Lord's generosity and, on occasion, his severity (Nah 1:5–8). Yahweh is seen as having the quality of intervening creatively or destructively depending on the occasion. The divine responses, however, are not arbitrary or capricious, but there is clearly the chance that God will, if provoked, respond negatively.

The holiness of God, described dramatically in Leviticus 11 and Isaiah 6:3–5, is one of the most nebulous of the divine attributes. Although it separates him from all else, the Israelites are invited to become holy because the Lord is holy (Lev 11:45). The cult place and the name of God are to be scrupulously reverenced, while heavy penalties are threatened for violations. Yahweh's passion may be turned against Israel if his holiness and his self-regard are notably affronted (Ezek 39:25–29).[25] Brueggemann maintains that in many instances it is difficult to foretell "whether the Lord will turn out to be a loose cannon or whether Yahweh's commitment to Israel will make a difference."[26] God can bring down terrible destruction and desolation, as was the case with the Northern Kingdom in 722 B.C. and with the Southern Kingdom in 587 B.C., but then his covenanted fidelity to Israel reasserts itself in the restoration and homecoming after the exile. Israel has no choice but to live with the rather enigmatic character of Yahweh.[27]

Brueggemann then turns his attention to the Old Testament wisdom tradition and freely admits that it has been problematic for twentieth-century biblicists. For him, there seems to be some disconnection between the wisdom writings and the rest of the Old Testament literature. Yahweh's presence and interventions in the life of his people are not the same in the wisdom corpus. He seems to have personally left the scene, and Wisdom becomes the operative force in the world. Sophia is personified as a female who acts as God's agent. In Proverbs 8:22–31 Wisdom appears as a created entity that holds a middle position between God and the world.[28] Especially in the postexilic writings, Yahweh is often surrounded by a number of secondary operatives who execute his commands but who do not in any way threaten the strong and persistent Old Testament emphasis on monotheism in Israel.

The wisdom writers present a kind of "natural theology," relying on their own experience to interpret for their readers and hearers what is required in order to live a righteous life. Brueggemann admits that these "sages" do not engage in direct conversation about God, but rather make judgments based on their life experiences.[29] They seem to have been a privileged class who portrayed Yahweh as the guarantor of order and right thinking. With Ben Sirach (ca. 180 B.C.) wisdom teaching is identified with the Torah and leads to the interpretations that characterize rabbinic Judaism.[30] Brueggemann points out that Jesus appears in the Gospels as a full and ready participant in the interpretative disputes that characterize first-century Judaism.

Roland Murphy

Before proceeding to the consideration of the revelation of God in the New Testament, the biblical scholar and former distinguished professor at North Carolina's Duke University, Roland Murphy (1917–2002), has something to add regarding the nature of Sophia as described by the wisdom writers.[31] In chapter 28 of the Book of Job, written after the exile, wisdom is described as being a quality or reflection of God that resides in the universe, although God alone seems to know her whereabouts (28:23). The Book of Proverbs, chapters 1–9, also a postexilic collection, introduces Wisdom (Sophia) as the first-born of Yahweh (8:22), coming before all the rest of creation. In chapter 8 Lady Wisdom speaks in her own name, but her identity is still unclear. Sophia is not Yahweh, but rather a creation of Yahweh. However, she does take the shape of a person, and she speaks as an agent of God (8:32–35).

It is likely that Ben Sirach wrote in Jerusalem and most likely was involved in a temple ministry of some sort. He was undoubtedly influenced by the Book of Proverbs. In chapter 24 he sketches a memorable portrait of Sophia, who traveled the world and eventually settled down in Jerusalem (24:11). She proceeded from the mouth of the Most High (24:3) and claimed for herself the gift of immortality (24:9). Murphy points out that Sirach has made an important contribution to the figure of Wisdom whom he directly identifies with the Torah (24:22–27).

The last and most stunning of the descriptions of Lady Wisdom is found in the Wisdom of Solomon, written in Greek and originating probably in Alexandria in the last century B.C. The depiction of Lady Wisdom (7:22–8:1) is indeed mystifying. In some sense Sophia is identified with God (7:25–26). Her divine qualities exceed the claims of Proverbs (8:22–25) and Sirach (24:3). She shares in the understanding of God, who allows her an active part in the process of creating, and she governs all things well (8:1). Roland Murphy's evaluation of Sophia is as follows: "In the biblical context the figure of Wisdom cannot be conceived as hypostasis or person because of the strict monotheism of the post exilic period."[32] However, Lady Wisdom and the spirit of the Lord referred to in 1:1–15 of the Book of Wisdom do not in Murphy's judgment seem to be distinct from the Deity.[33] Rather, they express various ways in which God is effectively present to the world and to humankind.

Observations

The God of the Israelites reveals Godself as utterly unique, a distinct and infinitely superior Deity who is to be ever present in their midst. God's "being there" defines him. The Lord, however, is "spirit," and humankind is like the grass of the field. He is loving and protective like a father and a mother, but a jealous Lord when his people show any interest in the "dead gods" of their neighbors. Yahweh leads his people by the hand to a gracious and unimaginable destiny, filling them with hope. Nonetheless, if the divine commands are disobeyed, Yahweh can respond with anger and severity. His mysterious and undefinable holiness will not be mocked, while his love for his people is compared to that of a forgiving husband for his wayward wife. The Israelites are assured again and again that he is their God and they are his chosen people. Yet in spite of his abiding presence and love, there is an element of unpredictability in the Lord's dealings with the Israelites.

After the Babylonian exile, Yahweh was more inclined to act through heavenly intermediaries. Two of God's most likely agents are his spirit and his word, and the two are closely associated. The Deity could dispatch his word and it would not return to him until its mission had been accomplished. The action of the spirit was subtler; it could move about imperceptibly to enlighten, strengthen, and confirm. The spirit and the word of God are portrayed at times as personalized beings, and on occasion they seem to be indistinguishable. In the latter wisdom literature, Sophia emerges as a privileged medium of revelation, almost a living personality distinct from Yahweh. Then, in other passages Sophia appears as a quality of the created world, the voice of order speaking out of the universe. Yahweh and his intermediaries constitute the intimations of Trinity in the Old Testament, but they do not emerge as distinct and equal personalities, for the rigid and uncompromising monotheism of the Jewish faith would not countenance such a development.

NOTES

1. Walther Eichrodt, *Theology of the Old Testament* (vol. 1; trans. J. A. Baker; Philadelphia: Westminster, 1961), 190.

2. Ibid., 206.

3. His first volume was published in German in 1933 and the second in 1939, with the English editions appearing in 1961 and 1967.

4. Walther Eichrodt, *Theology of the Old Testament* (vol. 2; trans. J. A. Baker; Philadelphia: Westminster, 1967), 59.

5. Ibid., 68.

6. Ibid., 80.

7. Gerhard von Rad, *Old Testament Theology* (vol. 1; trans. D. M. G. Stalker; San Francisco: Harper & Row, 1962), 180. Von Rad's work has been reprinted in paperback by Westminster John Knox as part of their *Old Testament Library Classics* with an introduction by Walter Brueggemann.

8. Ibid., 186.

9. Ibid., 441.

10. Ibid., 444.

11. Ibid.

12. Ibid., 449.

13. Ibid., 452.

14. Gerhard von Rad, *Wisdom in Israel* (Nashville: Abingdon Press, 1972).

15. Ibid., 147.

16. Ibid., 148.

17. Ibid., 153.

18. Ibid., 156.

19. Ibid., 163.

20. Ibid., 171.

21. Walter Brueggemann, *Theology of the Old Testament* (Minneapolis: Fortress, 1997). For a perceptive analysis of this work, see Richard Sklba's review in *Theological Studies* 59 (December 1998): 720–22.

22. Ibid., 41, 37.

23. Ibid., 180.

24. Ibid., 236.

25. Ibid., 294.

26. Ibid., 296.

27. Ibid., 311.

28. Ibid., 343.

29. Ibid., 681.

30. Ibid., 689.

31. Roland Murphy, *The Tree of Life: An Exploration of Biblical Wisdom Literature* (New York: Doubleday, 1990).

32. Ibid., 133.

33. Ibid., 143.

2

THE REVELATION OF GOD IN THE NEW TESTAMENT

The theological treatises on God as revealed in the Judeo-Christian tradition took a far different shape compared with the data in the Old Testament. Christian New Testament presentations have been customarily divided into two tracts entitled *On the One God* and *On the Trinity of Persons in God*. The first of these is largely a philosophical presentation dealing with the knowability of God as God is reflected in creation. Then, the possibility for human beings of some kind of supernatural knowledge or vision of the Divinity is found to be possible since that has been offered to humankind. That God can be known by human reason through the works of creation has been acknowledged by the majority of Christian thinkers over the centuries.[1] However, to what extent this possibility becomes a reality for men and women is not entirely clear. Moreover, God has directed human beings to a supernatural end and to share in the divine wonders that utterly surpass the comprehension of the human mind. Indeed, "Eye has not seen, nor has ear heard, nor have our hearts imagined what good things God has prepared for those who love him" (1 Cor. 2:9). The treatment of the one God then deals with the divine knowledge, which is affirmed by most to be perfect and detailed vis-à-vis the past, the present, and the future. And finally, the issues of divine providence and the question of predestination are addressed.[2]

The companion treatise on the persons of the Trinity sets out the scriptural warrants for the consubstantiality of the Father, the Son, and the Holy Spirit. It then traces the development of the trinitarian doctrines through the patristic period, the deliberations of the early ecumenical councils, and the more recent contributions. The four divine relations are then treated, along with the meaning of "person" in the Trinity, the names of the three persons, and finally, the missions of the Son and the Holy Spirit.[3]

Karl Rahner

A good many years ago, Karl Rahner (1904–84), the noted theologian who taught at Innsbruck and Munich, wrote a monograph in which he attempted to lay the foundation for a more biblically based treatment of the revelation of God in the New Testament that would correspond more fittingly to the Old Testament portrayal of the Deity.[4] He asks whether there is a considerable difference between the conception of God in the New and Old Testaments. There could well be, he replies, because of the notable variances of time and circumstance in the unfolding of the revelation. Inasmuch as the Old Testament's message of salvation is intrinsically related to the Christ event, there would have to be an inner connection, but the orientation of the Old Testament to the New is quite obscure. Yet we cannot interpret the Old Testament except in terms of the New. The revelation of God in the New Testament must necessarily be seen as the fulfillment of what has been disclosed before, because the whole pattern of saving history constitutes a continuous unfolding of God's saving acts.[5]

For Rahner, the Yahweh of the Israelites is a particular person with a proper name who created everything that is and who intervenes in the life of his people. The Jews came to know their God from their historical experience of him, and they became more and more familiar with him as he encountered them over the years, especially in their critical moments. Like the Israelites, the New Testament people never doubted God's existence. They required no demonstration of the Deity's existence or of God's concern for them. These truths they knew, not from rational proofs, but because they sensed that the Deity was somehow with them.[6] In the New Testament there is evidence that God can indeed be known from the world of creation (Rom 1:19–23), and this possibility creates in humankind a moral obligation to search out the Divinity. Ignorance of God is considered to be a moral fault.

Rahner attests that the New Testament contains abundant evidence that the pagan deities are no gods at all (Acts 19:26), and allegiance to them in many cases amounts to the worship of demons. The true guarantee of the existence of God is to be found in the fact that God has disclosed Godself within human history to the patriarchs and the prophets of Israel and finally through Jesus, his Son (Heb 1:1–2). There is ample witness in the New Testament to the uniqueness of God (Rom 3:30) as opposed to the many false deities.[7] This God alone is the cause of all things, "ordering the seasons, giving everyone life and breath" (Acts 17:24–26).

In the New Testament the Lord is identified as the God of Abraham, Isaac, and Jacob (Mark 12:26–27), as well as the God of Jesus Christ (Eph 1:3). God's self-manifestation is not just a disclosure of the wondrous deeds he has performed, but an announcement of the divine actions that will unfold in the future (Eph 1:11–14). Humankind can always rely on the fact that God is faithful to his promises (Rom 3:3).[8] God is forgiving (Mark 11:25), merciful (Luke 1:72), and infinitely loving (John 3:16). Our God is the God of hope (Rom 15:13), who in his compassion earnestly desires the salvation of all (1 Tim 2:4). Yet the awareness that we are loved by God must be accompanied by the consciousness that "our salvation must be worked out with fear and trembling" (Phil 2:12).[9] As was the case in the Old Testament, the New Testament reveals the Deity in and through God's activity—which is the way humankind has come to know God.

In the event of the Incarnation, God has taken a position that he will never abandon. Rahner affirms that the Lord will never withdraw from it nor ever go beyond it.[10] This constitutes God's definitive act for humanity (Heb 1:1–4) and the fulfillment of all that he had done before. All the virtues and qualities of God that are revealed in the Old Testament are still there for us to appreciate, but the mystery of the Deity's own personal life was not yet disclosed until the Incarnation. Nor was it clear before the Christ event that men and women who respond in faith and charity to Jesus would be allowed to enter into the very life of God.[11] Those who are conformed to the image of the Son will indeed be brothers and sisters in the image of the firstborn (Rom 8:28).

Our fellowship, Rahner declares, is with the Father and the Son (1 John 1:3) and is effected by the Holy Spirit through whom God's love has been poured into our hearts (Rom 5:5). The just become sharers in God's most intimate personal life through the Spirit who "testifies within our own spirit that we are the sons and daughters of God" (Rom 8:16). It is Rahner's conviction that the Trinity is reflected in the New Testament, although it is to be found there in very simple and undeveloped terms.[12] He holds that when the word "Theos" (i.e., God) is employed in the New Testament, it signifies the first person of the Trinity, and only when it is clear from the context does Theos apply to anyone else. There are passages in the New Testament where Theos clearly means "Father," for in the same verses Christ is referred to as being sent by this God (Heb 1:1–2). In other texts (e.g., John 1:1) the Logos is called God, and in John 20:28 the apostle Thomas declares of the risen Jesus, "My Lord and my God." Rahner lists several texts in which Christ is called Theos, for example, Romans 9:5; John 1:1, 18; 20:28; 1 John 5:20; and Titus 2:13.[13] These references, however, are relatively few compared with the number of times that the New Testament alludes to Christ's divine nature in other terms, not employing the word "Theos." He concludes that Theos is primarily associated with the Father, and only gradually and cautiously did it come to be applied to Christ. Rahner adds that Theos is never used to refer to the Holy Spirit.[14]

When Christ is called the Son of God or the Word of God, and when we encounter the phrase "the Father of Jesus Christ," the reference is clearly to the Father. Also, when the Holy Spirit is identified as the Spirit of God (Matt 3:16), God in this context refers to the Father. We encounter the same usage by the apostle Paul when we read that the Father of Christ destines us to become sons and daughters by adoption (Gal 4:4–6). We are indeed children of the Father rather than children of the triune God (Matt 18:19). According to the words of Christ, we enter into a relationship with the Father, who has freely chosen us to be his own (John 6:37–40).[15]

Rahner concludes his study by observing that the greatest number of passages using the term "Theos" clearly refer to the Father. The six texts discussed above in which Theos refers to the Son are "hesitant and restrictive," while Rahner reaffirms that Theos is never used in the New Testament to refer to the Holy Spirit.[16] Moreover, when Christ is called the Son of God, this always means the Son of the Father. John employs the term "Father" 102 times, while 23 of these appear as "my Father."[17] When God (i.e., Theos) is spoken of in the New Testament, it is the person of the Father who is referenced, the individual person who possesses the divine nature unoriginately. In Greek thought the unity and integrity of the divine nature flow out of the fact that it is the Father who communicates his nature to the Son and to the Spirit. For people like Justin Martyr, Irenaeus, and Tertullian, the Father is considered to be God par excellence.

The Cappadocians (i.e., Basil, Gregory of Nazianzus, and Gregory of Nyssa) looked on the Father as the absolute God or the divine *ousia*. Rahner observes that this Greek conception of the Trinity (wherein the Father is the source) is to be taken seriously because it is grounded in the Scriptures.[18] Furthermore, the prayers of the liturgy from earliest times are structured in such a way that it is the Father to whom we pray through the Son, and the Father is simply referred to as "Deus."

Raymond Brown

The outstanding American biblical scholar Raymond Brown (1928–98) has reviewed the references in the New Testament to ascertain how Christ and the Holy Spirit are related to God the Father.[19] He says that Jesus was never called God in the Synoptic Gospels, and that the Fourth Gospel does not portray Jesus as saying specifically that he is God.[20] Moreover, there does not seem to be any justification for asserting that Jesus is called God in the earliest layers of the New Testament traditions. Brown does hold that Paul believed in the divinity of Jesus, although he may have used other categories to explain himself.[21] The scholar claims that in the New Testament there are three reasonably clear instances in which Christ is affirmed as God (Heb 1:8–9; John 1:1; and John 20:28) and five other passages (Rom 9:5; John 1:18; Titus 2:13; 2 Pet 1:1; and 1 John 5:20) in which he is probably identified as God, although there is reasonable doubt in each of the five cases. Regarding the Holy Spirit, there is some uncertainty as to when the New Testament began to portray the Spirit as a personal agent.[22]

Even in the critical passage in John 1:1 where we read that "the Word was God," there is no explanation as to how the Word is related to God the Father, although Brown affirms that passages of this sort would eventually raise questions that would lead to the conclusion that between the Father and the Son there was more than a functional relationship. The Jesuit theologian John Courtney Murray has written:

> The Christology of the New Testament was, in our contemporary word for it, functional. For instance, all the titles given to Christ the Son—Lord, Saviour, Word, Son of God, Son of man, Prophet, Priest—all these titles, in the sense that they bear in the New Testament, are relational. . . . They do not explicitly define what he is, nor do they explicitly define what his relation to the Father is.[23]

Raymond Brown alleges that by the time of the Council of Nicaea (325), there had been a progression from a more functional understanding of Christ to an ontological one.[24] The fact that Jesus did not seem to be called God in the Palestinian communities in the first generation of Christians seems to suggest that this development could have been of Greek origin. In the New Testament passages that in all likelihood grew out of liturgical worship (e.g., Heb 1:8–9; 2 Pet 1:1; 1 John 5:20), Jesus is referred to somewhat more clearly in divine terms.

James D. G. Dunn

Another scholar whose views merit attention in this regard is James D. G. Dunn (b. 1939), a professor of divinity at the University of Durham in England. His evaluation of Paul's approach to the divinity of Jesus is somewhat more restrictive than that of Raymond Brown. Dunn's critique of Philippians 2:6–11 and 2 Corinthians 8:9 does not envision the notion of a preexistent person who descended from heaven as redeemer. For him these passages affirm that Christ's spotless earthly life was the very embodiment of grace from beginning to end, in sharp contrast to the selfishness and pride of Adam.[25] Even the affirmation in Hebrews 1:8–9 that Brown viewed so positively is not seen as more than a tentative affirmation of Christ's divinity by James Dunn. He does affirm, however, that Hebrews is the first of the New Testament writings to have embraced the notion of a preexistent divine sonship, but it is a good distance short of an expressly articulated position. Moreover,

> At the same time we must not overstate the significance of what the writer to the Hebrews has done. For in the evidence that we have reviewed the concept of pre-existence is a far from clearly formulated thought and seems to have emerged more as a corollary to the author's Platonic idealism than as a firm christological perception. It would certainly go beyond our evidence to conclude that the author has attained to the understanding of God's Son as having had a real personal pre-existence.[26]

Dunn then turns to the Johannine writings and declares at the outset that the formal purpose of John's Gospel is to lead his readers to a belief in Jesus as the Son of God. Dunn adds that this purpose is even more evident in 1 John. The intimacy of Christ's prayers to the Father in John (10:30; 14:7, 10) clearly substantiates Jesus' oneness with the Father. In the Fourth Gospel the divine sonship is indeed grounded in his preexistence, although Dunn reminds us that the issues of ontology and essence have not yet been addressed.[27] The Logos poem in John 1:1–18, however, presents the most striking Word Christology in the New Testament. For John the preexistent Logos is indeed a divine personal being and the only Son of the Father.[28] This blending of the Logos Christology and the Son of God Christology became, according to Dunn, the matrix from which evolved the Christologies of the following centuries.[29]

As Dunn sees it, the identification of Christ with the Word of God in such a direct and immediate manner (e.g., John 1:14) opens a new phase in Christian thought. He emphasizes that there can be no doubt that John the Evangelist had a distinct idea concerning the personal preexistence of the Logos-Son.[30] The Fourth Gospel represents the high point of the evolving christological thought of the first century of the Christian era. Dunn attests that the history of Christology is really the history of the church's efforts to comprehend John's Christology, inasmuch as the evangelist seems to present Jesus as "a being self-consciously distinct" from the Father.[31]

Dunn warns that we must always keep in mind the wide variety of christological thought that is characteristic of the first-century writings, and we must avoid overly simplistic solutions in an attempt to reconcile the diversity of approaches into one coordinated scheme. However, it is no doubt true that the high Christology of John (e.g., 5:17–18; 10:30–33), identifying Jesus with God, did prove unacceptable to the Jews of the late first century A.D. Nonetheless, the writer of the Fourth Gospel continued to believe that his Christology was consistent with Jewish monotheism, for to him Christ is the embodiment of God's ultimate self-revelation.[32] It could indeed be said that the Christology of the church is fundamentally Johannine, because without the Gospel of John, even the Pauline corpus would not have served as a base for the trinitarian doctrine we hold today.[33]

In a more recent study, James Dunn addresses the titles that the New Testament attributes to Christ. The classical title "Son of God," says Dunn, "at the time of Jesus had a much broader reference and simply denoted someone highly favored by God."[34] The many occasions on which Jesus speaks of God as his Father seem to enable the first Christians to call him Son of God. The fact that he almost certainly used the Aramaic word "Abba" (Mark 14:36) revealed an intimate familial relationship that his followers no doubt noted. Dunn affirms that in Paul the application of wisdom categories to Jesus was quite important. As the embodiment of divine Wisdom, Christ is the definitive self-expression of God (Col 1:19; 2:9). Whether his role in creation (e.g., 1 Cor 8:6) assumed his preexistence, or whether as the crucified one he assumed the role of preexistent Wisdom, Christ is identified by Paul as the definitive revelation and the final redemption of

God (2 Cor 5:19). According to Dunn, "The question whether Paul called Jesus 'God' does not provide much help on this point. For one thing, 'God' like 'Son of God' did not have such an exclusive reference at this stage even in Jewish circles. . . . And for another, the only clear occurrence comes in the later or deutero-Pauline literature (Titus 2:13)."[35]

In spite of the fact that Spirit is practically synonymous with Wisdom in pre-Christian Judaism (e.g., Wis 9:17), Paul did not identify Christ with the Spirit in the same way that he identified Christ with Wisdom. It is in the lived experience of Christians that Christ and the Spirit are seen as one, in that Christ is made manifest and accepted through the Spirit, who is frequently called the Spirit of Christ (e.g., Rom 8:9; Phil 1:19). Beyond this idea of the Spirit as the medium through whom Jesus establishes his relationship with believers, it is not clear that we can imply any further identification between Christ and the Spirit.[36]

Regarding the Christology of John, Dunn asserts that the new emphases in the Fourth Gospel must be seen as a notable development over the Christology of the Synoptics, and even of Paul. His view is that the concept "Word" was given preference over "Wisdom" largely because the masculine term "Logos" seemed more appropriate at the time, and also because "Word" could more effectively serve as a point of contact between Jewish monotheism and Greek religious thought.[37] In the context of Jewish wisdom theology, the Word is not considered to be other than God, but rather God in his self-disclosure. Christ is portrayed by John as the definitive revelation of divinity. In Dunn's judgment, "Jesus as God must not be understood as another, a second God, but as God himself incarnate, God making himself present and known to mankind."[38]

With John's Christology, the reshaping of Jewish monotheism by the Christian writers has begun. Also, this development was most likely what precipitated the split between Christian thought and rabbinic Judaism over what the Jews believed was the abandonment of monotheism on the part of the Johannine community. Moreover, the Spirit, according to the fourth evangelist, is depicted as the one who takes Christ's place after his death and resurrection. It is the Spirit who completes the revelation of Jesus for the disciples and animates them with their sense of mission. Dunn points out that the road to future development was provided by the Wisdom/Word Christology of Paul and especially of John, and he concludes:

The New Testament writings contained sufficient safeguards to prevent Christology from abandoning monotheism (Christ as God incarnate), but also sufficient dynamic in the relationship implied between God, the exalted Christ, and the Spirit of Christ to require a redefinition of that monotheism in a trinitarian direction. Whether subsequent formulations managed to take sufficient account of all the balancing elements in New Testament Christology, however, remains an open question.[39]

Yves Congar

Toward the end of his long life, the highly regarded French theologian Yves Congar (1904–1995) published his three-volume work on the Holy Spirit.[40] In the Old Testament, he says, God gave his Spirit to kings and prophets, animating them with discernment and wisdom, guaranteeing that the Lord's plan would be achieved through them. The prophet Joel (350–340 B.C.) foretold that God's Spirit will be poured out not just on certain chosen ones, but on all people (3:1–2). In the wisdom literature, Sophia is almost identified with the Spirit, whose function is to guide men and women in accordance with the divine will. Jewish monotheism permitted various dimensions of God's activity among the people to be considered as somehow distinct from him yet actually one with him. The Spirit and Wisdom were to a certain extent personalized in much of the postexilic literature.

The coming of the Spirit at Jesus' baptism is seen as his anointing for the messianic ministry.[41] After his baptism and the temptations in the desert, Jesus experienced the abiding presence of the Spirit with him (Acts 10:36–39). Congar notes that the writings of John and Paul contain numerous references concerning the Spirit. The gift of the Spirit fulfills the promise that was made to Abraham (Gal 3:14). Indeed, it is the Spirit who witnesses to our spirits that we are the sons and daughters of God (Rom 8:16). As a matter of fact, no one can confess that Jesus is Lord except through the Holy Spirit (1 Cor 12:3). Congar relates that there are forty or more quasi-trinitarian formulas in Paul, but there are no clear statements revealing a trinity of persons in the one divine nature.[42]

It is evident in Acts that this same Spirit who anointed Jesus quickens the missionary endeavors of the apostles after Christ's resurrection. This Spirit directs the growth of the church and appears in Acts as a personalized force, although not in the clear terms of the definition of the Council of Constantinople I (381). In the Gospel of John, the coming of the Spirit into believers was not to occur until after Christ's glorification (7:39). Following his death and resurrection, he gave the Spirit to his disciples to be their comforter and advocate (16:13–14) who would lead them into the full range of truth.

It is the Father who sends the Paraclete in Jesus' name (John 14:26). He is the other Advocate who will always be with them (John 14:16), but he will not come until Jesus departs (John 16:7). Congar judges that it is almost impossible to draw any real conclusions even from the Gospel of John regarding the dogma of the Trinity.[43] However, he adds that it is John's "trinitarian view" that inspired Ignatius (d. ca. 110), Justin (d. ca. 165), and Irenaeus (ca. 140–200). Although Athanasius (ca. 295–373) concluded from the baptismal formula that the Holy Spirit shared in the divine nature like the Father and the Son, both he and Basil the Great (ca. 330–79) stopped short of calling the Spirit "God" because they did not want to move beyond the data found in the Scriptures.[44]

Before concluding the discussion of the Trinity in the New Testament, something should be said about several of the doxological affirmations such as 1 Corinthians 12:4–6, 2 Corinthians 13:14, 1 Peter 1:2, 1 John 3:23–24, and especially Matthew 28:19. It is fair to affirm that these do not reflect the full-blown orthodoxy of the Councils of Nicaea (325) and Constantinople I. The enumeration of the Father, the Son, and the Holy Spirit by way of a blessing or an invocation says very little about how the sacred authors described or defined what has come to be known as trinitarian doctrine. Regarding Matthew 28:19, we are not to look for "a developed trinitarianism in the first gospel."[45] Although it is true that certain church fathers found in the baptismal formula a statement of the implicit equality of the three divine persons, that interpretation ventures beyond the parameters of Matthew 28:19. We seem to have in these "trinitarian" passages references to the many ways in which God is present to humankind. "The juxtaposition of the three modes in which God encounters us describes him as subject and author of all the favor and the love that has encompassed the world from all eternity and will continue to do so for all eternity."[46]

Observations

The revelation of God in the New Testament is nothing less than the completion, the fulfillment of what has been disclosed in the old dispensation. The Deity is identified again as the God of Abraham, Isaac, and Jacob (Mark 12:26–27), as well as the Father of Jesus (Eph 1:3). This God is forgiving (Mark 11:25) and infinitely loving (John 3:16) who desires the salvation of all (1 Tim 2:4), although all must work out their salvation "with fear and trembling" (Phil 2:12). The Incarnation is the definitive act of salvation for humanity (Heb 1:1–4), and those who pattern their lives after the image of Christ will be brothers and sisters of the firstborn (Rom 8:28). This undreamed-of fellowship is brought about by the Holy Spirit, through whom God's love has been poured out into our hearts (Rom 5:5). Although the Trinity is reflected in the New Testament, its traces are found there in a rather simple and undeveloped form. Theos regularly refers to the first person of the Trinity, and occasionally to the Son, but the term is apparently never used of the Holy Spirit.

Jesus is not called God in the Synoptic Gospels, nor does he specifically refer to himself as God in the Gospel of John. There is some dispute as to whether Paul unambiguously identifies Jesus as God, and there is some uncertainty as to when the New Testament began to feature the Spirit as a distinct personal agent. The Christology of the New Testament has been called functional in that Jesus' mission and message are rather strikingly portrayed, but his precise relationship to the Father and to the Holy Spirit is not explicitly articulated. By the time of the Council of Nicaea, the understanding of Christ had evolved from a functional to an ontological notion.

In the Johannine writings Jesus' intimacy and oneness with the Father are quite evident, grounded as they are in his preexistence (John 1:1–18); however, the issues of ontology and essence have not yet been addressed. Although the Fourth Gospel is the high point of the development of christological thought in the first century, it would be wrong to try to fuse the different New Testament approaches into a single uniform scheme. It must be said that the Christology of the church has been and continues to be essentially Johannine, for not even the Pauline writings could support the trinitarian doctrine we profess today.

A term like "the Son of God" did not have the inclusive meaning that it has today and could have simply denoted someone highly favored by God. Moreover, other than the idea of the Spirit as the medium through whom Christ establishes his relationship with believers, there does not seem to be any further precise identification between Christ and the Spirit in the New Testament. There is no abandonment of monotheism, but there is enough in the way of new indications regarding the relationships among the Father, Christ, and the Holy Spirit to call forth a refocusing of that monotheism in a trinitarian direction.

NOTES

1. H. Denzinger and A. Schönmetzer, *Enchiridion Symbolorum,* 32d ed. (Freiburg: Herder, 1963), no. 3026.

2. H. Lennerz, *De Deo Uno* (5th ed.; Rome: Gregorian University, 1955).

3. Charles Boyer, *Synopsis Praelectionum de SS. Trinitate* (Rome: Gregorian University, 1949).

4. Karl Rahner, "Theos in the New Testament," *Theological Investigations* (vol. 1; trans. Cornelius Ernst; London: Darton, Longman & Todd, 1961), 79–148.

5. Ibid., 89.

6. Ibid., 94.

7. Ibid., 101.

8. Ibid., 109.

9. Ibid., 115.

10. Ibid., 117.

11. Ibid., 122.

12. Ibid., 125.

13. Ibid., 136.

14. Ibid., 138.

15. Ibid., 143.

16. Ibid.

17. Ibid., 145.

18. Ibid., 147.

19. Raymond Brown, *An Introduction to the New Testament* (New York: Doubleday, 1997).

20. Ibid., 190.

21. Ibid., 183.

22. Ibid., 193.

23. John Courtney Murray, *The Problem of God* (New Haven, Conn.: Yale University Press, 1964), 40.

24. Raymond Brown, *An Introduction to New Testament Christology* (Mahwah, N.J.: Paulist Press,1994), 171.

25. James D. G. Dunn, *Christology in the Making* (2d ed.; Grand Rapids: Eerdmans, 1989), 121-25. See also Jerome Murphy-O'Connor, *Paul: A Critical Life* (New York: Oxford University Press, 1996), 225–27.

26. Dunn, *Christology in the Making*, 55–56.

27. Ibid., 58.

28. Ibid., 244.

29. Ibid., 245.

30. Ibid., 249.

31. Ibid., 250, 264.

32. Ibid., xxx.

33. Ibid., 351, n.142.

34. James D. G. Dunn, "New Testament Christology," in *Christology* (vol. 1 of *The Christ and the Spirit;* Grand Rapids: Eerdmans, 1998), 8.

35. Ibid., 16.

36. Ibid., 16-17.

37. Ibid., 24.

38. Ibid.

39. Ibid., 29.

40. Yves Congar, *I Believe in the Holy Spirit* (trans. David Smith; 3 vols.; New York: Seabury Press, 1983).

41. Ibid., vol. 1, 19.

42. Ibid., vol. 1, 39.

43. Ibid., vol. 1, 56.

44. Ibid., vol. 1, 74.

45. W. D. Davies and Dale C. Allison, *The Gospel According to Saint Matthew* (vol. 3; Edinburgh: T&T Clark, 1997), 686.

46. Eduard Schweizer, *The Good News According to Matthew* (trans. David Green; Atlanta: John Knox, 1975), 533–34.

3

THE FORMULATION OF THE
DOCTRINE OF THE TRINITY
IN THE WRITINGS OF THE FATHERS
AND IN THE EARLY COUNCILS

Developments before Nicaea

The journey to Trinity moves beyond the New Testament and finds its way into the early Christian literature, that is, the apostolic fathers and the second- and third-century fathers of the church. In the early fourth century, the Arian controversy initiated a whole new development that precipitated the doctrinal definitions of the early councils. These in turn triggered further discussions and theological controversies in the fifth through the eighth centuries. The story does not by any means end there, for the differences in trinitarian thought between East and West that were debated at the Council of Lyons II (1274) and at the Council of Basel, Ferrara, Florence (1431–45), have not exactly narrowed the rift. For some Eastern scholars (e.g., Vladimir Lossky), the divide in trinitarian doctrine renders mute the whole question of union between the Orthodox and the Roman Catholic Church until this issue is settled. For others (e.g., Sergius Bulgakov), these trinitarian differences are significant but do not constitute an absolute impediment to reunion. For this study, certain pivotal church fathers and the deliberations of several of the more important councils have been chosen as critical stepping stones in the appraisal of trinitarian thought. No doubt, some would have wanted other names and different conciliar gatherings to be dealt with, but these, I believe, will reliably trace the story of the growth of the doctrine of Trinity down through the centuries. We will begin with three critical voices from the second century.

Ignatius of Antioch

Ignatius of Antioch, the second bishop of that important see in Syria, was martyred in Rome during the reign of the Roman emperor Trajan ca. 110 A.D. On his way to Rome, Ignatius wrote six letters to various churches and one to his dear friend, Polycarp, bishop of Smyrna. Although his references to the Father and to Christ are frequent and his testimony concerning the divine character of Jesus is prominent (Ephesians 1, intro; 7,2; Smyrneans 1,1), his references to the Holy Spirit are quite rare. While Jesus is referred to as God and Savior, as well as the "perfect man" (Smyrneans 4,2), Ignatius's allusions to the Holy Spirit are infrequent. In Ephesians 9,1 the Father, the Son, and the Holy Spirit are mentioned as collaborators in the work of redemption, but their roles are not defined. In the letter to the Magnesians, a doxology of sorts enumerates three figures (13,1), and in the epistle to the Philadelphians, the Spirit is described as "from God" (7,1). Thus, a portrait of a Trinity of three divine and coequal figures is not evident in Ignatius.[1]

Justin the Apologist

When we encounter Justin the Apologist, who was martyred in Rome ca. 165 A.D., we discover more information concerning the Christian God, who now appears through the prism of Stoic and Platonic philosophy. Although every person in his or her reason possesses a germ or seed of the Logos, Christ possessed the Logos fully and completely.

Justin reports a trinitarian formula for baptism and points out that the eucharistic prayers are hymns of praise to the Father through the Son and of the Holy Spirit (*First Apology,* chap. 61). He affirms that next to God we worship and love the Word who is from the unbegotten and ineffable God, and who shared our sufferings that he might bring us salvation (*Second Apology,* chap. 13). It was Christ who was present at the Old Testament theophanies, appearing in various guises, for example, as an angel or a man, and even in the form of fire in the burning bush. According to Justin, Christ is called God in that he is the first begotten, the Son of the only, unbegotten, unutterable God (*Trypho,* chap. 126). He was begotten from the Father, not by abscission, as if the essence of the Father was divided (*Trypho,* chap. 128). Christ is an offspring numerically distinct from the one who begot him. The Holy Spirit is usually referred to as the Spirit of Prophecy, the one who inspired the Old Testament prophets to speak of the coming Messiah. Other than the liturgical references at baptism and the eucharist, Justin does not say much about a trinity of persons in God.[2] He taught that the Logos-Son is a divine person but is subordinate to the Father.

Irenaeus of Lyons

Irenaeus of Lyons is considered by the noted historian of primitive Christianity, J. N. D. Kelly, as the second-century theologian who "dominated Christian orthodoxy before Origen."[3] He was born ca. 140 A.D. and migrated from Asia Minor to Gaul, where he became bishop of Lyons in ca. 177. He died sometime after 200. Irenaeus's masterpiece, *Against Heresies,* represents a detailed treatment of gnosticism that enormously enriches our understanding of the latter half of the second century. The venerable bishop spent his life opposing gnosticism in all its various shapes and forms.

The heart of gnostic beliefs consists in the claim that those gifted with the gnosis (i.e., the special, singular knowledge) possess a privileged insight concerning God and human salvation from secret revelations that were never communicated publicly to Christian believers. Their efforts attacked the underpinnings of the church's message contained in the Gospels, the other New Testament writings, and the apostolic preaching that serve as the ground, the "canon," of Christian faith.

Irenaeus leaned very heavily on the New Testament writings of John, and especially of Paul. He was not a philosopher, but first and foremost a biblical theologian who took great pains to elucidate the Christian creed. Kelly notes that his exposition of the Godhead is "the most complete, and most explicitly trinitarian, to be met with before Tertullian."[4] Although the divinity of the Son is set forth in striking clarity again and again, the Spirit is nowhere expressly designated as God. Nonetheless, it is clear that Irenaeus does consider the Spirit as divine.

Robert M. Grant, another accomplished historian of the early church, describes how Irenaeus links together the various saving plans or "economies" of God that can be discerned from creation to the *parousia.* These movements repeat or recapitulate one another, forming a magnificent saving design. Christ, who stands in the middle, reverses the downward trend and recapitulates the human life course, transforming it and reversing its direction upward. For the bishop of Lyons, it was necessary for Jesus to live through all the stages of human life in order to transform it and change its course. Thus, he taught that the Lord must have lived into his fifties (i.e., old age), because otherwise the recapitulation would not have been complete.[5]

Irenaeus professes his belief in the Trinity throughout his work, *Against Heresies* (e.g., bk. 1, 10.1). He occasionally expresses his feeling through a doxology wherein he speaks of God the Father and Jesus the Son who gave us the gift of the Holy Spirit (bk. 3, 6.4). He points to the Scriptures as spoken by God's Word and his Spirit (bk. 2, 28.2), whom he refers to as "the hands of God" (bk. 5, 28.4). At other times Irenaeus refers to the Son as Word and to the Spirit as Wisdom, both of whom were with God at the creation (bk. 4, 20.1). In this context he cites Proverbs 8:22–25 to prove his point (bk. 4, 20.3). Although his articulation of the identity and mission of the Son in book 3, 9.1–3 is much more complete and represents a high point in the early development of Christology, the identity of the Holy Spirit is never as lucidly set forth. The work of the Spirit is described in terms of prophecy and sanctification. It is the Spirit who works, the Son who administers, and the Father who approves the task of the ongoing salvation of humankind (bk. 4, 20.6). Kelly notes that it was Irenaeus who literally "summed up the thought of the second century."[6]

Quintus Septimius Tertullian

Quintus Septimius Tertullian was born in North Africa of pagan parents ca. 160 and received a superb education as a jurist. After spending some time in Rome as an advocate, he returned as a Christian in ca. 195 to Carthage, where he embarked on an active literary career in the service of the church. He became frustrated by the mediocrity of religious practice among church members and left the church ca. 207 for the Montanist sect, where he remained until his death sometime after 220.[7]

Tertullian's doctrine of the Trinity is most fully formulated in his work, *Against Praxeas,* which exposes the errors of a teacher named Praxeas who came from Asia to Rome to join a number of others who were teaching a doctrine of modalism in various forms. These modalists, or monarchians, opposed the existence in God of a triad of persons. As a matter of fact, Praxeas held that it was the Father who was born of Mary and who personally experienced the passion and death. Modalism seemed to originate in Asia Minor and was transported to the West by Praxeas, Sabellius, and others in the early third century. Sabellius, who came to Rome from North Africa, taught that the one God operated under three modalities, that of the Father, the Son, and the Holy Spirit. Apparently there was no distinction of persons but only different modes of operation—creation, redemption, and sanctification—that were attributed to the one God.

In Rome at this time, there was much theological ferment and a great variety of opinions were espoused. During the pontificate of Zephrinus (198–217), modalism became extremely popular. It seems that Pope Zephrinus himself viewed the new talk of persons in God with suspicion. Actually the Roman presbyter, Hippolytus (d. 235), considered the pope a modalist, although this is contested by others. Hippolytus, who had been won over by the Logos theory of Justin, spoke emphatically about the real distinction between the Father and the Word within the divine nature. However, he seemed to be unwilling to call the Word "Son" until the Incarnation, and he left little room for the distinct personhood of the Holy Spirit.[8] While Pope Zephrinus's successor, Callistus (217–22), was somewhat sympathetic to the modalist position, he did eventually excommunicate Sabellius.

In the process of refuting the modalism or monarchianism of Praxeas, Tertullian provides the most complete exposition of the doctrine of the Trinity that the early church had produced up to that point. His rule of faith, outlined in chapter 2 of *Against Praxeas,* identifies the Father as the one from whom the Son proceeds. It is the Son who became man and who is called Jesus—being both man and God. The Holy Spirit was sent by the Father and Son and is the sanctifier of the faith of those who believe in the Father, Son, and Holy Spirit. Tertullian asserts that the divine monarchy is in no way destroyed by the Son and the Holy Spirit, who are members of the Father's own substance. The Son is from the substance of the Father, while the Holy Spirit proceeds from the Father through the Son (chap. 3). The Father and the Son are portrayed as two distinct beings. Before creation, God had within himself both reason and, inherent in reason, the Word. This power of divine intelligence was called Sophia in Proverbs 8:22–25. The Word is the Son, and a person who is second to the Father (chap. 7).

Tertullian refers to the Son as an emanation from the Father. He compares God the Father to the root, the Son to the tree, and the Holy Spirit to the fruits. The Son is second to the Father, while the Holy Spirit is third from the Father and the Son. The three divine figures are distinct from one another because they differ from one another in their mode of being. While the Father is the entire divine substance, the Son is a portion of the whole. "The Father is greater than I" (John 14:28). It is the Son who sends the Spirit, the Comforter, the Paraclete who is distinct from the Son. Tertullian asserts against the monarchians that these relations call for distinct persons (chap. 10). He refers to certain passages in Genesis (i.e., 1:26; 3:22), in which God speaks in the plural, as intimations of the distinction of persons in the Godhead. This distinction of persons is made on the basis of personality, not substance, and there is no suggestion of polytheism here.

The Father, the Son, and the Holy Spirit—each is God. The Son is in the second place and the Spirit is in the third place, but they comprise one undivided substance. In Tertullian's judgment, the Word is the divine person who was communicating with humankind from the beginning, as reflected in the Old Testament. Also, the divine administration from the outset of creation was in the hands of the Word. Then, as the Word was made flesh, he became visible as the Son. The Jews understood that Jesus made himself equal to God (John 5:17), and that was why they intended to kill him.

In chapter 25, Tertullian directs his attention to the Holy Spirit.

> "He shall receive of mine," says Christ [John 16:14], just as Christ himself received of the Father's. Thus the connection of the Father in the Son, and of the Son in the Paraclete, produces three coherent Persons, who are yet distinct from one another. These three are one essence, not one Person, as it is said, "I and my Father are one," in respect of unity of substance, not singularity of number.[9]

Citations from the other Gospels are introduced to further demonstrate the distinction of persons and the relationships among the divine figures (e.g., Matt 28:19; Luke 20:9–19). Regarding Jesus, Tertullian affirms that he shares "a twofold state," or nature, which is joined in one person. Each nature or substance has its own operations, with the divine nature being responsible for the miracles and the mighty deeds, and with the human nature exhibiting the affections and actions proper to it. In conclusion, Tertullian refutes Praxeas when he declares that it was the Father who suffered. The Father was in no way associated with the sufferings of the Son, nor did the Holy Spirit suffer (chap. 29).

"Persona" for Tertullian connotes individuality, that is, one who speaks and acts. The one divine substance has three figures, forms, persons. The Logos always possessed a particular state or persona in God, and since the Incarnation the person of the Son has possessed a twofold state—divine and human. Tertullian introduced the concept of person into trinitarian thought, although he does not explain how the person of Christ operates in and through two states or natures. Prior to creation, God was not really alone, for he possessed within himself his reason, or his Word, which was immanent until creation. After the creation, the Word could be called "Son" and God could be called "Father." The Spirit, the Son's Advocate, proceeds from the Father through the Son. Thus, there are three persons, individuals, in the Divinity, and this is in no way opposed to the essential unity of God.[10] However, it must be said that "Tertullian could not shake off entirely the influence of subordinationism."[11] The distinction between the Word immanent in God and the Word emitted or spoken by God seems to portray the divine generation as taking place gradually. Although the internal Word is eternal, the Son, the uttered Word, does not seem to be eternal. Further, the Father is the whole divine substance, while the Son and the Holy Spirit are only a portion of the whole.[12] In spite of these limitations, Tertullian's contribution to the development of trinitarian theology was truly noteworthy.

Origen

Probably the most intriguing of the early church fathers is Origen, who was born in Alexandria ca. 185. The eminent patrologist John Quasten calls him "the outstanding teacher and scholar" of the early church. He is described as a man of "spotless character" and "encyclopedic learning."[13] Origen headed the catechetical school at Alexandria from 203 to 231. He was ordained at Caesarea in Palestine in 231 without the permission of Bishop Demetrius of Alexandria. This prompted his excommunication by the bishop and the clergy of his native diocese. Origen then left for Caesarea, where he founded a new school and presided over it for twenty years. He died in Tyre in 253 at the age of sixty-nine. Although his literary output was prodigious, the controversy surrounding his teaching and that of his followers, the Origenists, during the three hundred years after his death, resulted in the disappearance of many of his writings.

Origen's most significant work on the subject of the Trinity, *On First Principles,* was written during his latter years at Alexandria. Although only a small portion of the study is extant in Greek, it has survived entire in a free Latin rendering by Rufinus (ca. 345–410), an Italian monk and translator. The first book of the treatise deals with the oneness and the spirituality of God, as well as the hierarchy of the three divine persons. Quasten points out that the main defect of the study is the predominant influence of Neo-Platonic philosophy.[14] Origen had attended the lectures of Ammonius Saccas in Alexandria. Considered the father of Neo-Platonism, Ammonius later taught Plotinus (ca. 205–70), who was the founder of the Neo-Platonic school.[15] In spite of its imperfections, *On First Principles,* which deals with the fundamental tenets of the Christian faith, represents a critical development in the history of Christian thought. It was Origen who coined the word *homooúsios* to describe the substantial unity between the Father and the Son. Yet although his doctrine of the Logos is a significant contribution, Origen refers to the Son as "a second God."[16] The issue of his subordinationist views has been affirmed by some (e.g., Jerome) and denied by others (e.g., Athanasius).[17] Aloys Grillmeier notes that although many call him the first of the systematic theologians, no substantial agreement can be reached concerning the direction of his theology.[18]

Origen is not particularly interested in the ontological constitution of Christ. The Logos is said to proceed from the will of the Father, while the Holy Spirit issues from the Father and becomes a subsisting hypostasis by means of the Logos. The Spirit is in the third place after the Father and the Son.[19] After emphasizing the absolute simplicity of the Father, Origen points out that Christ possesses a multiple constitution, and thus a number of descriptive titles can be attributed to him. It is in and through Christ that the transcendent properties of the Father are revealed. Origen has been called the theologian of the human soul. For him the soul facilitates the union between the human body and the Logos. In Grillmeier's judgment, Origen assumes that the union established between Christ and the Logos is an ontological one, although he never formally addresses the issue.[20] Like all the human souls in Origen's Neo-Platonic schemes, the soul of Jesus existed from eternity before his body came into being. However, unlike other human souls who might be inhabited in some fashion by the Logos, in Christ the Logos was entirely in control. Grillmeier observes that in the middle of the third century, the beginnings of speculative theology were inconclusive indeed.

Origen's Neo-Platonist philosophy allowed him to offer a different view of the mystery of the Trinity. According to J. N. D. Kelly, for Origen only God the Father is God in the full sense. The Son who was begotten from eternity is a derivative Deity, as is the Holy Spirit who is brought into existence by the Logos.[21] "The Son and the Spirit are also in their degrees divine, possessing though derivatively, all the characteristics of the Deity; distinct from the world of creatures, they cooperate with the Father and mediate the divine life flowing from him."[22] Not withstanding the subordinationist tenor of Origen's thought, there is a strong pluralist cast in his trinitarian position. There is no doubt that for him the three persons are eternally and really distinct. Kelly insists, however, that Origen's Neo-Platonism assumes that the Son and the Spirit are the first beings in the chain of emanations from the unoriginate Father.[23]

Perhaps the foremost authority on Origen in our day is Henri Crouzel, who has spent his entire career researching and writing about the Alexandrian scholar. Crouzel affirms that the work *On First Principles* should not be considered as a "summa theologica" because Origen does not presume to speak dogmatically. Rather, it was his custom to set forth several solutions to certain theological problems, allowing his readers to decide for themselves. He wanted the intelligent Christians to discover answers to problematic issues so they would not find their way into the gnostic sects.

God the Father is described as a simple intellectual nature who nonetheless feels the passion of love that is the source of the redemption. Origen emphasizes that there is but one God, that is, the creator God (Old Testament), who is the Father of Jesus Christ (New Testament). Against the gnostics he proclaims the goodness of the creator God. It is actually the Father's goodness that is the ground out of which the Son is born and from which the Holy Spirit proceeds.[24] The Son's generation from the Father is eternal, for the Father never existed without his Logos. According to Crouzel, the Son is both subordinate to and equal to the Father inasmuch as the Father is the source of both the Son and the Spirit. Although the Father's simplicity does not allow for the possibility of his assuming several distinct roles or titles, the Son assumes many roles, for example, Wisdom, Logos, Truth, Light, Firstborn, which describe the various facets of the redemptive mission of Christ. The Son is the intelligent instrument of the Father in creation. According to *On First Principles,* the Father's role is to impart being, the Son's mission is to make being rational, and the function of the Spirit is to impart sanctity.[25]

The soul of Christ, in Origen's judgment, existed long before the Incarnation. He was the bridegroom of what he terms the preexistent church, which included all rational souls. When most of the members of the preexistent church turned their backs on the presence of God, Christ did not abandon them. Rather, he sent the patriarchs and the prophets to Israel and personally appeared through various theophanies in preparation for his coming in the flesh. When the time predetermined by the Father came to pass, Christ relinquished the form of God to assume the form of a servant (Phil 2:6–7).[26] Although Origen offers a number of explanations for the redemption of Jesus that were also discussed by other early fathers, he presents a doctrine of the "restoration of all" that is rather uniquely his. The renowned patrologist Berthold Altaner explains the theory:

> After death the souls of those who have sinned on earth enter a purifying fire, but gradually all, even the devils, ascend from step to step and will finally, completely purified, rise again in ethereal bodies when God will once more be all in all. This restoration *(apokatástasis)*, however, does not mean the end of the world, but only a preliminary conclusion. Other worlds existed before this world, and others will come after it. He taught with Plato that one world follows the other in endless succession. Hence Origen denied the eternity of hell.[27]

Henri Crouzel observes that prior to ca. 360, there was not a great deal of theological ferment regarding the Holy Spirit. This was when the pneumatomachians, that is, those fighting against the Spirit, and the Macedonians, who formally denied the divinity of the Holy Spirit, began to attract attention. Before that time the church professed the divine character of the Holy Spirit, and it was never specifically contested, except in a general way by the subordinationists (who held that the Father is superior to the Son and the Holy Spirit), and the modalists (who taught that the one God merely manifests himself in three different ways). According to Origen, the Holy Spirit is associated with the Father and the Son in dignity and is described as an individual intelligent being, although neither the word "person" nor the word "God" was explicitly applied to him. However, there are three subsistent realities—the Father, the Son, and the Holy Spirit—but only the Father received the Godhead from no one else. Only the Son is son by nature, and the Spirit needs the mediating function of the Son to subsist individually. The Holy Spirit receives his existence and everything that he is from the Father through the Son.[28]

In spite of Origen's rather unique theological turns, Henri Crouzel calls him the first great Christian theologian. The subordinationism attributed to Origen is not, according to Crouzel, contrary to orthodoxy, because it does not assume an inequality of power among the divine persons. Origen's views on the Trinity—apart from the preexistence of

Christ's soul—represent for Crouzel a considerable advance over the thought of his predecessors.[29]

One of the exponents of Origen's trinitarian teaching was Dionysius, the bishop of Alexandria. In response to an outbreak of Sabellianism (i.e., modalism) in the Libyan Pentapolis, the bishop went too far in distinguishing the Father and the Son, making the Son appear as a mere creature. When Pope Dionysius (260–68) was informed of the bishop of Alexandria's position, he wrote to the Egyptian church to clear up what he thought were subordinationist tendencies in the teaching of the bishop of Alexandria. The pope's exposition of trinitarian doctrine has been preserved in a work of Athanasius on the decrees of the Council of Nicaea. According to the fragment, Pope Dionysius proclaimed the distinction of persons—Father, Son, and Holy Spirit—in the unity of the Trinity.[30]

> That admirable and divine unity therefore must neither be separated into three divinities, nor must the dignity and eminent greatness of the Lord be diminished by having applied to it the name of creation, but we must believe in God the Father Omnipotent, and in Jesus Christ his Son and in the Holy Spirit. . . . Thus doubtless will be maintained in its integrity the doctrine of the divine Trinity and the sacred announcement of the monarchy.[31]

The bishop of Alexandria responded to the pope, declaring that his position was the same as the Roman pontiff's, so the matter was closed. The pope's declaration of trinitarian theology on this occasion was quite possibly the most important brief statement on the Trinity by a Roman pontiff in the third century.

In the East after Origen, considerable opposition developed concerning his doctrine of the preexistence of souls. Also, more and more skepticism arose regarding his affirmation of a real human intellect in Christ, since this was seen as destroying the unity of his being. During the first three centuries of the Christian era, practically all the approaches to the clarification of the mystery of the Trinity were tinged with some degree of either subordinationism or modalism. The modalist tendencies were most quickly diagnosed as heterodox and labeled as such (e.g., Sabellius). The subordinationist tendencies were more difficult to confront because the pervasive constructs of Middle Platonism (ca. 100 B.C. to 300 A.D.) were so widely accepted that they had become a part of the thought patterns of most educated people.

Justin and the Apologists, Tertullian, Hippolytus, and Origen were all affected in one degree or another by subordinationist thinking.

According to Middle Platonism, the supreme principle or hypostasis is God, the source from whom all being derives. This process, called emanation, does not affect "the One" or God in any way, but whatever else exists is an overflow or emanation of the One. Crouzel observes that although Origen espoused a subordinationist worldview even with regard to the divine persons, this did not affect his orthodoxy, because he insisted that all three divine persons possess an equality of power.[32] There was thus what Grillmeier calls a tolerable, unclarified subordinationism that was quite common in the early Christian centuries, and an intolerable brand that surfaced, for example, in the Alexandrian priest Arius after 318. Arius (ca. 250–336) was a subordinationist who, in the judgment of many of his contemporaries, went clearly over the line. In ca. 320 he submitted a letter to his bishop, Alexander of Alexandria, expressing to his ordinary his views, especially concerning the relation between the Father and the Son.

For him God the Father alone is uncreated and eternal. He brought forth the only begotten Son, who did not exist before he was brought forth. The Son is not a part of the substance of the Father, nor does he have identical being with the Father. Arius refers to three hypostases—Father, Son, and Holy Spirit—but for him only the first hypostasis is God. The Son and the Spirit are creatures.[33] In the exposition of Origen, the Son is eternal, but he remains in the bosom of the Father until the Incarnation. For Arius neither the Son nor the Holy Spirit existed eternally. Rather, they came into being when the Father willed to create them. Thus, there was a period when neither the Son nor the Holy Spirit existed. Arius also denied that there was a human soul in Christ. It was the created Logos, the second hypostasis, who assumed human flesh. If indeed the Logos was divine, such a union with a human body would have been utterly inconceivable. Grillmeier affirms that we need not assume that Arius ever altered his views on these matters.[34]

Nicaea and Constantinople I

Council of Nicaea—325

The turmoil caused in the East by the teaching of Arius prompted a widespread call for a general council to settle the controversy. In early 325, fifty-nine bishops gathered at Antioch to condemn Arius. However,

Emperor Constantine soon intervened and summoned the Council of Nicaea, which opened in June of 325 with more than three hundred bishops in attendance. According to Eusebius of Caesarea (ca. 265–339), who participated in the gathering, Constantine himself directed the course of the deliberations. Ossius of Cordova and the two presbyters who represented the Roman pontiff were apparently the only westerners present. It is unfortunate that no official record of the council was produced. The most important contribution of the first ecumenical council was the formulation of a creed that could claim universal authority. The text of the profession of faith was probably an adaptation of a baptismal formula that was current in Palestine, although there were several critical additions. For example, the Son is described as originating "from the substance of the Father" and is called "true God of true God." Also, the term "consubstantial" *(homooúsios)* was applied to the Son and has been the source of endless disputes from that day forward. The profession of faith reads as follows:

> We believe in one God the Father all powerful, maker of all things both seen and unseen and in one Lord Jesus Christ, the Son of God, the only begotten from the Father, that is from the substance of the Father, God from God, light from light, true God from true God, begotten not made, consubstantial with the Father, through whom all things came to be. . . . And in the holy Spirit.[35]

The Arians could either sign the profession or be sent into exile. Nonetheless, at the request of the emperor, many of the Arians were later received back into the church. The main point of contention at Nicaea was the term *homooúsios,* which the council agreed upon, because every biblical turn of phrase can be interpreted in their favor by the Arians. But even *homooúsios* was open to a variety of interpretations. Constantine wanted a creed that as many Christians as possible could accept. A number of influential Eastern bishops, for example, Eusebius of Caesarea and Eusebius of Nicomedia, were not happy with the Nicene formulation because it ran counter to their subordinationist theologies. On the other hand, many bishops who were bitterly opposed to the Arians did not like the unbiblical terms employed in the council's profession of faith.

Nicaea did not settle the christological controversy by any means. As a matter of fact, for thirty years after the council, the term *homooúsios* was hardly used. Actually, Cyril of Jerusalem (ca. 315–86) was always uneasy about employing the Nicene terminology.[36] Athanasius does not mention *homooúsios* in his work, *On the Incarnation,* written prior to 325, and it was not until his writings after 350 or so that he became an outspoken proponent of the Nicene formula.[37] One of the causes of the problem over *homooúsios* was that the representatives at the council added no explanation as to the manner in which the term was to be understood.[38] Hence, after Nicaea there were continuous debates as to how the one substance of the Father and the Son could be reconciled with the distinction affirmed between them.

Athanasius of Alexandria

A major voice in the debate was Athanasius of Alexandria (ca. 295–373), whose career experienced many ups and downs. He was present at the Council of Nicaea as a deacon and succeeded to the patriarchate of Alexandria in 328. From that time to the day of his death, he was exiled on five occasions from Alexandria largely because of his anti-Arian stance. Athanasius returned to Alexandria to stay in 366. There he lived out his life in relative peace until his death in 373. During the reign of Emperor Constantius (337–61), there were numerous Eastern synods proclaiming a variety of declarations of faith—many of them sympathetic in some degree with the Arian position. Athanasius, however, stood firm, upholding the single and indivisible nature of the Father and the Son, although for many years he avoided using the term *homooúsios*. By the mid-fourth century, though, he espoused and publicized the authentic homooúsian position and terminology. In his understanding of Christ, the soul of Jesus seemed to play no part in his inner human life. The Logos was the source from which all life and movement came.[39] The sole motivating principle in Christ seemed to be the Logos.

In spite of the efforts of Athanasius and other adherents of Nicaea, the latter years of the reign of Constantius witnessed a return of Arianism in the East. (For the record, the West was not deeply engaged in the Arian disputes either at the time of the Council of Nicaea or for some years afterward.) In addition to the Arians who continued to hold that the Son was unlike the Father, there were the Semi-Arians who taught that the Son was of a similar nature to the Father (i.e., *homooúsios*), that the Son was like the Father in substance. After the Nicene Creed became more widely known and appreciated in the West, Pope Liberius (352–66) addressed the emperor and requested that he convoke a universal synod for confirming the decrees of Nicaea. Constantius, however, continued to advocate the position that the Son is like the Father, rather than consubstantial with him. A synod held at Constantinople in 360 rejected all the previous professions of faith, affirming that "the Son is like the Father, as the divine scriptures say and teach."[40] According to J. N. D. Kelly, this became the official version of what was henceforth to be recognized as Arianism, especially among the barbarians on the fringes of the Roman Empire.[41]

Council of Constantinople I—381

The Council of Constantinople I met in May 381. It was called by the emperors Gratian (West) and Theodosius I (East) to oppose especially the Arians and the pneumatomachians (who denied the divinity of the Holy Spirit). Unfortunately, the council's doctrinal pronouncements have not survived. We do have, however, the synodical letter of the synod of Constantinople of 382, which spelled out these doctrinal enactments in summary form. Included in the acts of the synod were seven canons, of which six dealt with disciplinary and administrative matters. Canon 1 enumerated all the heresies that the 150 fathers at Constantinople I condemned, including the Arians, the pneumatomachians, and the Apollinarians.[42]

It is widely agreed that the profession of faith of the 150 fathers in 381 was not a newly composed creed, but perhaps a local baptismal formula that reflected the Nicene definition. Although the delegates at Constantinople I added other phrases to the formula they employed, they did not see themselves as promulgating a new profession of faith. They included additional items clarifying their opposition to certain heterodox tendencies that had become more troublesome after Nicaea. Specifically, their expansion of the third article of the creed regarding the Holy Spirit was an attack against the pneumatomachians and Macedonians who denied the full divinity of the Spirit. The third article of the 381 creed declares that the Spirit is "the holy, lordly and life-giving one, proceeding from the Father, co-worshipped and co-glorified with the Father and the Son, the one who spoke through the prophets."[43] Yves Congar points out that according to the faith profession of 381, the Spirit is "neither God nor consubstantial with the Father and the Son, but is the Lord and life-giver proceeding from the Father, the object of the same worship and same glory with the Father and the Son."[44]

In the letter of the bishops gathered for the synod of Constantinople in 382 and addressed to Pope Damasus (366–84) and a number of Western bishops, the consubstantiality of the three divine persons is clearly articulated. Also, the errors of Sabellius, Arius, and the pneumatomachians are again proscribed.[45] This synod of 382 confirmed that the object of Constantinople I was to eradicate once and for all the various errors that stood in the way of the faith professed at Nicaea. Both the Arians and the Sabellians, as well as those who denied the full divinity of the Holy Spirit, were branded as heretical. Constantinople I did not employ the term *homooúsios*, preferring to use biblical terminology. According to J. N. D. Kelly, "not all in the orthodox ranks felt easy about the frank description of the Holy Spirit as God, and as consubstantial with the Father and the Son."[46] Both Athanasius and Basil of Caesarea were rather cautious about declaring explicitly that the Holy Spirit was of the same substance as the Father and the Son. As a matter of fact, Gregory of Nazianzus affirmed at the time of the council that some of those who believed the Spirit was fully divine kept this as an opinion to themselves.[47]

The Cappadocians: Basil, Gregory of Nazianzus, and Gregory of Nyssa

In addition to Athanasius of Alexandria, the Cappadocians—Basil (ca. 330–79), Gregory of Nazianzus (330–89), and Gregory of Nyssa (ca. 335–94)—paved the way for the definition of 381. Basil's treatise, *On the Holy Spirit,* written in 375, cautiously prepared the way for the declaration of the consubstantiality of the Holy Spirit, although Basil did not call the third person "God." Gregory of Nyssa affirmed the oneness of nature shared by the Father, the Son, and the Holy Spirit, and Gregory of Nazianzus employed the term "consubstantial" regarding the Holy Spirit.[48] The explanation of the origin of the third person was most strikingly set forth by Gregory of Nyssa, Basil's brother, who taught that the Spirit proceeds out of the Father and also "receives" from the Son. The Father is the cause, the Son is directly produced by the Father, and the Spirit proceeds from the Father and derives his being from the Son. Kelly contends that after Gregory of Nyssa, "the regular teaching of the eastern church is that the procession of the Holy Spirit is 'out of the Father through the Son.'"[49] Gregory of Nyssa affirms that all divine activity proceeds from all three persons: "The divine action begins from the Father, proceeds from the Son, and is completed in the Holy Spirit; none of the persons possesses a separate operation of his own, but one identical energy passes through all Three."[50]

Hilary of Poitiers

Trinitarian development in the West moved much more slowly. Hilary of Poitiers (ca. 315–67), who was elected bishop of his native city in 350, was exiled to Asia Minor by Emperor Constantius because of his efforts to organize resistance against the Arians in Gaul. During his three years in Asia Minor, Hilary wrote his principal theological treatise, *On the Trinity*. After returning to Poitiers, he spent the rest of his life struggling against the Arians until his death in 367.

His work, *On the Trinity*, was largely directed against the positions of the Arians, although it can be considered as the most complete synthesis of the mystery thus far produced in the West. Hilary centers his attention on the distinction between the Father and the Son and on the equality of the two persons in the one Godhead. The term *homooúsios* is seldom employed by him because of the widely differing interpretations that the term had been given. His treatment of the Holy Spirit is rather infrequent compared with the ample consideration of the Father and the Son whose unity in the divine nature he consistently affirms. Moreover, he seems unwilling to speak of the Holy Spirit as a person, viewing him as the gift from the Father through the Son. This rather "imperfect alignment" of the Holy Spirit with the Father and the Son detracts from the strength of his presentation; however, given the fact that the work is for the most part a polemical treatise against the Arians, it served as a valuable source for his successors in the battle against that pervasive heresy.[51]

Another Western contributor to the discussion on the Trinity is Marius Victorinus, who was born in Africa and came to Rome in his later years (ca. 350) as an instructor of rhetoric. In ca. 355 he was converted to Christianity and began immediately to enter into debates with the Arians. He was a Neo-Platonic philosopher who, as a Christian, made a number of sweeping modifications in the Neo-Platonic paradigm. His doctrine of the eternal generation of the Son was an important contribution. For Victorinus the Father is the divine essence, absolute and unconditioned, invisible and unknowable. The Son is the eternal object of the Father's will and the image by which he knows himself. The Spirit, who is given less attention by Victorinus, is described as the link between the Father and the Son who completes the circle within the Divine Being. The character of the three persons (whom he prefers to call "subsistences") can be summed up as Existence, Life, and Understanding. These three characteristics are shared by all three so that in God there is only one substance, one will and life, and one knowledge.[52] The work of Victorinus served as an important source of the momentous trinitarian contribution of Augustine.

Observations

The practice of baptism in the name of the Father, the Son, and the Holy Spirit—which became the norm in the second century—propelled the development of trinitarian theology. The early fathers such as Justin and Tertullian tended to subordinate the Son and the Holy Spirit to the Father, and even Irenaeus never clearly articulated the divinity of the Holy Spirit. Origen, the first great Christian theologian, has been accused by some for having inserted subordinationism into his portrayal of the Trinity, although this has been denied by others. He did insist, however, on the existence of a human soul in Christ and on the eternal distinction of the three divine persons. During the third century, the approaches to the Trinity were, for the most part, tinged with either modalism or subordinationism. The latter was more difficult to detect because of the Neo-Platonic mind-set that was so pervasive at the time.

Arius preached what has been called an intolerable subordinationism, and this precipitated the Council of Nicaea (325). At this first ecumenical gathering, the consubstantiality of the Father and the Son was defined. Between Nicaea and Constantinople I (381) there were interminable debates especially in the East over the meaning of *homooúsios*. The second ecumenical council condemned again those denying the full divinity of Christ, and it proclaimed that the Holy Spirit is to be worshiped and glorified along with the Father as a single Godhead. The Spirit, however, was not explicitly called "God," nor was the Spirit explicitly termed "consubstantial" with the Father. Gregory of Nyssa, among the Eastern church fathers, gives us the clearest description of the divinity of the Holy Spirit, who "proceeds out of the Father through the Son."

NOTES

1. Michael W. Holmes, ed., *The Apostolic Fathers* (2d ed.; trans. J. B. Lightfoot and J. R. Harmer; Grand Rapids: Baker, 1989), 79–118.
2. Justin, *First Apology; Second Apology; Dialogue with Trypho* in *The Ante-Nicene Fathers* (vol. 1; ed. A. Roberts and J. Donaldson; repr., Grand Rapids: Eerdmans, 1989), 163–270.

3. J. N. D. Kelly, *Early Christian Doctrines* (San Francisco: Harper & Row, 1978), 104.

4. Ibid., 107.

5. Robert M. Grant, *Irenaeus of Lyons* (New York: Routledge, 1997), 46–53.

6. Kelly, *Early Christian Doctrines*, 104.

7. The Montanists were revivalists who believed that the end of the world was near. They stressed fasting and other forms of asceticism and disregarded the organizational dimensions of the Church.

8. William La Due, *The Chair of Saint Peter* (Maryknoll, N.Y.: Orbis, 1999), 30.

9. *The Ante-Nicene Fathers* (vol. 3; ed. A. Roberts and J. Donaldson; repr., New York: Scribner's, 1926), 621.

10. Kelly, *Early Christian Doctrines*, 110–13.

11. Johannes Quasten, *Patrology* (vol. 2; Westminster, Md.: Christian Classics, 1990), 286.

12. Ibid., 324–27.

13. Ibid., 37.

14. Ibid., 58.

15. Henry Crouzel, *Origen* (trans. A. S. Worrall; San Francisco: Harper & Row, 1989), 10.

16. Quasten, *Patrology*, 78.

17. Ibid., 76.

18. Aloys Grillmeier, *Christ in Christian Tradition*, (vol. 1; trans. J. Bowden; Atlanta: John Knox, 1975), 139.

19. Ibid., 140.

20. Ibid., 146.

21. Kelly, *Early Christian Doctrines*, 128–31.

22. Ibid., 131.

23. Ibid., 132.

24. Crouzel, *Origen*, 185.

25. Ibid., 191.

26. Ibid., 193.

27. Berthold Altaner, *Patrology* (trans. H. Graef; New York: Herder and Herder, 1960), 233–34.

28. Crouzel, *Origen*, 202.

29. Ibid., 203.

30. La Due, *The Chair of Saint Peter*, 40. Dionysius, the bishop of Alexandria (d. 264–65), was not related to Dionysius of Rome who was pope from 260–268.

31. *The Ante-Nicene Fathers*, vol. 7 (ed. A. Roberts and J. Donaldson; repr., New York: Scribner's, 1926), 365–66.

32. Crouzel, *Origen,* 203.

33. Grillmeier, *Christ in Christian Tradition*, vol. 1, 225–26.

34. Ibid., 227.

35. G. Alberigo et al., *Decrees of the Ecumenical Councils*, vol. 1 (ed. N. P. Tanner; Washington, D.C.: Georgetown University Press, 1990), *5.

36. J. N. D. Kelly, *Early Christian Creeds* (3d ed.; New York: Longman, 1972), 256.

37. Ibid., 258.

38. Grillmeier, *Christ in Christian Tradition,* vol. 1, 270.

39. Ibid., 310.

40. Kelly, *Early Christian Creeds*, 293–94.

41. Ibid., 294.

42. Alberigo et al., *Decrees,* *31.

43. Ibid., *24.

44. Yves Congar, *I Believe in the Holy Spirit*, vol. 1 (trans. D. Smith; New York: Seabury Press, 1983), 75.

45. Alberigo et al., *Decrees,* *28.

46. Kelly, *Early Christian Creeds*, 343.

47. Ibid.

48. Kelly, *Early Christian Doctrines*, 259–61.

49. Ibid., 263.

50. Ibid., 267.

51. *Patrology* (vol. 4; ed. A. Di Berardino; trans. P. Solari; Westminster, Md.: Christian Classics, 1991), 54–61.

52. Kelly, *Early Christian Doctrines,* 270–71.

4

AUGUSTINE OF HIPPO AND CONCILIAR TEACHING TO 681

Augustine

Augustine of Hippo (354–430) wrote his masterful treatise on the Trinity over a period of some twenty years (400–420). He began it as a young man and completed it when he was elderly.[1] Although his *Confessions* and his *City of God* are more widely read and well known, his "description of the trinitarian image in man was adopted as standard in scholastic textbooks."[2] Its long years of preparation account for some of the unfinished qualities in the work, but it stands as a study of incomparable genius. *On the Trinity* was not intended as a polemical piece, but rather represents Augustine's lifelong personal spiritual quest for the triune God. Unlike Hilary's *De Trinitate,* which focused principally on the demonstration of the divinity of the Son, the bishop of Hippo stressed throughout the equality of the three persons, each of whom possesses the whole substance of the Godhead.

The philosophical background is the Neo-Platonism of Plotinus (205–70), who began with the One, from whom the Mind proceeds; the self-conscious Mind then serves as the point of departure for the rest of his grand design. However, we are reminded by the theologian David Coffey that it is possible that Augustine discovered the concept of trinitarian relations from Gregory of Nazianzus (d. ca. 390), who spoke of the divine persons' bearing toward one another as relations.[3] One of Augustine's more critical contributions consists in the distinction between substantive and relative terms in the discussion of the Trinity. For him some predicates point to substance while others refer to unchangeable relations. Father and Son are related to each other through generation, and the Spirit is related to the other two as Gift.[4] According to Coffey, Augustine "insists, first, that there can be no distinction in God according to substance, and second, that the distinctions that do exist, those among the persons, pertain to relation, which must therefore be a different kind of relation, a non-accidental kind."[5] Augustine had not advanced to the point where he affirmed that the persons of the Trinity are actually subsistent relations, but he was certainly moving in that direction. Perhaps his most important contribution was his insight that, searching within the nature of the human soul, one can discover something of a reflection of the Trinity, for God is indeed manifested "in the things that are made" (Rom 1:20). In our own being, our knowledge, and our love, we can discern an image of the Trinity. Augustine proposes a couple of triads that reflect the triune life of God, but perhaps the most revealing is that of memory, understanding, and will—that is, the mind's remembering, understanding, and willing itself.[6]

Memory is the first term, understanding the second, and willing the third. Our insight into the Trinity is possible to the extent that divine grace facilitates our discovery of the image of the triune God within our own souls. "The human trinity of memory, understanding, and will: these are three specific functions which make up or constitute the spiritual being of a man, and they differ from one another essentially in themselves. . . . Augustine discerns a real image of the Father in memory, of the Son in understanding, and of the Spirit in will."[7] The Son is the expression of the Father, and in taking human flesh, he became the spoken Word. The Spirit can best be understood as Gift, whose role is to unite the Father and the Son. Thus, the Spirit can be called the bond of mutual love wherein the Father and the Son love one another.

In book 7 of *On the Trinity*, Augustine delves into the question of the relationships among the divine figures. The terms "Father" and "Son" describe the relationship between the first and second persons. Also, when the second person is called the "Word," this connotes a relationship. The Holy Spirit is the supreme charity joining together the Father and the Son. Moreover, the Holy Spirit brings devout Christians into union with the three divine persons.[8] The word "person" is simply a term of convenience so that we can answer the question, "Three what?" Augustine affirms that while the Greeks speak about one being and three substances in the Trinity, the Latins talk of one being or substance in three divine persons. When we ask the question, "Three what?" we attempt to discover some name that can be attributed to all three, and no such name comes quickly to mind. The differing usage in the East and the West was largely developed to deal with heretical conflicts. The three divine figures are often called substances in the East and persons in the West. Augustine expresses his own preference for the term "person" rather than "substance" as applied to the three.[9] If we do not reserve one particular word for signifying the three individuals, we would then be reduced to silence.

In the concluding book of *De Trinitate*, after bringing together the images he has so deftly drawn, Augustine confesses that the reflection of the Trinity in human nature is nonetheless not at all adequate to portray the splendid reality of the divine Triad. The Son is understanding, begotten from the understanding of the Father. The Holy Spirit does not have the Father for memory and the Son for understanding, but remembers and understands as a distinct individual. Accordingly, the Holy Spirit is not just related to the Father nor to the Son, but is the Spirit of both of them. This implies that the Spirit is the common charity by which the Father and Son love each other.[10] For the bishop of Hippo, each of the divine figures possesses memory, understanding, and charity as his own. Augustine adds the following:

> In this triad only the Son is called the Word, and only the Holy Spirit is called the gift of God. And only the Father is called the one from whom the Word is born and from whom the Spirit principally proceeds. I added "principally" because we have found that the Holy Spirit also proceeds from the Son. But this too is given to the Son by the Father. . . . He [i.e., the Father] so begot him that their common gift would proceed from him too and the Holy Spirit would be Spirit of them both.[11]

In a memorable article written many years ago for the *Dictionnaire de theologie catholique*, Eugène Portalié (1852–1909) gives a stunning portrait of Augustine and his work that has hardly been surpassed throughout the twentieth century. He asserts that Augustine's most notable contributions in the area of trinitarian theology are these: (1) He sets out the concept of the divine nature before a study of the persons; (2) he insists that all the divine actions and operations outside the Divine Being are to be attributed to the entire Trinity; and (3) he provides a strikingly ample explanation of the divine processions.[12]

Augustine deals with and investigates the divine nature before he analyzes the three persons. For him the term "God" means first of all the Godhead, whom he describes personally but not in terms of any of the three persons in particular. The symbol called the *Quicumque Creed*, which begins by professing faith in the Godhead common to all three persons, was inspired by the work of Augustine.[13] According to his approach, the oneness of the Divinity is immediately apparent in that the absolute perfections of the divine nature are set forth first, prior to a consideration of the persons, for example, the divine omniscience, omnipotence, and divine providence. The Eastern authors, on the other hand, begin with the Father—thus tending to create the impression that the Father alone is God in the fullest sense. While the danger of the Eastern approach is that there seems to be an ingrained tendency toward subordinationism vis-à-vis the Son and the Holy Spirit, the problem with Augustine's presentation (and after him, with all of Western theology) is that there is a danger in portraying the Godhead independently of the three persons. This can create the impression of a fourth individual in God, or the risk of absorbing the three persons into a new version of Sabellianism.[14]

In dealing with the divine activities outside the Godhead, Augustine asserts that one can attribute to each of the divine persons a role in the external operations, in accordance with the particular manner in which each person possesses the divine nature. The Greek fathers seem to stress the part that each person performs in the external divine actions, almost to the point where each is portrayed as having a distinctive role. For example, only the Son was responsible for the appearances to the patriarchs in the Old Testament, and the Holy Spirit alone descended at Pentecost. For Augustine the manifestations outside the Deity are the work of all three divine persons, although certain roles can be "appropriated" to one or the other because of the particular nature of the appearance.

Augustine emphasized the psychological approach to the understanding of the divine processions, and Thomas Aquinas refined it. The Son was born of the Father in terms of an act of understanding, while the Holy Spirit proceeds from the Father and the Son as the substantial term of their love.[15] With these two processions, the fullness and the richness of the Divine Being is revealed. The approach that Augustine inaugurated through his acute and sensitive analysis of the operations of the human soul—the mind, the memory, the intellect, and the will—opened up for Christian believers a spectacular portrait of the triad of interrelated individuals in the divine nature.

Cyril of Alexandria

In the East at this time, we witness the rise of Cyril (ca. 375–444), who became patriarch of Alexandria in 412. No one less than Athanasius had been his principal mentor. Cyril's theological debate with Nestorius, the patriarch of Constantinople, began shortly after Nestorius was promoted to the patriarchal see in 428. In Nestorius's judgment, it was improper and incorrect to call Mary the mother of God *(theotokos)*, for she was only the mother of Christ. The respected Christian historian Karl Baus notes that in Cyril's second letter to Nestorius (430), the bishop of Alexandria reminded him that he must conform his teaching to the time-honored pronouncements of the Fathers. It was they who called Mary the *theotokos* because she had given birth to the body to which the Logos was united.[16] Nestorius's response harshly rejected the term *theotokos*, because for him it implied that the divine nature itself was born and died—subjecting it to change. This eventually led to the Council of Ephesus in June 431.

Council of Ephesus—431

Nestorius's position was reviewed by the bishops assembled at the Council of Ephesus and judged to be heretical. Nestorius was therefore stripped of his episcopal dignity and removed from office. The synod then formally prohibited the production or promulgation of any creed other than the one defined by the holy fathers at Nicaea.[17] Over the next one hundred years, there was a notable migration of Nestorian Christians into Persia. This congregation survives today as the Assyrian Church of the East, with members in Iraq, Iran, Syria, Lebanon, and elsewhere.

The years between 431 and the Council of Chalcedon in 451 were stormy indeed. The Antiochians sometimes insisted on the absolute integrity of the human nature of Christ to the point at which the substantial unity of the two natures in the one person was apparently compromised. For example, Nestorius in several contexts seemed to hold that each of the two natures in Christ had its own *prosopon* (i.e., a fully individualized concrete nature), which would have made it difficult to understand how there could be any substantial unity in Jesus. The Alexandrians, on the other hand, stressed the unity of the divinity and the humanity of Christ, occasionally to the extent that his humanity was all but swallowed up in his divinity. Cyril, for example, frequently spoke of the "one nature" of the Word incarnate. Thus, the parties waged a twenty-year battle between the two ecumenical councils.

The teachings of Theodore of Mopsuestia (d. 428) of the Antiochian school were pitted against the writings of Cyril of Alexandria, and the debates were interminable. Tensions crystallized around a monk named Eutyches (ca. 378–454), who was the abbot of a large and influential monastery in Constantinople. The abbot also had a considerable following among the monks of the capital. For Eutyches the doctrine concerning Christ could be articulated in a simple proposition: "I confess that before the union our Lord consisted of two natures, but after the union I confess one single nature."[18] That is, the original components for the Incarnation were the divine Word and an integral human nature, but in the union of the two natures, the divine so predominated that in Christ there is only one nature, and that divine.

Council of Chalcedon—451

After Eutyches was condemned by a local synod in 448, he appealed to Rome, Alexandria, and Jerusalem. Emperor Theodosius II (408–50) exonerated Eutyches, and a synod at Ephesus in August of 449 declared him to be orthodox. Pope Leo I's *Tome to Flavian*, written to the patriarch of Constantinople in June 449, outlined the orthodox doctrine and pointed up the errors of Eutyches that were eventually ignored by the synod. Thus, the way seemed ready for the victory of monophysitism in the East.[19] Emperor Marcian (450–57) ordered the convocation of a new ecumenical council to settle these doctrinal conflicts. He wanted the delegates gathered for the Council of Chalcedon in October 451 to draft a new creedal formula that would counter the errors of both Nestorius and Eutyches, after the prelates in attendance had heaped praise upon Pope Leo I and Patriarch Flavian.

> We all with one voice teach the confession of one and the same Son, our Lord Jesus Christ: the same perfect in divinity and perfect in humanity, the same truly God and truly man, of a rational soul and a body; consubstantial with the Father as regards his divinity, and the same consubstantial with us as regards his humanity; like us in all regards except for sin; begotten before the ages from the Father as regards his divinity, and in the last days the same for us and for our salvation from Mary, the virgin God bearer [*theotokos*], as regards his humanity . . . acknowledged in two natures which undergo no confusion, no change, no division, no separation . . . the property of both natures is preserved and comes together into a single person and a single substantial being.[20]

In February 452 the emperor promulgated legislation enforcing the decisions of Chalcedon as imperial law. Henceforth there were to be no more public meetings or public discussions concerning the conciliar definition. Within a few months, however, dangerous pockets of resistance to the definition erupted in Constantinople, Jerusalem, and especially in Alexandria.[21] The Alexandrians were not willing to accept the doctrinal definition, and hence the church was on the threshold of a devastating schism. The wording of Chalcedon provided only a sketch of what was needed to heal the divisions. Terms like *homooúsios* and *hypostasis, physis* and *prosopon,* had been introduced into the dogmatic statements, but they were not clarified or defined. Grillmeier notes that although all of the conciliar formulas must be retained, no one of them can be considered as the definitive articulation of the constitution of Christ. "The demand for a complete reappraisal of the church's belief in Christ right up to the present is an urgent one."[22]

The Alexandrian school regarded the definition of Chalcedon as Nestorian. Reactions in Egypt and Palestine were "immediate and violent."[23] Several years after the council, the emperor called together the metropolitans of the East and the West to inquire about the reception of the definition, and the testimony of the Eastern prelates created much concern. As a matter of fact, there were in the East demands that the enactments of Chalcedon be repealed.[24] Emperor Zeno (474–91) made a special effort to address the religious divisions that were tearing the East asunder. He drafted an imperial constitution, the *Henotikon*, which purported to downplay the definition of Chalcedon and thus win back the monophysites who were certain that Chalcedon had exaggerated the distinction between the divinity and humanity of Christ. An exchange of excommunications between Pope Felix III (483–92) and the patriarch of Constantinople, Acacius, in ca. 484 created a schism between Rome and Constantinople that lasted until 519.

Council of Constantinople II—553

In the patriarchates of Antioch and Alexandria, there were sizeable majorities against Chalcedon, and during the sixth century those sees were the center of resistance. Neither Emperor Justin I (518–27) nor his favorite nephew and successor, Justinian (527–65), was able to heal the deep doctrinal divisions in the East. The Council of Constantinople

II was called by Justinian in May 553 to address the conflicts between the Alexandrians and the Chalcedonians. The majority of those invited were Eastern prelates. In the course of the deliberations, certain writings of Theodore of Mopsuestia, Theodoret, and Ibas were taken out of context for the most part and condemned as heretical in order to placate the Alexandrians. However, the delegates did condemn both Apollinarius (or Apollinaris) and Eutyches for their unwillingness to posit a full and integral human nature in Jesus. Theodore of Mopsuestia and Nestorius, on the other hand, were condemned for allegedly asserting that the union of the human and divine in Christ was merely an accidental and not a substantial one.[25]

Constantinople II declared that "the union between the Word of God and human flesh was a union of subsistence . . . without confusing the elements that came together." The delegates affirmed that "there is only one subsistence or one person." Further, "the holy synod of Chalcedon has thus made a formal statement of belief in the subsistence of our lord Jesus Christ. . . . Each of the two natures remained what it was, and in this way we understand that the Word was united to human flesh."[26] Pope Vigilius (537–55), who was not in attendance, withheld his consent for about six months before approving the acts of the council and the condemnation of Theodore of Mopsuestia and two others. Most of the churches of the West severed relations with Rome over the pope's condemnation of Theodore. Resentment over Vigilius's condemnation simmered in the West for many years. In the East the moderate Chalcedonians of Constantinople II did not win over many of the multitudes who had espoused or who were tending in the direction of monophysitism. "After Constantinople II, the canons of orthodoxy were asserted as the four gospels and the four ecumenical councils."[27]

Council of Constantinople III—680–81

The Council of Constantinople III (680–81) disposed of hybrid theories like monoenergism (one energy or principle of action in Christ) and monotheletism (one will in Christ) that became popular in the East in the seventh century. The council was rather sparsely attended because Egypt, Africa, Palestine, Syria, and most of Asia Minor were at that time overrun by the Muslims. The council fathers did, however, define that there are two wills and two natural principles of action in Christ. The acts of the council were approved by Pope

Leo II (682–83), and Emperor Constantine IV promulgated the decrees throughout the empire.

Observations

Augustine's outstanding work in the West insisted on the equality of the three persons. He penetrated within the human soul to find a stunning reflection of the Triad in the human memory (the Father), the understanding (the Son), and the will (the Holy Spirit). He also developed the approach to the distinction among the divine persons as one based on the concept of relation. (Thomas Aquinas then perfected the notion of the three divine persons as three subsistent relations.) Meanwhile in the East, the Council of Ephesus (431) condemned Patriarch Nestorius (a follower of the school of Antioch) for his views on the moral (rather than substantial) unity of the two natures in Christ. Cyril of Alexandria, on the other hand, repeated again and again that there was "one nature of the Word incarnate." The Alexandrians and Antiochians heatedly debated their differences until the battle was formally joined at the Council of Chalcedon (451). There Christ was pronounced as truly God and truly man—consubstantial with us and with the Father. Many of the Alexandrians opposed the definition of the council and severed communion to form the monophysite churches. The attempts of Constantinople II (553) and Constantinople III (680–81) to effect a reunion with the monophysites were unsuccessful.

At the end of the seventh century, it was commonly held in the East and the West that the authentic teachings concerning the Incarnation and the Trinity were to be found in the four Gospels and in the pronouncements of the first four ecumenical councils. We may be inclined to agree with Grillmeier that although the statements of the general councils are always to be preserved and reviewed, there is great need for a restatement in our day of the central doctrines of the Incarnation and the Trinity. In conclusion, in those early years christological and trinitarian developments were almost inseparable, and hence the one can hardly be treated without reference to the other.

NOTES

1. Augustine of Hippo, *The Trinity* (ed. J. Rotelle; trans. E. Hill; Brooklyn, N.Y.: New City Press, 1991), 20.

2. Ibid., 19.

3. David Coffey, *Deus Trinitas* (New York: Oxford University Press, 1999), 68. Gregory's *Theological Orations*, Sermons 27–31 date from 380, and are perhaps his finest reflections on the Trinity. It must be kept in mind, nonetheless, that Augustine's knowledge of Greek was quite limited.

4. Augustine of Hippo, *Augustine: Later Works* (trans. and ed. J. Burnaby; Philadelphia: Westminster, 1955), 21.

5. Coffey, *Deus Trinitas*, 69.

6. Augustine of Hippo, *Augustine: Later Works*, 27.

7. Ibid., 31.

8. Augustine, *The Trinity*, 224.

9. Ibid., 228.

10. Ibid., 418.

11. Ibid., 419.

12. Eugène Portalié, *A Guide to the Thought of Saint Augustine* (trans. R. J. Bastian; Westport, Conn.: Greenwood Press, 1960), 130.

13. The *Quicumque* Creed is a summary of doctrine characterizing the Latin approach to the mystery of the Trinity. It was an original Latin composition that dates from the end of the fifth century. The author is unknown.

14. Portalié, *A Guide to the Thought of Saint Augustine*, 132.

15. Ibid., 133–34.

16. Karl Baus, "Part Two: The Theological Disputes in the East and West to the Middle of the Fifth Century," *History of the Church* (vol. 2; ed. H. Jedin and J. Dolan; London: Burns & Oates, 1980), 101–2.

17. G. Alberigo et al., *Decrees of the Ecumenical Councils*, vol. 1, ed. N. P. Tanner (Washington, D.C.: Georgetown University Press, 1990), *65.

18. Baus, "Part Two," 111.

19. Aloys Grillmeier, *Christ in Christian Tradition*, vol. 1, trans. J. Bowden (Atlanta: John Knox Press, 1975), 528.

20. Alberigo et al., *Decrees*, *85.

21. Aloys Grillmeier, *Christ in Christian Tradition* (vol. 2, pt. 1; trans. P. Allen and J. Cawte; Atlanta: John Knox, 1987), 98, 105.

22. Grillmeier, *Christ in Christian Tradition*, vol. 1, 556.

23. A. H. M. Jones, *The Later Roman Empire 284–602* (vol. 1; 1964; reprint, Baltimore: Johns Hopkins University Press, 1990), 334.

24. Grillmeier, *Christ in Christian Tradition*, vol. 2, pt. 1, 241.

25. Alberigo et al., *Decrees,* *114–16.

26. Ibid., *116-18.

27. Aloys Grillmeier with Theresia Hainthaler, *Christ in Christian Tradition* (vol. 2, pt. 2; trans. J. Cawte and P. Allen; Louisville, Ky.: Westminster John Knox, 1995), 475.

5
TRINITARIAN DEVELOPMENTS IN THE EARLY MIDDLE AGES

The fallout after Ephesus (431) and Chalcedon (451) was enormous. In the second half of the fifth century, many of those attached to Theodore of Mopsuestia and Nestorius separated themselves from the adherents of Ephesus and Chalcedon. After the condemnation of Theodore at Constantinople II in 553, a separated Nestorian church began to take a more discernible form. The Nestorians and their bishops could not accept the condemnation of their beloved Theodore, nor could they give their allegiance to the doctrine of *theotokos.* Eventually the Nestorians found a more amenable home in the Persian kingdom.

The losses to the monophysites in the sixth century were even more devastating. Large numbers of Christians within the patriarchate of Alexandria found the definition of Chalcedon unacceptable because of the affirmation that the two discreet natures in Christ experienced "no confusion, no change." This for them amounted to a return to Nestorianism because it severed the unity in Christ that their great teacher, Cyril, had affirmed so unambiguously. The monophysite church of Egypt actively evangelized in Ethiopia and other surrounding regions. During the Middle Ages, this grouping of communities came to be called the Coptic church. Another extremely active monophysite church arose in Syria during the reign of Justinian (527–65) under the leadership of Jacob Baradai, an untiring evangelizer. These "Jacobites" migrated to Persia and undertook the conversion of a number of Arab communities.

The church in the West also was not without its doctrinal crises in the area of trinitarian teaching. A wealthy Spanish gentlemen named Priscillian popularized in the latter fourth century a Sabellian view of the Trinity, whereby the Father, Son, and Holy Spirit were to be considered merely as three modes or facets of the same Deity. Priscillian's teaching spread throughout Spain and even won over several Spanish bishops. Thus, the Priscillianist sect became extremely influential in Spain in the second half of the fourth century, and it was not until Priscillian and several of his colleagues were brought to trial at Trier on criminal charges that the principal agents of the movement were taken out of circulation. The first synod of Toledo (ca. 400) issued anathemas dealing with Priscillianism, including a strong condemnation of its Sabellian views on the Trinity.

It is not clear whether or not the creed that was supposedly adopted at this synod actually contained the reference to the Holy Spirit as proceeding from the Father and the Son.[1] In any event, the symbol set forth at the third synod of Toledo in 589 declares in explicit terms that the Holy Spirit proceeds from the Father and the Son.[2] The *filioque* formulation became quite common in Gaul and was formally adopted by the Frankish church at the Council of Aachen in 809. Pope Leo III (795–816), however, was not willing to add it to the recitation of the creed in Rome. After Photius became patriarch of Constantinople in 858, the issue of the insertion of the *filioque* into the creed surfaced as a controversy of major proportions between East and West. The procession of the Holy Spirit as articulated by the solemn profession of faith at Constantinople I (381) had affirmed that the Spirit proceeds from the Father.[3]

In 867 the patriarch of Constantinople, Photius, accused Pope Nicholas I (858–67) of heresy for imposing the *filioque* on the Bulgarian church. In fact, the patriarch attempted to excommunicate and depose the pope for having unilaterally added the *filioque* to the creed. For Photius this amounted to the destruction of the Father's role as the sole principle in the Trinity. Actually, the Latin missionaries in Bulgaria were the ones who had brought the modified creed, and this was all Photius needed to accuse the pope of heresy.[4] It seems that Benedict XIII (1012–24) was the first pope to insert the *filioque* into the symbol of faith used in Rome. At the general Council of Lyons II (1274), which was to discuss reunion with the Byzantines, the procession of the Holy Spirit was formally decreed as proceeding from the Father and the Son.[5] The Byzantine emperor Michael VIII and his ecclesiastical representatives agreed to this declaration because the emperor urgently required the military assistance of the West to fight off the threats of Charles of Anjou. His clergy and his people back home, however, refused to go along with the doctrinal concessions that the emperor had made, and the addition of the *filioque* to the symbol of Nicaea and Constantinople I was firmly rejected by the Eastern faithful. At the Council of Ferrara-Florence (1438–42), the Byzantine delegates were once again pressured to agree to the procession of the Holy Spirit from the Father and the Son, rather than from the Father alone.[6] The Byzantine clergy and faithful spurned the agreement, retaining their traditional belief in the procession of the Spirit from the Father alone. The same can be said of the decree for the Jacobites, which insisted on the *filioque*. In the estimate of most historians of the Eastern church, these decrees did not have much tangible effect.

Augustine's trinitarian theology promoted the *filioque*, for he affirmed that the Father endowed the Son with the capacity to coproduce the Holy Spirit. Although the Father is the one from whom the Spirit proceeds principally, Augustine taught that the Son is also responsible for the procession of the Spirit. This approach was widely accepted in the West in the fifth and sixth centuries. The text that was often cited is John 16:14: "He [the Spirit] shall receive of mine." In the East, on the other hand, the thinking was quite different. Gregory of Nyssa (ca. 335–94), for example, insisted that the Father "stood in the relation of cause to the other two."[7] It was considered absolutely incontrovertible that the Father alone is the fountainhead and sole source of the Deity. From the Council of Ferrara-Florence to the twentieth century, the *filioque* issue was hardly addressed. The Eastern churches remained convinced that in any case, the issue should have been settled jointly and after a free and full deliberation according to the procedure of the early general councils. Prominent Orthodox scholar Boris Bobrinskoy points out that in 1981, at the sixteenth centennial of the Council of Constantinople I, Pope John Paul II recited the creed without the *filioque*.[8]

From the time of Maximus the Confessor (580–662) and John of Damascus (675–749), the Eastern theologians have been offended by the Western doctrine of the *filioque*. For them the Father is the sole cause of the Son and the Holy Spirit.[9] This was true of Gregory of Cyprus (1241–90), who condemned the *filioque* declaration of the Council of Lyons II. Gregory of Palamas (1296–1359), the archbishop of Thessalonica, insisted that the person of the Spirit proceeds from the Father alone, as did Mark of Ephesus (1392–1444), the last representative of the Byzantine tradition on the eve of the fall of Byzantium (1453).[10]

Among modern Orthodox scholars, some hold to a strict traditionalism going back to Photius, while others are not so adamantly opposed to the *filioque*. Based on texts such as John 15:26, in which the Spirit is said to proceed from the Father, the Orthodox tradition feels that it is incorrect to think of the begetting of the Son first and then to address the procession of the Spirit. For the Orthodox, "the Holy Spirit proceeds from the Father alone, in a complete simultaneity of origin with the Son."[11] They do not believe that the Father transmitted to the Son the power to be coprinciple of the Holy Spirit. In terms of the eternal processions, the Son proceeds from the Father alone, and so does the Spirit. Regarding the temporal missions of the divine persons, the Father sends the Son who sends the Spirit. Or from another perspective, Eastern theology sees the Father dispatching the Spirit who sends the Son.[12]

Whereas the highly regarded Orthodox theologian Sergius Bulgakov (1871–1944) does not consider the *filioque* an absolute obstacle to the reunion with Rome, his eminent counterpart Vladimir Lossky (1903–58) teaches that the notion of the procession of the Holy Spirit from the Father and the Son is simply unacceptable to Orthodox theology.[13] Listen to the words of Lossky:

> The positive approach employed by the filioquist triadology brings about a certain rationalization of the dogma of the Trinity. . . . One has the impression that the heights of theology have been deserted in order to descend to the level of religious philosophy. If in the former approach [i.e., the Western] faith seeks understanding in order to transpose revelation into the plane of philosophy, in the latter approach [i.e., the Eastern] understanding seeks the realities of faith, in order to be transformed by becoming more and more open to the mysteries of revelation. . . . It is understandable that a divergence in this culminating point, insignificant as it may seem at first sight, should have a decisive importance. The difference between the two conceptions of the Trinity determines, on both sides, the whole character of theological thought.[14]

In Lossky's judgment, causality within the Divine Being is to be predicated of the Father alone. The Western description of processions through the intellect and through the will is for him a philosophical anthropomorphism.[15] For Lossky such deductions only obscure matters. Orthodox theology posits an important distinction between the essence of God and his energies. While the hypostatic procession is from the Father alone, the energetic procession is from the Father to the Son and goes forth in the Holy Spirit. When the Eastern fathers speak of the Son as image of the Father and the Holy Spirit as image of the Son, this refers to the order of divine manifestation. In the realm of divine manifestation, it is indeed possible to establish an order of persons—from the Father to the Son and then through the Spirit.[16] Lossky concludes by affirming that the *filioque* is a diriment (i.e., invalidating) impediment to the reunion of East and West, until "the West, which has been frozen so long in dogmatic isolation, ceases to consider Byzantine theology as an absurd innovation and recognizes that it only expressed the truths of tradition, which can be found in a less explicit form in the fathers of the first century of the church."[17] The theology of the Trinity still stands as one of the disputed issues between East and West.

Early Creedal Expressions in the West

Symbol Quicumque

The trinitarian development in the West after Augustine was greatly influenced by the *Symbol Quicumque*, a rhythmical Latin composition from the latter fifth century, composed by an unknown author. Probably written in southern Gaul, it embodies the Augustinian approach by speaking first of the one God and then of the divine persons, who are portrayed as equal in glory and equally eternal. Each of the persons is God, yet they are not three gods, but one God. The Father is uncreated, the Son is begotten by the Father alone, and the Holy Spirit proceeds from the Father and the Son.[18] The *Quicumque* was widely used in the Latin liturgies and therefore had considerable influence in the shaping of popular faith in the West.

Creed of the Eleventh Council of Toledo—675

Another creed that was extremely important in the development of trinitarian faith in the West was the creed of the Eleventh Council of Toledo in 675. It built on the previous declarations of trinitarian faith promulgated by earlier synods held in Toledo from the year 400 on. The symbol of the eleventh synod articulates in authentic fashion the Latin approach to the mysteries of the Trinity and the Incarnation. It is said to reflect "the deepest insights and the clearest affirmations ever proposed by any document of the West, as regards these two mysteries."[19] It begins by professing faith in the one Trinity of three persons. The Father is identified as the source and origin of the Godhead, who has begotten the Son from his own substance. At no time did the

Father exist without the Son, who is equal to the Father. One and equal with the Father and the Son is the Holy Spirit, who proceeds from both and is known as the love and sanctity of the Father and the Son. While they are called three persons in view of their relations, belief in the one divine nature or substance is proclaimed. Although the persons are distinguished, the Godhead is not divided. Each of the persons has distinctive characteristics. The Father has eternity without birth, the Son has eternity with birth, and the Holy Spirit has eternal procession without birth.[20]

From Anselm to the Council of Lyons II—1274

Anselm of Canterbury

With the rise of scholastic theology in the eleventh century, a new surge of activity occurred in the area of trinitarian thought. Perhaps the most important theologian of the eleventh century was Anselm of Canterbury (1033–1109), who can be considered a disciple of Augustine. The Benedictine abbot perceived in the Divine Being a memory, an understanding, and a love of itself, in which he recognized the Father, the Son, and the Holy Spirit. Their essence is identical, but they are distinguished in that one essence by virtue of the fact that there is a *genitor*, a *genitus*, and a *procedens*, that is, one who generates, one who is generated, and one who proceeds. Thus, they are identical in the one essence, yet they are not confused.[21] Anselm concludes that "there is a unity because of the unity of essence; a trinity because of the three I know not what."[22] It was difficult for the abbot to speak of three "persons" because, according to his understanding of the term, persons exist separately from each other. In his judgment, persons must be considered individual substances.

For Anselm the Father, Son, and Holy Spirit are equally God. The only differences are those relationships due to origin or procession. It is impossible to be identical with the one from whom one has one's being. The opposition of relationship is what establishes the differences within the unity of God.[23] Moreover, Anselm affirms that the Spirit proceeds equally from the Father and the Son as from one principle. This teaching, according to Yves Congar, "does not really contain the traditional idea of the monarchy of the Father and it is a long way from the Greek understanding of the mystery."[24] Congar also points out that Anselm's understanding of the formula "from the Father through the Son" manifests his unawareness of the importance that approach had in Greek patristic literature. For Anselm the Holy Spirit proceeds immediately from the divinity of the Father and immediately from the divinity of the Son. He calls the Eastern formulation misguided. Congar further notes that the *filioque* issue was dispatched rather quickly by Anselm, "as has frequently been the case in Western Catholic circles until our time."[25]

Richard of St. Victor

Another important medieval contributor to the development of trinitarian thought is Richard of St. Victor (d. 1173), who wrote a magnificent monograph, *On the Trinity*, toward the end of his life. Richard was a monk in the celebrated Abbey of Saint Victor in Paris, the center of rich theological speculation in the twelfth century. For Richard it is essential that there be a plurality in God through the existence of a second person, who must be the equal of the Father in order to be the term of the Father's perfect love.[26] He proceeds to show that the concept of perfect love or charity can open for us an understanding of the second and third persons of the Trinity. The Father represents love that is simply given, that is, gratuitous love, while the love that is received and given is the Son. And finally, the love that is purely received is the Spirit.[27] Richard insists that where there is no plurality of persons, there can be no charity. He defines "person" as one who exists in himself alone, according to a certain mode of reasonable existence. Each of the three is differentiated from the other by a property that cannot be communicated. Although he distinguishes among the persons by means of their principle of origin, he further employs an analysis of love in its absolute perfection: "This special way of existing which characterizes the divine Persons consists in the manner of living and realizing Love. That Love is either pure grace or it is received and giving, or it is purely received and due."[28]

Observations

After the doctrinal decisions at Ephesus (431) and Chalcedon (451), the Nestorians and the monophysites left the great church in droves, establishing themselves as distinct Christian communities in Africa, the Middle East, and Persia. Under the influence of Augustine, belief in the procession of the Holy Spirit from the Father and the Son (i.e., the *filioque*) became popular in Spain and Gaul but did not enter the creed recited in Rome until the eleventh century. The ecumenical

Councils of Lyons II (1274) and Ferrara-Florence (1438–42) forged agreements with the Eastern Orthodox over the *filioque* issue, but these agreements were soundly rejected by the clerics and the faithful in the East. Many Orthodox theologians today continue to find the *filioque* position unacceptable.

NOTES

1. H. Denzinger and A. Schönmetzer, *Enchiridion Symbolorum*, 32d ed. (Freiburg: Herder, 1963), no. 188.

2. Ibid., no. 470.

3. G. Alberigo et al., *Decrees of the Ecumenical Councils*, vol. 1 (ed. N. P. Tanner; Washington, D.C.: Georgetown University Press, 1990), *24.

4. Hans-Georg Beck, "Part Four: The Early Byzantine Church," *History of the Church* (vol. 2; ed. H. Jedin and J. Dolan; London: Burns & Oates, 1980), 189.

5. Alberigo et al., *Decrees*, vol.1, *314.

6. Denzinger and Schönmetzer, *Enchiridion*, no. 1300.

7. J. N. D. Kelly, *Early Christian Creeds* (3d ed.; New York: Longman, 1972), 359.

8. Boris Bobrinskoy, *The Mystery of the Trinity* (trans. A. P. Gythiel; Crestwood, N.Y.: St. Vladimir's Seminary Press, 1999), 282–83.

9. Ibid., 285.

10. Ibid., 288–90.

11. Ibid., 296.

12. Ibid., 298–99.

13. Ibid., 302.

14. Vladimir Lossky, "The Procession of the Holy Spirit in Trinitarian Theology," *Eastern Orthodox Theology* (ed. D. B. Clendenin; Grand Rapids: Baker, 1995), 170.

15. Ibid., 175.

16. Ibid., 179.

17. Ibid., 182.

18. J. Neuner and J. Dupuis, eds. *The Christian Faith* (5th ed.; London: Harper Collins Religious, 1990), 11.

19. Ibid., 110–114.

20. Ibid.

21. Yves Congar, *I Believe in the Holy Spirit* (vol. 3; trans. David Smith; New York: Seabury Press, 1983), 97.

22. Ibid. Congar is quoting a passage from Anselm's *Monologium*, written ca. 1070.

23. Ibid., 98.

24. Ibid., 99.

25. Ibid., 100.

26. Ibid., 103.

27. Ibid., 104.

28. Ibid., 105.

6

THOMAS AQUINAS, THE REFORMATION, AND THE ENLIGHTENMENT

Thomas Aquinas

Among the scholastics the undisputed high point of trinitarian theology is achieved in the work of Thomas Aquinas (1225–74). In his *Summa Contra Gentiles,* written between 1258 and 1264, he deals with the Trinity in book 4, chapters 1 through 26. His approach in the work is primarily that of an apologist, treating the most critical issues separating Christians from Muslims, Jews, and heretical Christians. Aquinas's definitive work on the Trinity is found in his *Summa Theologiae,* composed from 1266 to the end of his life. In the first part of his masterpiece, he deals with the Trinity in questions 26 through 43. The divine processions are his first concern. He asserts that processions in God remain within the Divine Being. Moreover, the procession of the Word reproduces the likeness of its originator. This procession is therefore called generation, and the Word proceeding is called the Son.[1]

In the spiritual world, says Aquinas, only two kinds of actions remain within the agent, that is, those of the intellect and those of the will. While the Word's procession corresponds to the action of the intellect, the procession of love is the other inward procession and corresponds to the act of the will. This second procession is not envisaged in terms of likeness, but rather of motion toward something. What proceeds as love receives the divine nature and yet is not said to be born. This procession is called "spiration," that is, the procession of the Holy Spirit. In a spiritual nature—even a divine nature—only two such actions remain within the agent. Thus, in God there are only two processions.[2]

In question 28 Aquinas deals with the issue of real relations in God. He insists that when certain actual entities are connected with and attracted by each other, such relations must be real ones. Because processions in God are in the very same divine nature, the relations rising out of the divine processions must be real. In God an existing real relation (e.g., Father/Son) is completely identical with the divine nature. Existentially, nature and relation are not two things in God but one and the same. Relation implies reference to another such that the two things stand in relative opposition to each other. Such opposition implies distinction. For example, while both fatherhood and sonship are really identified with the divine nature, their proper meanings imply opposite relationships. Finally, Aquinas affirms that in the divine nature there are four real relationships flowing out of the two processions, that is, fatherhood, sonship, spiration, and procession.[3]

Question 29 explores the meaning of the word "person" as applied to God. Aquinas teaches that individual beings with a rational nature are called persons. And since the word "person" refers to that which is most perfect in all of nature, the word can be used of God, but not in the same sense in which it is used of creatures. To subsist in a rational nature is really what it means to be a person. Although the dignity of the divine nature infinitely surpasses all others, it is still fitting to use the term "person" of God. Inasmuch as distinction in God arises only through the relation of origin, a relation in God is not an accidental entity, but is rather the divine nature itself. "Person" in this context signifies relation directly and nature indirectly. Thus, when we ask, "Three what?" the answer is "three persons." The word "person," however, when applied to God does not have precisely the same meaning that it has when it is applied to rational creatures.[4]

In question 30 Aquinas asks about the number of persons in God. He responds that because there are several real relations, it follows that there are several subsistent persons in the divine nature. Since the absolute attributes of God (e.g., goodness, wisdom) are not opposed to one another, no real distinction is drawn between them; however, the relative attributes of God (e.g., fatherhood, sonship) are both subsistent and distinct from one another. Hence, it follows that there are several subsisting figures, that is, persons, in the divine nature. These several persons are subsistent relations that in reality are distinct from one another. Thus, for example, fatherhood and sonship must belong to two persons, that is, the Father and the Son. The other two relations (i.e., spiration and procession) are in contrast to neither of these but are contrasted to each other. We conclude therefore that spiration belongs both to the Father and the Son; consequently, procession must belong to another person who is called the Holy Spirit, who proceeds as love from the other two. Thus, we conclude that there are precisely three persons in God. Each of them subsists in the divine nature and is distinct from the other two. The word "person," then, is common to all three divine figures.[5]

In his presentation of the theology of Trinity, Aquinas leans very heavily on the work of Augustine. He does advance beyond Augustine, however, in that he is able to distinguish more clearly between the two processions. Aquinas follows the bishop of Hippo in calling the Father the principle and the unbegotten one. The Son is appropriately named the Word because he proceeds from the knowing of the one who conceives him, that is, the Father. The second procession, the coming forth of the Holy Spirit, is discussed only briefly by Thomas because it is difficult to say anything meaningful about it. This procession—unlike the generation of the Son—has no specific name, and hence it is referred to by the generic term "spiration." Thus, the name of the person proceeding by love is not distinctive.

For David Coffey, Aquinas's approach to the divine processions can be set forth as follows. Generation produces a being "with a likeness in the nature of the same species." An example of this is a son proceeding from his father. The same likeness is realized in the word produced by the human intellect in the act of self-knowledge. Thus, Aquinas concludes that the procession of the divine Word can rightly be called generation, and the Word can be termed God's Son. The procession from the will, on the other hand, results in the production of "an urge or motion toward something." Therefore, what proceeds from the will in God is not generated as a son, but rather proceeds as a spirit, a vital motion or impulse. This is the case when someone is moved by love to accomplish something, and in God, what comes forth from the divine will is none other than the Holy Spirit.[6]

Aquinas insists that the Holy Spirit proceeds from both the Father and the Son, for if he did not proceed from the Son as well, he would not be distinct from the Son. He cites John 16:14, where Christ promises, "He [the Spirit] will glorify me because he shall receive of mine." The procession of spiration is the same in the Father and the Son. Thus, the Spirit proceeds from the two as the love uniting them, that is, the medium joining the two and proceeding from both. Because there are two divine processions, there are four real relations in God: paternity, filiation, spiration, and procession. The three divine persons are subsistent relations within the divine nature, really distinct from one another but only conceptually distinct from the one divine nature. In God, essence and person are not different realities, yet there is a real distinction among the persons who are identified with the one divine essence.[7]

Question 42 of the *Summa* affirms in some detail that the three divine persons are equal in that each of them is equally eternal and none exceeds the other in terms of power or magnitude. Moreover, it must be emphasized that the Father is in the Son and vice versa. Since the essence of the Father is in the Son, the Father is in the Son. Also, because the Son is identified with his essence, he is in the Father, for the Father shares the same essence. The very same kind of indwelling of persons can be predicated of the Holy Spirit, because all three share the same divine essence.

In question 43 the temporal missions of the divine persons are addressed. Although it would be inappropriate to speak of the temporal mission of the Father, it is indeed fitting to speak of the missions of the Son (John 10:36) and of the Holy Spirit (John 15:26), who are said to dwell in the souls of the just. Two elements are required for a temporal divine mission. The divine person must proceed from another divine person or persons and also must have the capacity to exist in a new way in creatures. This can be said of both the Son and the Holy Spirit. Although he did not espouse Richard of St. Victor's pervasive model of trinitarian love,

> Thomas along with other medieval theologians endorsed the radical, loving interconnectedness (*circumincessio*) of the three divine persons, something better expressed in Greek as their *perichoresis*, or reciprocal presence and interpenetration. Their innermost life is infinitely close relationship with one another in the utter reciprocity of love.[8]

Aquinas has attempted to conceive of three distinct persons in the one divine being, for that is what God has revealed to us about Godself. Following Augustine, he has drawn an analogy from the internal life of humankind to the infinite and eternal life of God. He has thus set out a portrait of the Trinity wherein the First Person is the source of divine life, the Son is the one eternally begotten from the Unoriginate Source through a process somewhat akin to human generation. The Unoriginate Source or Father, and the begotten one, the Son, bring forth eternally the term of their boundless love who is the Spirit. This Triad lives in an infinitely close relationship in the endless reciprocity of love that the Greeks term *perichoresis*. Then, through the missions of the Son and the Spirit, the divine life is continuously offered to humankind in various ways, making it possible for humans to participate in the return of love for love.

From the Reformation to the Enlightenment

Lateran Council IV—1215 and Council of Lyons II—1274

Yves Congar has pointed out that the trinitarian declarations of Lateran IV (1215) and Lyons II (1274) have not been accepted by the East.[9] At Lateran IV the Holy Spirit was said to proceed from both the Father and the Son equally and eternally, without beginning or end. The Son is identified as coequal, consubstantial, co-omnipotent, and coeternal, who is with the Father and the Spirit as one principle of all things.[10] Lyons II added that the Holy Spirit proceeds from the Father and the Son, not as from two principles, but as from one principle; not by two spirations, but by one single spiration.[11] Even the definition of the Council of Florence (1439), which involved the procession of the Holy Spirit eternally from the Father and the Son as from one principle and a single spiration, was not accepted by the Byzantine faithful.[12]

Therefore, Congar reminds us:

> It [the Roman Catholic Church] can, however, reasonably be expected to recognize that the Western formulae do not express everything that the Catholic Church believes, . . . and that it is possible for other expressions of the same faith to exist, taking different insights as to the point of departure and using other instruments of thought. There is a need to invite Orthodox theologians to engage in an analogous critical hermeneutical examination of their own doctrines. In other words, we must re-create the situation of the church fathers, who were in communion with each other while following different ways and admit the possibility of two constructions of dogmatic theology, side by side, of the same mystery, the object of the same faith.[13]

The respected historian of dogma Bertrand de Margerie notes that the Council of Florence almost completes the essential core of the Catholic Church's efforts toward trinitarian clarification.[14]

The Reformation

During the Reformation of the sixteenth century, there was surprisingly little discussion concerning the doctrine of the Trinity. Although Martin Luther's early views on the subject could be considered controversial, the *Augsburg Confession* (1530) prepared by Philip Melanchthon for the Diet of Augsburg in 1530 laid out a rather conventional approach to the Trinity. In the section entitled, "Articles of Faith and Doctrine," we read the following:

> There is one divine essence, which is called and which is truly God, and there are three persons in this one divine essence, equal in power and alike eternal: God the Father, God the Son, God the Holy Spirit. All three are one divine essence, without division, . . . of infinite power, wisdom, and goodness, one creator and preserver of all things visible and invisible. The word "person" is to be understood as the Fathers employed the term . . . , not a part or property of another but as that which exists of itself.[15]

The *Confession* goes on to say that the Son became man, and the two natures, divine and human, were inseparably united in one person. There is one Christ, true God and true man.[16] Christ sanctifies through the Holy Spirit and comforts all who believe in him, that he may bestow on them life and every grace and blessing.[17]

John Calvin's *Institutes*, which went through several editions from 1536 to 1559, sets out a similar view of the Trinity. After reviewing the differences in terminology between the East and the West, Calvin declares:

> Although they, whether Greek or Latin, differ among themselves over the word [i.e., person, substance, hypostasis], yet they quite agree in the essential matter. . . . The Father and the Son and the Spirit are one God, yet the Son is not the Father, nor the Spirit the Son, but they are differentiated by a peculiar quality. . . . When we hear "one" we ought to understand "unity of substance"; when we hear "three in one essence" the persons in the trinity are meant.[18]

Council of Trent—1545–63

In session three of the Council of Trent (February 4, 1546), the creed of Nicaea and Constantinople I was formally affirmed, with the addition of the *filioque* for the procession of the Holy Spirit.[19] It seems that no other effort was made to address the Trinity formally from 1546 through the end of the twenty-fifth session in December 1563, indicating that the doctrine of the Trinity was not a disputed issue for the Reformers.

The Enlightenment

The seventeenth century ushered in a whole new world of thought in Europe. René Descartes (1596–1650), Francis Bacon (1561–1626), Isaac Newton (1642–1727), and John Locke (1623–1704) were the major forerunners of the movement referred to as the Enlightenment. The age of the Enlightenment, which matured after 1700, communicated a confidence in the power of the human mind that was considerably enlarged by the scientific revolution. It also generated a new faith in the capacity of human reason to evaluate and challenge the time-honored standards of tradition and of the Christian churches. The *philosophes,* such as Voltaire (1694–1778) and Diderot (1713–84), attempted to apply the new canons of reason to the social, religious, and political institutions of their day in order to free humankind from all arbitrary power and influence, especially that of the ecclesiastical institutions. One of their chief goals was to communicate a new sense of confidence in the capacity of humans to lift themselves up without the aid of God and organized religion.[20]

The *Encyclopedia,* organized by Diderot and d'Alembert (1717–83)—which on completion boasted of seventeen volumes in 1772—presented the most advanced critical thought in philosophy, religion, science, and politics. It was intended to secularize the various disciplines of learning and to unleash the potential of humans and their resources so that a secularized society could bring peace and prosperity to humanity. The movement especially embraced France, England, and Germany but also found followers elsewhere in Europe and America. For the *philosophes* the greatest enemies of humankind and a formidable obstacle to human emancipation and improvement were the Christian churches. Moreover, the churches were deeply involved in the political machinery of Europe. They owned huge tracts of land and controlled vast resources in the largely agrarian economy. The clergy were seen as supporting and defending the status quo, which was frustrating great numbers of people who were yearning for something more.

Among the disciples of the Enlightenment, the most popular religious belief was deism, which held that God is the great artisan and watchmaker who created the universe and endowed it with fixed laws. The deists professed a belief in the existence of God that could be arrived at from the study of nature. They also expressed faith in life after death. Furthermore, there was a pervasive feeling that if deism became more and more popular, all the fanaticism, the rabid exchanges, and the bitter rivalries of the various Christian bodies might finally come to an end. Then there would be little need for the priestly and ministerial classes, who incited and encouraged hatred and division among the citizenry. This was for the *philosophes* the strongest motivation for their attacks on the clergy and the churches.

Indeed, the Western world had changed a great deal in the seventeenth and eighteenth centuries. Isaac Newton and his discovery of the laws of universal gravity called forth a great deal of new enthusiasm concerning the physical sciences. John Locke proceeded—on the basis of Newton's physics—to limit human knowledge to the realm of empirical experience. While the seventeenth century witnessed the creation of impressive philosophical systems by such thinkers as Descartes, Leibniz (1646–1716), and Spinoza (1632–77), the eighteenth century became the age of analysis and criticism. The *philosophes* focused their attention on religion and political institutions that they felt were enslaving people. They were largely deists who believed in God and life after death but who reduced the content of religious affirmation to those truths that were comprehensible to reason. As the eighteenth century progressed, the *philosophes* moved to skepticism and then, in some instances, to atheism.

David Hume (1711–76) shattered the fabric of deism by asserting that religion has no rational foundation. He was an atheist and a skeptic who doubted, among other things, the validity of the principle of causality. Hume exercised an enormous influence on the thinkers of the Enlightenment. In fact, Immanuel Kant (1724–1804) credited Hume for awakening him from his dogmatic slumbers. For a good number of years, Kant had been a disciple of Leibniz and Christian Wolff (1679–1754). Under the influence of Hume, however, he considerably limited the historical pretensions of human reason through his *Critique of Pure Reason* published in 1781. Although the existence of God, the immortality of the human soul, and the existence of human freedom cannot be arrived at analytically through the use of pure reason, Kant considered these truths to be dictates of the practical reason. It is impossible, he thought, to study the world and not believe in a supreme being, nor can one live a moral life and refuse to believe in his or her own freedom and immortality. One must believe in God and the afterlife, for otherwise virtue will never be finally rewarded, nor sin definitively punished.

Kant's contribution was highly significant in curtailing the influence of the Enlightenment in the latter years of the eighteenth century. By ca. 1750 secularization among the Christian clergy was pervasive. In the 1780s and 1790s, there was a serious decline in religious fervor and church attendance in many European countries. When the French Revolution broke out, a new spirit was ignited in most of the areas that had been deeply affected by the spirit of the Enlightenment. England, Germany, and France especially experienced a renewed emphasis on feelings and the imagination. Methodism in England, Goethe and Herder in Germany, and Rousseau in France embodied this new élan called Romanticism that was spreading across the Western world. Its effects could be felt notably in literature, music, philosophy, history, theology, and even religious practice.

Observations

In the West, Anselm (1033–1109) and Richard of St. Victor (d. 1173) each contributed to the development of trinitarian theology, but it was Thomas Aquinas (1225–74) who brought it to maturity with his refinements of the notion of divine procession, the real relations, and the divine persons as subsistent relations within the one divine essence. During the Reformation in the sixteenth century, Luther and Calvin did not alter the scholastic approach to the Trinity. Moreover, the Council of Trent simply affirmed the creed of Nicaea and Constantinople I, along with the addition of the *filioque*. With the Enlightenment of the eighteenth century and the influence of such thinkers as Voltaire, Hume, and Kant, there came a dramatic decline in the content of Christian belief and in religious practice across Western Europe and elsewhere.

NOTES

1. Thomas Aquinas, *Summa Theologiae*, Prima Pars (Madrid: Biblioteca de Autores Cristianos, 1978), Q. 27, art. 1–2. For an excellent English translation of *Summa Theologiae,* see Thomas Aquinas, *Summa Theologiae* (6 vols.; Latin text and English trans.; London: Blackfriars; New York: McGraw-Hill, 1964).
2. Ibid., Q. 27, art. 3–5.
3. Ibid., Q. 28, art. 1–4.
4. Ibid., Q. 29, art. 1–4.

5. Ibid., Q. 30, art. 1–4.

6. David Coffey, *Deus Trinitas* (New York: Oxford University Press, 1999), 29.

7. "The three really distinct real relations in God are identical with the divine essence (Denzinger-Schönmetzer, *Enchiridion,* no. 804) and so subsistent. Hence the real relation as relation is a mode of being; but the relation as subsistent is a person." Bernard Lonergan, "Christology Today: Methodological Reflections," *A Third Collection* (ed. Frederick E. Crowe; New York: Paulist Press, 1985), 99.

8. Gerald O'Collins, *The Tripersonal God* (New York: Paulist Press, 1999), 147.

9. Yves Congar, *I Believe in the Holy Spirit* (vol. 3; trans. David Smith; New York: Seabury Press, 1983), 129.

10. G. Alberigo et al., *Decrees of the Ecumenical Councils*, vol. 1 (ed. N. P. Tanner; Washington, D.C.: Georgetown University Press, 1990), *230.

11. Ibid., *314.

12. Ibid., *525–26.

13. Congar, *I Believe,* 131.

14. Bertrand de Margerie, *The Christian Trinity in History* (trans. E. J. Fortman; Petersham, Mass.: St. Bede's Publications, 1982), 199.

15. John Leith, ed., *Creeds of the Churches* (3d ed.; Louisville, Ky.: John Knox, 1982), 68.

16. Ibid.

17. Ibid., 69.

18. Hugh Kerr, ed., *Calvin's Institutes: A New Compend* (Louisville, Ky.: Westminster John Knox, 1989), 36–37.

19. Alberigo et al., *Decrees,* vol. 2, *662.

20. For insight into the period of the Enlightenment, see Ernst Cassirer, *The Philosophy of the Enlightenment* (trans. F. Koelln and J. Pettegrove; Princeton, N.J.: Princeton University Press, 1968); and Peter Gay, *The Enlightenment: An Interpretation* (2 vols.; New York: W. W. Norton & Co., 1977).

7

FRIEDRICH SCHLEIERMACHER AND THE NINETEENTH CENTURY

Friedrich Schleiermacher

It has been said that modern Protestant theology began with Friedrich Schleiermacher (1768–1834). Due to the influence of his Moravian upbringing, he emphasized the importance of religious feeling and emotional response over doctrinal refinements. Schleiermacher, who has also been called the father of liberal theology, taught at the Universities of Halle and Berlin. His masterpiece, *The Christian Faith,* appeared in 1821–22 and was revised in 1830. The presentation of the Trinity was problematic for him, because he felt that the utterances of Jesus and the apostles did not firmly ground this doctrine. The exegesis that was meant to establish firmly the trinitarian belief has never been able to rest secure because of the constant attacks leveled against it over the centuries.[1] Furthermore, our faith in Christ and our fellowship with him would be the same even if we had no knowledge of the doctrine of the Trinity. In fact, Schleiermacher argues that it is wiser to establish the doctrine of Christ independently of our belief in the Trinity, because "there is danger that each of the divine persons will be conceived as existing independently by themselves."[2]

For Schleiermacher Jesus is distinguished from the rest of humankind by the constant potency of his God-consciousness, which was a veritable existence of God in him.[3] Whereas in believers there is an imperfect God-consciousness that is not pure and does not assert itself in activity, in Christ the God-consciousness is in his self-consciousness continually and exclusively, determining his actions every moment and thus constituting the perfect dwelling of the supreme being in him. In Schleiermacher's judgment, Christ is "the only 'other' in whom there is an existence of God in the proper sense."[4] He insists that the ecclesiastical assertions and definitions concerning the person of Jesus must be reviewed continually inasmuch as they are often products of bitter argumentation and controversy. He affirms that in Christ the divine nature and the human nature are combined into one person. The New Testament, however, tells us nothing about the divine nature of Jesus from the viewpoint of its existence from all eternity. Even the expression "Son of God" is to be used "only of the subject of this union, and not of the divine element in it before the union."[5]

For Schleiermacher every active state in Christ arose from the existence of God in him. Jesus was impelled by this divine presence "permeating his soul with the variety of its functions."[6] Every impulse of Christ was determined by this unique God-consciousness described as "the perfect indwelling of the supreme being."[7] Schleiermacher complains about the scholastic doctrine of Christ that is overloaded with a multitude of definitions and distinctions that grew largely out of the heated controversies of the past, and he questions how many of those formulations are still viable and how much has to be jettisoned in favor of a more contemporary portrayal.

Schleiermacher asserts that in the original drafts of Protestant theology in the sixteenth century, the old formulas were simply carried over. Thus, there is need for the development of a new and revised statement of Christology that is adapted to our times. The many attempts to present a unified picture of Christ have vacillated between the opposite errors of mixing the two natures to form a third and making one nature less important than the other.[8] The being of God in Christ is such that everything that comes forth in him is purely human, yet "every moment also reveals the divine in Christ as that which conditions it."[9]

This Pietist theologian offers a minimalist view of the resurrection and the ascension. He says that the disciples recognized Jesus as the Son of God without having the slightest awareness of these coming events. Thus, our own faith in Christ can be valid without an awareness of these facts, because they did not constitute an indispensable element in the original Christian belief. If we feel, however, that the resurrection and the ascension are adequately attested in the New Testament, we certainly may express our credence in them. Regarding the attributing of divine titles to Christ, Schleiermacher reminds us that Jesus himself alerted us against such practices: "What is the use of ascribing divine titles to Christ, if he himself calls attention to an improper use of the word 'God'? (John 10:34–36)."[10]

Schleiermacher's initial theorem regarding the Holy Spirit sets the scene for his presentation of the third divine person. He believes the

Holy Spirit is the union of the divine essence with the community of Christian believers, animating and directing their common life and their apostolic endeavors. He insists that we put aside the question of whether or not the Spirit is a figure relatively distinct in the divine essence. Indeed, he recommends that we consider the Holy Spirit simply in terms of the relationship between the divine essence and human nature "insofar as in its operations, it meets us within our Christian consciousness."[11] He continues, "This explains the testimony of the first possessors of the Holy Spirit, who describe him as a specific divine efficacious working in believers, though not one to be separated from the recognition of the being of God in Christ."[12]

No one, Schleiermacher explains, can achieve the new life except in the fellowship of the Holy Spirit, who acts as a common consciousness. His union with believers is not what he calls a person-forming union, for if it were, it would be indistinguishable from the union of natures in Christ. This union of the believer and the Holy Spirit does not uniformly penetrate the entire being of the faithful Christian. It is "a mingled separation and union of the divine and human."[13] Without this union of the worthy believer and the Holy Spirit, there can be no living fellowship with Christ. In fact, sharing in that Spirit and our bond with the living influence of Christ are one and the same thing. The work of the Spirit is to bring Christ into our lives. The Holy Spirit creates within the believer a divine incentive to realize the standard of Christ in our lives.[14] In this manner the Christian church, assisted by the Holy Spirit, becomes the perfect representation of the Redeemer.

Schleiermacher makes no attempt to integrate or to organize in any way his views on the Trinity. Actually, the subject is dealt with in the concluding pages of his most important treatise, *The Christian Faith*. He observes that it is not a primary utterance of our Christian faith, but rather a joining together of several primary utterances that focus on the divine presence in Christ and on the continuing presence of the divine consciousness in the believing community. The union of the divine essence with human nature, both in the person of Christ and in the common Spirit of the church, constitutes the essential element in the doctrine of the Trinity.[15] Initially, it had no other purpose but to equate, as forcibly as possible, the unity of the divine nature with the human nature of Christ and with the community of Christian believers. According to Schleiermacher, what is essential in the teaching concerning the Trinity is to equate as clearly as possible the divine essence united to the human nature of Christ to the divine essence itself.

Beyond this, he urges, we must call a halt to further trinitarian speculations. We should not assume, for example, that there are indeed eternal distinctions in the supreme being. "Who would venture to say that the impression made by the divine in Christ obliges us to conceive such an eternal distinction as its basis?"[16] Referring to the statements in John's Gospel purporting to reveal an eternal distinction between the Father and the Son, Schleiermacher questions why the Holy Spirit was not pointed out in that context as the other member who was in the beginning with God and who was God. It seems that only after these distinctions in the Divine Being had been transposed into eternal distinctions did there arise the need to defend the traditional doctrine from the accusations of polytheism.

Positing three distinct persons within the divine essence and affirming that each is equal to the other two is impossible for Schleiermacher, for the persons can be represented only in such a way that one is necessarily subordinated to the other. If the Father is the one who eternally begets the Son and is himself unbegotten—and no such begetting power exists in the Son—one is led to conclude that there is a relationship of dependence between the Father and Son.[17] If one follows the Greeks or Latins regarding the procession of the Spirit, the Father is still superior to the other two persons. Then the only question is whether the Son and the Spirit are equal to each other. "The pre-eminence given to the Father proves that he is conceived as standing in a different relation to the unity of the essence. . . . This can be traced back to the idea of Origen that the Father is God absolutely while the Son and the Spirit are God only by participation in the divine essence."[18]

Schleiermacher points out that it is somewhat surprising that the doctrine of the Trinity has remained stationary so long in the rather unsatisfactory position in which it found itself after the first several ecumenical councils. He urges, therefore, that we move forward with a thoroughgoing evaluation of the doctrine "in its older form" so that we can reconstruct it in such a way that will make it more intelligible for our times.[19] Schleiermacher includes his views of the Trinity at the end of his study, because discussing it at the beginning, he says, would presuppose that faith in this doctrine is a necessary prerequisite for Christian belief and redemption—which he attests is not the case. Finally, he questions whether the Sabellian hypothesis could ever be placed on a par with Athanasius's approach, which has carried the day since the fourth century. Or is it possible to devise a formula that can explain the two unions of the divine essence with human nature (i.e., in

Christ and in the Christian community) without positing real distinctions in the essence of God?[20] These questions, claims Schleiermacher, make it impossible at this stage to draft an acceptable presentation of the doctrine of the Trinity.

Catholic Traditionalism and Rationalism

In the early 1800s, Catholic theology was in a rather deplorable state. The institutional devastation left in the wake of the Napoleonic wars, a century of the pervasive Enlightenment, and the dramatic spread of Kantian philosophy had created a pressing need for restoration. Scholasticism had ceased to be a force in France, Germany, and most of Italy. Thus, the first two or three decades of the nineteenth century constituted a period of major rebuilding.

In France, for example, a strong strain of traditionalism developed in the area of religious thought. Individual human reason was deemed incapable of achieving any certain knowledge regarding religious and moral matters. Instead, according to traditionalism, these kinds of truth had been communicated to the human race at the outset by a special act of divine revelation, and tradition preserves and infallibly relays these truths to successive generations. The individual acquires his or her knowledge of these truths from the society that has handed them down for generations and generations. All knowledge of religious and moral truths is ultimately derived from God's primitive revelation.[21] Theologians Louis Boutain (d. 1867) and Augustine Bonetty (d. 1876) were required by the Vatican authorities to disavow their positions, because they were too pessimistic regarding the possibility of men and women arriving at certain religious truths from reason alone. Included among these truths were the existence of God and the immortality of the human soul.[22]

The problem in Germany was a resurgence of rationalism, with Georg Hermes (d. 1831) and Anton Günther (d. 1863) as the two most notable thinkers. Both were concerned with the problem of the relationship between faith and reason. The work of Hermes, a celebrated professor of theology at Münster and then Bonn, was condemned by Rome shortly after he died.[23] The errors of Anton Günther of Vienna were condemned in 1857 by the Congregation of the Index; consequently, Günther submitted to the ecclesiastical authorities and never wrote again.[24]

For Günther the point of departure for philosophy consisted in the soul's self-awareness as a limited spirit together with its simultaneous awareness of the absolutely perfect being that it was not. Limited perfection, he held, can be known only in terms of its necessary correlate, that is, absolute perfection.[25] In Günther's judgment, the fundamental structure of reality has its roots in the interplay between the finite spirit and the absolutely perfect being. He felt that he could reason his way to human nature's need for redemption, the Incarnation of the divine Logos in human flesh, and even to the triune character of the Godhead. He concluded that God must be a self-conscious being, and as self-conscious, the Divinity needs to be triune. The Father knows himself and thus emanates the Son. The Holy Spirit proceeds intelligibly from both the Father and the Son, and through the procession of the Spirit, God becomes aware of himself.

> Thus the opposition between them [the Father and the Son] must be sublated by a subsequent act of knowledge in which the being of the Father and the being of the Son is seen to be identical. This subsequent act of knowledge is the Holy Spirit which, as the known identity of the Father and the Son, the knower and the known, proceeds intelligibly from both. Through the procession of the Holy Spirit God becomes aware of himself. He knows his unitary essence *(Wesen)* through the intelligible emanations which constitute the processions of the Trinity. Therefore a self-conscious God must be triune.[26]

Gerald McCool, a respected historian of dogmatics, observes that this was much more than Hermes had ever affirmed, and Hermes had been condemned for semirationalism in 1831. Although Günther taught that the processions in the Trinity were necessary, he insisted that the manner in which the processions occurred remains a profound mystery. This qualification, however, did not avert his condemnation in 1857, when his books were placed on the Roman Index.

Catholic Ontologism

In Italy a philosophical approach called ontologism attempted to reconcile the relationship between faith and reason after the ravages of the Enlightenment and the Kantian revolution. Vincent Gioberti (d. 1852) held that the idea of being was nothing less than the infinite divine reality immediately present to the soul. For Gioberti metaphysics is "a scientific reflection upon the intellect's primitive intuition of the Necessary Being," and this is what impels humankind to search out unlimited truth.[27] Although Gioberti lost interest in scholarship and left the church in 1848 to enter politics, another Italian philosopher, Anthony Rosmini (d. 1859), also attracted a good deal of attention. McCool says, however, that more recent scholarship does not classify Rosmini's philosophy as ontologism in the strict sense.[28] His idea of being that is immediately intuited by the human mind belongs somehow to the divine nature. Does the being whom humankind intuitively sees pertain in some way to the necessary and eternal Being who is God? His response is that his Ideal Being presupposes God but is not God himself. In 1887 the Holy Office condemned forty propositions from his later works. The condemnation reaffirmed that our natural knowledge of God is not intuitive.[29]

Neo-Thomism

Between 1855 and 1887, traditionalism, Günther's rationalism, and ontologism were condemned by the Roman authorities. This left scholasticism, that is, Neo-Thomism, as the only remaining option for the systematic articulation of Catholic theology. Scholars such as Matthew Liberatore and Joseph Kleutgen spearheaded this movement in Rome in the mid-nineteenth century. The Neo-Thomists insisted that the days of eclecticism in Catholic thought were at an end. Kleutgen emphasized that the new scholastic method effectively addressed all the modern questions, and hence there was no need to abandon it. His work had a profound influence in Catholic academic circles throughout Europe.

Pope Leo XIII (1878–1903), with the aid of Joseph Kleutgen, a Jesuit, and Thomas Zigliara, a Dominican, published the encyclical *Aeterni Patris* in August 1879. This document asserts that scholastic philosophy is the single metaphysical system that can adequately represent the essence of patristic thought that preceded it. McCool comments that *Aeterni Patris* gave "a decisive and irreversible orientation to Catholic philosophy and theology."[30] He adds, however, that nineteenth-century Thomism had its weaknesses in the areas of history, exegesis, and positive theology. The trinitarian theology of Aquinas's *Summa Theologiae* (outlined earlier) was recognized as the standard presentation in the schools and gained in popularity and influence from the second half of the nineteenth century, especially after *Aeterni Patris*.

David Friedrich Strauss

Among the growing adherents of Protestant liberal theology in the nineteenth century, scores of lives of Jesus were written, and many of them were widely read. David Friedrich Strauss (1808–74), who studied at Tübingen and Berlin, published a highly controversial work in two volumes, *The Life of Jesus Critically Examined* (1835–36). According to his portrayal, the Gospels were largely mythical constructions based on Old Testament stories and events.

> The resultant picture was of a thoroughly historical and human figure about whom we have very little reliable information. We know, for example, of his home in Galilee, his baptism by John (certainly not including heavenly voices), his mission in Galilee, his claim to be the Messiah, his rejection at Nazareth, the cleansing of the temple (as recorded by Mark), and his trial and crucifixion. Everything else, if not properly called mythical, is at least surrounded by serious historical difficulties.[31]

Strauss's life of Jesus created such a negative reaction within the scholarly community of Europe that his prospects for a promising academic career were all but shattered. The depiction of Jesus as a human being and nothing more constituted a direct attack against traditional trinitarian beliefs.

Ernest Renan

Another life of Jesus (1863), written by Ernest Renan (1823–92), a professor of Semitic languages at the Collège de France, was extremely popular in Europe. Although Renan firmly denied the divinity of Christ, he portrayed Jesus as an exemplary teacher who was gentle and approachable. After Jesus was rejected by the leadership in Jerusalem, says Renan, Jesus turned into something of a revolutionary, and his preaching became harsher and more strident. He then attempted to promote his cause by performing miracles (which were vigorously repudiated by Renan). Finally, according to Renan, when Jesus came to realize that his ministry was unsuccessful, he was anxious for martyrdom. As was the case with Strauss, Renan's effective denial of Christ's divinity eroded belief in the Trinity among his extensive readership.[32]

Adolf von Harnack

The last and perhaps most influential of the nineteenth-century liberal Protestant theologians was Adolf von Harnack (1851–1930), who was born in northeastern Germany and studied at Erlangen, Dorpat, and the University of Leipzig. He taught at Giessen, Marburg, and the University of Berlin. At Berlin he lectured on ecclesiastical history for thirty-three years. Among his pupils were such notables as Karl Barth and Dietrich Bonhoeffer. Harnack completed his three-volume masterpiece, *History of Dogma,* in 1890. In English translation, the work was published in seven volumes from 1896–99. According to Lutheran scholar Wilhelm Pauck, Harnack's *History of Dogma* "will have a permanent place among the masterpieces of theological literature."[33] Fearing that his magisterial work would not be read by students, Harnack produced a one-volume summary, *Outlines of the History of Dogma,* that was published a year or two after *History of Dogma.* The English version of *Outlines* appeared in 1893.

The stated purpose of Harnack's three-volume history is to chart the transformation of gospel Christianity through the influx of Greek philosophy that hardened that primitive faith into dogma. His overriding interest is the development of Christian institutions, and his goal is to liberate the church from dogmatic Christianity. The Reformation, in his judgment, rediscovered the gospel and reaffirmed its primacy, but the dogma was left largely untouched. Thus, the Reformation must carry on, for Christians need to be liberated from what he terms "doctrinal authoritarianism." Harnack asserts that Logos Christianity, the Nicene dogma of the Trinity, and the Chalcedonian dogma of Christ are the products of "acute Hellenization" that need not be continued forever.[34]

For Harnack authentic Christianity consists in the disposition that the Father of Jesus awakens in believers' hearts through the gospel. Beyond this he never articulated what he believed the nature of Christianity to be. He insists, however, that no historical representation of Christianity should be absolutized once and for all as normative. Modern historical theology must complete what the Reformation began and sketch out the guidelines for "an undogmatic Christianity." Christians should not make statements regarding Christ's nature, especially his divine nature; neither should they make any affirmations regarding the Trinity. Harnack says that Christians must be content with the New Testament "and leave room for the same diversity of thought and speech which the early Christians displayed in their understanding of the lordship of Christ."[35]

In a memo to the Lausanne Conference on Faith and Order in 1927, Harnack wrote: "Should we not be satisfied with this consensus as it is expressed in the confessional affirmations that Christ is the 'Son of God,' the 'God-Man,' the 'Image of God,' 'Our Lord'? In my judgment this should be sufficient, and the churches would leave it to every Christian how he might further conceive the person of Christ."[36] Wilhelm Pauck adds that the conference did not follow Harnack's advice.

Although it is true that from the first century there was a persistent profession of faith in the Father, the Son, and the Holy Spirit, Harnack argues that in the third century the majority of church fathers viewed the Holy Spirit as a power rather than a person. Those who taught that the Spirit was divine in the full sense (e.g., Irenaeus) considered it a power, while those who conceived the figure as personal (e.g., Tertullian, Origen) judged him to be someone subordinate to the other two in the Triad.[37] Harnack attests that at Nicaea (325) the Holy Spirit is simply mentioned without any addition or explanation whatsoever, while after 358 Athanasius of Alexandria directed his full attention to establishing the divinity of the third person. He argued that since he must be worshiped, he is God—*homooúsios*—like the Son. In the East, however, the Arians and the Semi-Arians, who comprised almost ninety percent of Eastern Christians, considered Athanasius's position a clear innovation.

The Cappadocians forged the orthodox doctrine of the Trinity (i.e., the three coequal subjects in the one divine essence), which served as a preparation for the Council of Constantinople I (381). Even the Cappadocians, however, were very cautious and circumspect about openly proclaiming the Holy Spirit as *homooúsios*.[38] After 381 it was no longer possible to teach that the Spirit is subordinate to the Son. Harnack points out that for the Orthodox Christians the consubstantiality of the Spirit seemed adequately grounded only when this person is said to proceed from the Father alone. He attests that a semblance of subordinationism remained embedded in the trinitarianism of the easterners as a consequence of their traditional insistence on the monarchy of the Father.[39]

Harnack concludes that the East and West drew rather diverse portraits of the Trinity, and these portraits remain diverse today. In the East the Father is viewed as the root of the other two persons. The full reciprocity of all three appeared to the Orthodox Christians to jeopardize the monarchy, while the procession of the Spirit from the Son as well as from the Father seemed to compromise the *homooúsios*. In the West from the time of Augustine, there has always been a strong affirmation of the procession of the Spirit from both the Father and the Son. In the two centuries after Augustine, this affirmation precipitated the addition of the *filioque* to the creed in the West. The bishop of Hippo completely eliminated every remnant of subordinationism and paved the way for the transformation of the three persons into subsistent relations within the one divine essence. For Harnack this approach smacks of modalism. He insists that the Athanasian Creed, that is, the *Symbol Quicumque*, grew in popularity in the West during the Middle Ages and was eventually proclaimed Christian dogma. Thus, for him the *Quicumque* ("He who will be saved must believe this . . .") transformed the doctrine of the Trinity into ecclesiastical law so that if one wants to be saved, the trinitarian dogma must be believed.

Many of Harnack's more personal religious convictions are expressed in his *What Is Christianity?* This short work, which reproduces the scholar's lectures at the University of Berlin during the winter semester of 1899–1900, enjoys great popularity even today. It catches the spirit of liberal Christianity that still attracts a good number of adherents. Harnack identifies dogma as the work of the Greek spirit, recasting the baptismal confession into a rule of faith and then setting out a theological exposition of the rule of faith against gnosticism.[40] He actually suggested in 1892 that the creed of Nicaea-Constantinople could be replaced by a brief confession that more clearly expressed the understanding of the gospel achieved by the Reformation.[41] He was convinced that Jesus wanted no other belief in his person than the keeping of his commandments.

In Harnack's judgment, the title "Son of God" simply grew out of Jesus' unique awareness that he experienced God as Father, and how Jesus came to that realization was his secret. Moreover, believes Harnack, we will never fathom the inward development of Jesus from the awareness that he is the Son of God to the consciousness that he is the promised Messiah.[42] After Jesus' death and resurrection, his followers came to believe that he had performed a definitive work for humankind and that he still lives in heaven. The primitive Christians stood in an immediate relationship with God through the Spirit, and they lived in expectation of Christ's near return.[43] What came from within was soon joined by elements from without, that is, law, discipline, ritual, doctrine. Around 200 the living faith seems to have been transformed into a religion of law and form. By 330, according to Harnack, Hellenism had infiltrated into every corner of the church, and the initial living faith had been transformed into a philosophy of religion.[44]

Harnack has little to say about the mystery of the Trinity. Not much can be said about the nature of Jesus' relationship with God the Father, except that he sensed an absolutely unique filial closeness to God. Harnack did not want to speak about Jesus as divine, except that in him the divine appeared in as pure a form as it can appear on earth.[45] In Harnack's writings the Holy Spirit seems to be more a power or a force than a person, a power coming out of God, serving as the vehicle for the deification of believers. The Christian church is held together by the Holy Spirit and by faith, thus forming a spiritual community of brothers and sisters. Harnack reveals the marrow of his own inner faith when he deflects the reproaches raised against the Protestant divisions by saying, "We do not wish it otherwise; on the contrary, we want still more freedom, still greater individuality in utterance and doctrine."[46]

Observations

The romanticism of the early nineteenth century, with its emphasis on religious feelings and emotion, counterbalanced the rationalism of the Enlightenment. The new movement was captured by Friedrich Schleiermacher, who taught that faith consisted in the feeling of total dependence on God, and he refused to engage in trinitarian speculation.

Within Catholicism the Kantian shock waves brought forth traditionalism, several forms of rationalism, and ontologism—all of which were opposed by the Vatican. Neo-Thomism remained standing as the only viable nineteenth-century philosophical system that could serve the church's theological enterprise. Leo XIII's encyclical of 1879 endorsed Neo-Thomism and encouraged its adoption in all academic institutions of higher learning throughout the Catholic world.

The last and perhaps most influential of all the nineteenth-century liberal Protestant theologians was Adolf von Harnack, whose *History of Dogma* remains a classic in the field. Harnack asks a number of hard questions that those working in the area of historical theology are still challenged to answer.

NOTES

1. Friedrich Schleiermacher, *The Christian Faith* (ed. H. R. MacKintosh and J. S. Stewart; English trans. of the 2d German ed.; Edinburgh: T&T Clark, 1986), 741. Although there are references to Christ and the Holy Spirit in Schleiermacher's early work *On Religion: Speeches to Its Cultured Despisers* (1799), there is no explicit treatment of the Trinity as such in the study. His concern is to indicate to his readers the importance of belief as such.

2. Ibid., 399–400.

3. Ibid., 385.

4. Ibid., 388.

5. Ibid., 392.

6. Ibid., 409.

7. Ibid., 388.

8. Ibid., 394.

9. Ibid., 409.

10. Ibid., 424.

11. Ibid., 569.

12. Ibid., 572.

13. Ibid., 573.

14. Ibid., 576.

15. Ibid., 738.

16. Ibid., 739.

17. Ibid., 743.

18. Ibid., 745.

19. Ibid., 749.

20. Ibid., 750.

21. Gerald McCool, *Nineteenth-Century Scholasticism* (New York: Fordham University Press, 1989), 46–56, 129–30.

22. H. Denzinger and A. Schönmetzer, *Enchiridion*, 32d ed. (Freiburg: Herder, 1963), nos. 2765–69, 2811–14.

23. Ibid., nos. 2738–39.

24. Ibid., nos. 2828–31.

25. McCool, *Nineteenth-Century Scholasticism*, 93.

26. Ibid., 103.

27. Ibid., 118.

28. Ibid., 120.

29. Gregory Baum, "Ratzinger Explains How Condemnation Was Right Then, Wrong Now," *National Catholic Reporter* 38 (25 January 2002):18. In a *nota* from the Congregation of the Doctrine of Faith, dated July 1, 2001, the condemnation of these forty propositions has been lifted. Cardinal Joseph Ratzinger explains that a condemnation made in one historical context can be reviewed and altered in another historical context. When interpreted in light of his own philosophical work, Rosmini's statements are apparently not contrary to the Catholic tradition.

30. Ibid., 236.

31. Claude Welch, *Protestant Thought in the Nineteenth Century* (vol. 1; New Haven, Conn.: Yale University Press, 1972), 149.

32. Owen Chadwick, *The Secularization of the European Mind in the Nineteenth Century* (Cambridge: Cambridge University Press, 1975). Chadwick gives a brief sketch of Renan and his work on pages 212–23. For informative sketches of both Strauss and Renan, see Albert Schweitzer, *The Quest of the Historical Jesus* (New York: Macmillan Publishing, 1968), 68–95, 180–92.

33. Wilhelm Pauck, "Adolf von Harnack," in *A Handbook of Christian Theologians* (ed. Martin E. Marty and Dean G. Peerman; Nashville, Tenn.: Abingdon, 1984), 88.

34. Adolf von Harnack, *Outlines of the History of Dogma* (trans. E. K. Mitchell; Boston: Starr King Press, 1957), 99.

35. Pauck, "Adolf von Harnack," 109.

36. Ibid., 109–10.

37. Harnack, *Outlines,* 267.

38. Ibid., 268.

39. Ibid., 270.

40. Harnack, *What is Christianity?* (trans. T. B. Saunders; Philadelphia: Fortress Press, 1986), 179.

41. Welch, *Protestant Thought,* 181.

42. Harnack, *What Is Christianity?* 138.

43. Ibid., 170–72.

44. Ibid., 203.

45. Ibid., 146.

46. Ibid., 276.

8

RECENT CATHOLIC CONTRIBUTIONS TO TRINITARIAN THEOLOGY

In the past two generations we have witnessed some rather startling developments in trinitarian theology. Among Catholic scholars, Karl Rahner triggered a change of direction that served as a point of departure for other theologians such as Walter Kasper, John O'Donnell, and Catherine Mowry LaCugna. There are, of course, a good number of others who have made notable contributions,[1] but these four can be considered representative of the mainstream of the Catholic effort since World War II. The purpose of this chapter is to set out in summary form the work of the four above-mentioned scholars so that their various positions can be compared in this critical area of Catholic thought.

Karl Rahner

In the first volume of his *Theological Investigations,* Karl Rahner (1904–1984) included an article entitled "Theos in the New Testament."[2] This paper was first delivered to a group of scholars in Vienna and was intended as a foundation for future study and discussion. He traces the difference between the notion of God in the Old and the New Testaments. Yahweh is seen again and again in the Old Testament as intervening in the history of the people of Israel. This Yahweh is a free person who is active in the world. He calls and chooses certain Israelites to perform definite missions on his behalf, guiding their activity, and yet this God remains entirely transcendent.

In the New Testament, God *(ho Theos)* is always assumed to be present in the background. No effort is made by the sacred authors to prove or explain his presence. Their concern is focused on how this God acts and deals with the people. Although the New Testament writers simply assume that the hearers of the Word are familiar with

God's behavior (Rom 1:18–21), the authentic and full knowledge of God is not possible without faith in Jesus, since God definitively disclosed Godself in his Son. The New Testament speaks of the God and Father of Jesus Christ (Rom 15:6; 2 Cor 1:3) who has revealed himself in the Son and in the Spirit. The manifestations of God are clearly personal, and he is frequently addressed in the New Testament as "Thou."

In the Old Testament, although Yahweh is revealed as the one who loves, this personal relationship is for the most part with his people as a whole. It is in Christ that God's love is really disclosed in the full and total sense (Rom 8:28–30). Those who accept Jesus as Lord are granted fellowship with God through the agency of the Holy Spirit (2 Cor 13:13). Rahner points out that in the New Testament, *ho Theos* almost always refers to God the Father. The Logos, however, is called Theos (John 1:1) and the only begotten God (John 1:18). We observed in chapter 2 that Rahner cites six New Testament texts in which Christ is called Theos but never *ho Theos*.[3] Also, there are several texts in which Christ's divine nature is affirmed in some fashion without the explicit use of the word "Theos." As stated earlier, the term "Theos" is apparently never used in the New Testament for the Holy Spirit. In the so-called trinitarian formulas (e.g., Matt 3:16–17; Rom 15:30; 1 Cor 12:4–6), God, for the most part, stands for the Father. Moreover, Rahner contends that nowhere in the New Testament is there a text in which *ho Theos* certainly refers to the triune God existing in three persons.[4] The early patristic evidence also attests that *ho Theos* exclusively refers to the Father. Finally, in the official prayers of the liturgy, it is the Father to whom we pray through the Son in the unity of the Holy Spirit. The Father is the person who is simply called God.

After Vatican II Rahner produced a monograph on the Trinity that proved to be highly influential in Catholic circles.[5] He objects to the fact that we occasionally hear of theologians and preachers assuming that any person of the Trinity could have become incarnate, rather than just the person of the Logos. From Augustine on, this thesis has been frequently articulated by theologians who were thereby neglecting the fact that our salvation comes from the incarnate Word, and that the grace coming from Christ is the grace of the Word. Rahner states that the treatise on the Trinity has often been isolated and, as a result, has precious little connection with the other dogmatic tracts. In fact, when the treatment of the triune God is concluded, this subject matter is rarely referred to again in the other theological courses.

In the West after Aquinas, the first issue dealt with is the one divine essence, and only afterward the three divine persons. On the other hand, the Greeks customarily begin with the unoriginate God who is identified as Father even before the treatment of the processions of generation and spiration. From the vantage point of salvation history, it is the Father who sends the Son and who gives himself to us in the Spirit. Although there are intimations in the Scriptures concerning two divine processions, as well as a suggestion that these may be related somehow to the spiritual operations of knowing and loving, Rahner is not particularly fond of the psychological speculations found in Augustine's *De Trinitate*. The attempts of the older classical apologists to discover vestiges of the Trinity in the Old Testament are not especially popular today.

Rahner insists that only the Logos can assume a human nature because he and only he is per se the Father's revelation. Otherwise our graced identification as sons and daughters of the Father would have nothing to do with the filial relation of the Logos to the Father. It is the peculiar nature of the second person that makes him the only suitable vehicle for this particular kind of divine self-communication. Rahner affirms that the thesis that declares that each of the divine persons can become man can claim no dogmatic authority. The human nature of Christ is the authentic symbol of the Logos. Jesus reveals through his words and actions the very reality of the Logos. It is indeed true that each of the divine persons communicates Godself to the believer in his own personal particularity, and this is called uncreated grace, which is no less than a communication of persons. The Father gives himself as Father, and in uttering himself he communicates the Son as his own self-revelation. Moreover, Father and Son welcome each other in love, and this mutual subsistent love is the Holy Spirit.

Karl Rahner does make note of the vague reflection of the Trinity in the Old Testament. Yahweh discloses himself through the Word and by the Spirit who assists in the understanding and acceptance of the Word. These two mediators reveal themselves as divine agents and thus represent a foreshadowing of the New Testament revelation of Father, Son, and Spirit. It is important to avoid the idea that there are in God three distinct consciousnesses and centers of activity. Rahner attests that the concept of person is fraught with several difficulties when applied to the triune God. Although he prefers to speak of the threefold divine personality, he grants that because the word "person" has been used for more than fifteen hundred years in our tradition, we have little choice but to retain it. The terms "person" and "essence" are never fully explained in the church documents, and hence the assumption is that they do not require clarification. The concept "person," however, has witnessed a rather considerable development since the fifth century. If today's widely accepted understanding of person as a distinct center of consciousness and activity is applied to the Trinity, we would find ourselves involved in the heresy of tritheism.

God is confessed as Yahweh in the Old Testament, and in the New Testament he is most specifically identified as Father when Jesus declares himself to be the Son. The Son is the historical self-communication of the Father. This historical revelation of the distinction between Father and Son reflects an eternal differentiation in God so that our understanding of the immanent Trinity comes from the economic Trinity. The *immanent Trinity* refers to the Deity considered apart from humankind and creation, while the *economic Trinity* is identified as the Divine Being revealed in creation and in human history. The Holy Spirit proceeds from the Father and the Son through an eternal communication of the divine essence. Although distinct from the Father and the Son, the Spirit is equally God. This procession of the Spirit from the Father through the Son is understood to be the expression of the mutual love of Father and Son.

It is the concept of relation that allows us to avoid the pitfalls of tritheism and modalism. These three really distinct subsistences, each of whom is identical with the one simple essence of God, are relations of opposition. They are distinct by virtue of their relation to one another. Each subsistent relation is real only through its identity with the divine essence, and because of its identity with the divine essence, each subsistent relation (or person) is as perfect as the other two. The opposed relations (e.g., Father/Son) must be really distinct from one another, just as the Spirit is distinct from the Father and the Son. However, these three subsistent relations are really identified with something absolute, that is, the divine essence. In the words of the Council of Florence (1439–42): "These three persons are one God, and not three gods, because there is one substance, one essence, one nature, one divinity, one immensity, one eternity. In every respect they are one where there is no opposition of relationship *(ubi non obviat relationis oppositio)*."[6]

Regarding the external activities of God, there is only one outward operation of the Divinity, exercised as one and the same by all three, according to the unique manner in which each of them shares the Godhead. Although Rahner affirms that the difference between the Incarnation and the descent of the Spirit as saving realities is not especially clear, it is the Son who appears in history as man and it is the

Spirit who disposes the world for this divine self-communication. If God chooses to express himself outside himself, he must create a spiritual being who has the obediential potency to receive such a communication. Although spiritual personal subjects (i.e., angels) could be considered as possible recipients of the divine self-communication, God chose in fact to direct his self-revelation to humankind. Christian angelology therefore must fit in with the event of the God-man.

God's self-offering to the world could occur only in a decisive and once and for all manner when made through the one whom Rahner calls the Absolute Bringer of salvation, that is, Jesus Christ. This divine self-communication comes to us as truth, which when accepted by the recipient becomes love and generates love in the believer. This divine overture itself creates the possibility of its acceptance, and when accepted, opens out toward the absolute future. Rahner points out that to the extent that relations are seen as the "most unreal" of realities, there is no doubt that they are not as well suited to help us understand a Trinity that is most real.[7]

Rahner returns to the notion of person and asks how well suited it is to be applied to the three subsistent relations in the Trinity. Although Aquinas's concept of person (i.e., that which subsists as distinct in a rational or intelligent nature) has found its way into our understanding of the triune God, we are not able to speak of three persons in the same way that we do elsewhere. What subsists as distinct and with its own individual self-consciousness is considered by us to be a distinct nature. The expanded meaning of the term "person" over the centuries was not something the church could control. Although the term originally carried the connotation of a distinct subsistence, now in addition there is a spiritual subjective element that has become an integral part of the notion of the term. A traditional concept such as "person" cannot be eliminated at will by a theologian acting on his or her own.

Rahner, however, prefers to speak of the three persons as three distinct manners of subsisting. This terminology suggests that the one God is tripersonal and does not seem to infer that we are dealing with three distinct divine natures or essences. The Father, Son, and Holy Spirit are distinct as relations of opposition and thus in their manner of subsisting. Employing this approach along with the traditional concept of person seems to avoid the problems that arise when the term "person" is used alone. When we say that God has two basic activities, knowledge and love, we can then conclude that there are two processions within the Godhead. The Father speaks the Word because he knows, and the movement of love between the Father and the Word brings forth the Spirit. Father, Son, and Spirit constitute three distinct manners of subsisting in the one divine essence.

In 1976 Karl Rahner published in German his *Foundations of Christian Faith*, which was translated into English in 1978. The theologian David Tracy has referred to this work as the clearest and most systematic expression of Rahner's position.[8] The German scholar reemphasizes the unlimited transcendentality of the human spirit, since humankind's basic orientation is toward absolute mystery. The radical openness to the mystery of God is a permanent quality of human beings as spiritual subjects. This ever-present, original orientation toward God constitutes the permanent ground out of which the more systematic knowledge of God arises. Vatican I (1869–70) declared that God can be known at least in principle by the light of natural reason without the aid of special divine revelation.[9] Rahner affirms that we do not know God as one object among others, but only as "the term of transcendence."[10] Humans have a primal and radical orientation toward the absolute mystery who is God. The unlimited horizon beyond our limited experiences is the absolute mystery, and this is what constitutes our fundamental experience of God. The Divinity is the absolute being, the absolute and ultimate horizon within which our human existence is lived out in freedom.

According to Rahner, if anything can be said of God, the notion of personality must be attributed to him because we are approached with knowledge and love by the absolute mystery. Rahner then initiates a description of what he calls an a priori doctrine of the God-man.[11] He reasons that matter and spirit have a great deal in common. Matter has the capacity to become more, to initiate a leap into something higher. God's self-communication is answered by free acceptance on the part of free subjects. The Absolute Savior who can be identified as God's absolute and definitive self-communication to the spiritual world must be part of the cosmos, a human born of woman, born under the law (Gal 4:4).

The incarnation of the Word is a privileged moment in the process wherein the divinization of all spiritual creatures is achieved. The hypostatic union makes the proclamation and the offer of salvation to us a reality of God himself. It is through the Incarnation that the mystery of the triune God is made available to us. According to the Greek tradition beginning with the Fathers, there is an insistence on the truth that only the Word of God can initiate human history in which the triune Deity is disclosed. When the Logos assumes a human nature, humanity itself has reached the point toward which it was tending by virtue of its transcendental orientation toward the infinite mystery. The Incarnation constitutes the highest actualization of the essence of humanity, since human nature possesses what Rahner terms an obediential potency for the hypostatic union.

Despite the fact that God is unchangeable,[12] the Logos—without a change in itself—assumes a created reality that does undergo change, that is, the human nature of Jesus. God truly can become something new in something else. He can give himself to what is not God and have his own history in the other as his very own history. The man Jesus is the self-revelation of God not only through his words and actions, but through who he is, inasmuch as he is the privileged expression of God. Thus, Rahner summarizes his outline of what he terms an a priori doctrine of the God-man. His position is based on two theses—the almost infinite perfectibility of human nature on the one hand, and God's boundless desire to share his life with rational creatures on the other. Through the Logos, God has the real possibility of offering his very self to us in our history.[13] Because Christ is identified as the Absolute Savior who is God's definitive offer of God's own self and, at the same time, the full and free acceptance of this offer, Rahner concludes that the one who expresses himself and offers himself in this manner is preexistent. This ability of God to express Godself in history through the Word belongs essentially to the Divinity and hence is inner-trinitarian. He adds that the Spirit who proceeds from the Father and the Son brings the justifying faith of Christ into the world.

At another point in his *Foundations,* Rahner stresses the idea of God's free self-communication, which he describes as the very heart of Christianity.[14] He emphasizes that what is communicated is really God's own being, so that humankind can know and possess God. This justifying sanctification comes through the Holy Spirit who works from within, shaping and directing the individual believer. The Spirit communicates its own divine reality, making it a central element in the fulfillment of the creature. This is the true essence of what establishes the ontological relationship between God and the believer. Spiritual creatures are so constituted that they are the possible addressees of this divine self-communication. The emptiness of the creature is due to God's creating this emptiness to communicate Godself into it. God is present to us in the Holy Spirit and in the Word, who is God's Son. All human beings are open to the experience of God's self-communication, at least as a gratuitous offer of salvation.

This original experience of God can be so universal and "unreligious" that it can occur to anyone anywhere.[15]

Karl Rahner suggests that he might have occasion to discuss the doctrine of the Trinity in connection with his treatment of the Incarnation in his *Foundations of Christian Faith,* but he fails to do so.[16] He confesses that the church's teaching concerning the Trinity is nearly unintelligible to believers today, causing misunderstanding and frustration. The terms "person," "essence," "hypostasis," and "nature" are not as meaningful in our day as they apparently once were. For example, our contemporary understanding of the idea of person necessarily involves the notion that each person is a free and distinct center of conscious activity. This definition could not apply to the divine persons because they share a single consciousness and a single freedom, although each gives a unique dimension to that divine consciousness and freedom.

The psychological explanation of the divine triune life popularized by Augustine and employed regularly in scholastic thought is seen as unhelpful by Rahner. It sidesteps the work of the Trinity in the economy of salvation "in favor of an almost gnostic speculation about what goes on in the inner life of God."[17] He stresses once again that the immanent and the economic Trinity are one and the same. It is only through the missions of the Son and the Spirit that the immanent Trinity is revealed to us. The Holy Spirit divinizes us in the very center of our existence. In Jesus, one and the same God is present and active in our history and in our world. Finally, God the Father is the origin of the coming to us of the Son and the Holy Spirit. Although these three possess the same divine essence, there are real differences in their modes of presence to us that must be somehow distinguished and appreciated. "In the economy and history of salvation we have already experienced the immanent Trinity as it is in itself."[18] This for Rahner represents our surest and truest access to our understanding, albeit limited, of the mystery of the Trinity.

His various approaches to the subject of the triune God do not reflect the same level of interest and detail that is evident in his numerous studies in the field of Christology. It is clear that he sensed the need for a thorough revision of the tract on the Trinity and that there must be a much closer identification between the presentation of the immanent and the economic Trinity. However, Rahner was apparently not ready to deal with the subject in any detail in his *Foundations of Christian Faith*, the last systematic treatment of his thought.

Walter Kasper

Formerly a professor of dogmatics at the Universities of Münster and Tübingen and bishop of Ruttenburg–Stuttgart in Germany, Walter Kasper (b. 1933) was appointed Roman cardinal on January 21, 2001, and shortly thereafter was chosen as president of the Pontifical Council for Promoting Christian Unity. He published *The God of Jesus Christ* in 1982, which was translated into English in 1984.[19] After dealing at some length with a wide range of contemporary questions concerning God, and particularly with the problem of the rise of atheism in our day, Kasper addresses the subject of divine revelation. He asserts that a religious person sees certain pivotal human experiences as signs through which what he terms "the divine mystery" are disclosed. In the Old Testament, revelation is seen as a special type of divine communication that is observable in the prophetic literature (Isa 6:9–10; Jer 2:2ff) and also in certain passages of the Pentateuch (e.g., Exod 20:2–17). The same is true in the later books in which God speaks through Wisdom's mouth (Sir 24:8ff). Then in the New Testament, "God has spoken through his Son whom he made heir of all things" (Heb 1:1–2).

The response to this divine self-revelation is faith, whereby men and women give themselves unreservedly to God. The hiddenness of God is made manifest in Jesus, and the divine self-communication is made present to us in the Spirit. Kasper points out that in our day we have experienced a notable diminution in the image of "father," who is seen by many of our contemporaries more as a source of domination and control. This was clearly not the case in either the Old or the New Testament. Israel's divine sonship was considered the most precious of its privileges (Rom 9:4–5). The prophet Hosea reminded the Israelites that they are the sons and daughters of the living God (Hos 2:4). This love was also interpreted as the love of a mother for her children (Isa 66:13). In the New Testament, "Father" becomes the name for God inasmuch as Jesus referred to God as Father 170 or more times in the Gospels.[20] Only through Jesus is it disclosed that God is the Father of all humanity (Matt 5:45).

Jesus recapitulates and exceeds all of the Old Testament hopes. He adopts the long-standing notion of the kingdom of God as his very own (Matt 11:5) and reveals that his reign is a reign of nonviolent love. His miracles and cures are the evidence of a world in the process of reconciliation. He speaks with authority as one who has power over the Mosaic law (Matt 5:24–48), and he gathers his disciples who are asked to leave all in order to follow him (Mark 10:28). Jesus is the living instrument through whom the love of God dwells among humankind, the only Son who makes us sons and daughters of God (Rom 8:14–17). Kasper affirms that the mission statements (Phil 2:6–11; Gal 4:4) presuppose the preexistence of the Son and that in John the divinity of the Son is clearly affirmed (e.g., 20:28). Despite the subordinationism evident in some of the early church fathers (i.e., Justin, Tertullian, Origen), the Council of Nicaea (325)—through the use of metaphysical, nonbiblical language—declared that the Son is of the same substance as the Father, true God of true God.

After Nicaea the question of the capacity of the divine Son to undergo suffering became a troubling problem. How can one reconcile the impassibility of the Son with his suffering on the cross? Was Jesus, as divine, absolutely untouched by the agony that was experienced so deeply in his human nature? The Fathers seem to be affected more by Greek philosophy than by the pain that Yahweh experienced in dealing with the people of Israel, as reflected in the Old Testament narratives. Kasper suggests that after Martin Luther (1483–1546) and his emphasis on the theology of the cross, God's suffering came to be seen more as an expression of his freedom, which allowed suffering to touch him. It was asserted that God could enter into suffering without being overcome by it. The distinction between Father and Son is what opened up the possibility of God's self-emptying in the Incarnation, while the work of the Spirit is to unite the Father and the Son, lover and beloved.

The Spirit was defined at Constantinople I (381) as the one who proceeds from the Father and the Son and who is adored and glorified in the same manner as the Father and the Son.[21] In the Old Testament, Yahweh's Spirit is said to be the creative power of all life. It was the Spirit who spoke through the prophets. Not only were Moses, Saul, and David anointed by the Spirit, but the writing prophets received their inspiration from the Spirit as well (Isa 61:1). Joel proclaimed that in the last days there would be a general outpouring of the Spirit on all humankind (3:1–2). The Holy Spirit descended on Jesus at his baptism (Matt 3:16). In his inaugural sermon in the synagogue at Galilee, Jesus announced that the Holy Spirit was resting on him to guide him throughout his mission (Luke 4:16-19). After the resurrection Christ sent the Spirit into his disciples (John 20:22), and the Holy Spirit is the one who would remind the disciples of all that Jesus had taught them (John 14:26).

The early church fathers were aware that the Spirit was active in the body of believers, and they identified the Spirit as the preserver of the tradition (e.g., Irenaeus, Hippolytus) and the one who makes Jesus continuously present. It is the Holy Spirit who pleads on our behalf with God (Rom 8:26) and distributes the spiritual gifts as he chooses (1 Cor 12:11). It did indeed take several centuries before the Spirit was formally given equal status with the Father and the Son. This was accomplished largely through the efforts of Athanasius and the Cappadocians, whose labors were crowned with success at the Council of Constantinople I. In the East the Holy Spirit was believed to proceed from the Father as from a single principle, and little was said about the relation between the Son and the Spirit. In the West, however, the movement of trinitarian life was completed, or rounded off, in the Holy Spirit, and the Son was given a role in the procession of the third divine person. The Westerners reasoned that if the Son has a share in the sending of the Spirit in history (John 14:16), he also must have a share in the intra-trinitarian procession of the Spirit.

The *filioque* that was developed in the West in the sixth and seventh centuries was eventually embedded in the Roman creed in the eleventh century and reinforced at Lateran IV (1215) and Lyons II (1274).[22] This development eventually proved to be unacceptable to the Eastern Orthodox, who were more concerned about maintaining the monarchy of the Father. Kasper argues that while the East is not clear about the relation of the Spirit to the Son, the West has experienced difficulty in distinguishing the relation of the Spirit to the Son from the relation of the Spirit to the Father. For the Greeks, the *filioque* represents an unacceptable insertion of philosophical thought into the triune mystery. The theology of the Holy Spirit must begin with the experience of the Spirit in history. It is the Spirit through whom the love of God is poured out into our hearts (Rom 5:5). Paul reminds us that it is only through the Spirit that we can address God as Father (Rom 8:15). The love of God moves beyond Godself through the indwelling of the Holy Spirit, and thus we are made partakers in the divine nature (2 Pet 1:4). In *The Pastoral Constitution on the Church in the Modern World* of Vatican II, we are taught that the activity of the Holy Spirit can be seen in the various religions of humankind as well as in the progress of human culture (nos. 26, 38).

In Kasper's judgment, we do not find anywhere in religious history a replication of the Christian idea of one Divinity in three persons. He reasons further that without a multiplicity in unity of this sort, God would be an isolated being who would need the world as a complement and thus would lose something of the divine character. Although the Old Testament offers only hints of God as triune, the New Testament reveals Jesus as God's Son who belongs to the eternal being of God, and the Spirit as the being who establishes believers as sons and daughters of the Father. The trinitarian structure of the baptismal mandate (Matt 28:19) remains the most significant foundation for the theological development of the doctrine. Also, Galatians 4: 4–6, 1 Corinthians 12:4–6, and 2 Corinthians 13:33 reveal Paul's trinitarian faith. Kasper attests that chapters 1–12 of John's Gospel dramatically delineate the relation of the Son to the Father, while chapters 14–17 describe the sending of the Holy Spirit. He further notes that the structure of the later creed already began to take shape in the last third of the second century.[23]

The tendency toward subordinationism (e.g., Tertullian, Origen) that developed in the disputes against gnosticism eventually lost favor after the Council of Nicaea (325). Christ was then confessed as true God and true man, and Constantinople I (381) declared that the Holy Spirit was to be adored and glorified in the same manner as the Father and the Son. Even before Constantinople I, Pope Damasus in 374 spoke of three persons in one divine substance.[24] Over the centuries the emphasis on the presentation of the immanent Trinity resulted in the portrayal of God as an independent entity who is not always connected with the central tenets of salvation. This tended to push the trinitarian doctrine into the background of Christian belief. As a result, after Kant and Schleiermacher, it was viewed by many as something of an appendix to the main creedal system of Christianity. As the Enlightenment grew more hostile to the concept of mystery, the trinitarian faith of Christians became less and less central to their religious profession.

Among Catholic theologians, Karl Rahner insists that the immanent Trinity can be clarified for us only in light of the economic Trinity. The one is simply the other, as Kasper explains.[25] Salvation cannot be viewed as a created gift of God that is distinct from God. It involves our becoming sons and daughters of the Father through the Spirit. In the outpouring of the Spirit, the economy of salvation is brought to its fulfillment. Rahner's purpose in uniting the immanent and the economic Trinity is to overcome the nonfunctionality of the doctrine.[26] Were it not for the fact that the three divine persons were actually disclosed in the course of history, the differences within the Trinity might then be seen as nothing more than modal distinctions.

Kasper firmly advocates that our approach to the triune God must begin with the missions and then advance to the processions. The Son is sent by the Father and the Spirit is sent by the Father (Gal 4:4–6). The missions—which are realized in time—presuppose the eternal processions that are only intimated in the New Testament (John 8:42; 15:26). The relation of the Father to the Son has been identified in tradition as *generation,* while the relation of the Father and the Son to the Holy Spirit has been termed *spiration.* Three of these relations are really distinct from each other, that is, fatherhood, sonship, and passive spiration.[27] These are mutually distinct relational realities. The mutually opposed relations in God are objective expressions of the three divine persons who are distinct from one another by means of their unique properties, that is, fatherhood, sonship, and passive spiration.

Kasper addresses the problem of the expanded meaning of the word "person" in modern times. Aquinas's understanding of person as that which subsists as distinct in a rational or intelligent nature has been superseded since John Locke (1632–1704). From the eighteenth century, the concept "person" necessarily features the notion of independent and individuated self-consciousness. A person has come to be understood as a freestanding center of action, and this new comprehension makes the idea of three distinct persons in one and the same nature very difficult to reconcile. Kasper finds that Karl Rahner's definition of person as a distinct manner of subsisting is cumbersome and rather unintelligible. In fact, since this understanding can be readily comprehended as modalist, we have no choice but to retain the term "person" and interpret it to believers as best we can.[28] The three divine subjects are conscious of themselves by means of the one single divine consciousness. Each of the three persons possesses the same divine consciousness in his own proper way. It goes without saying that there is an immeasurably greater interrelationality among the three divine subjects than there is in human interpersonal relations.

The theology of the Trinity concerns itself with the self-communication of God. It makes the point that the one God is by no means a solitary Divinity. The modern era has frequently portrayed a theistic impersonal God who is something of a projection of the human ego. The oneness of God, however, cannot be understood to mean that the Divine Being is a solitary figure. This is the fundamental reason why the theistic notion of a unipersonal God is unsustainable. According to Kasper, this would bring about a necessary relation between God and the world that would destroy the freedom of the Divinity in dealing with the created universe.[29]

In Kasper's judgment, chapter 17 of John's Gospel opens a window into the revelation of the mystery of the Trinity.[30] Jesus asks the Father to glorify him, that he, the Son, may glorify the Father (John 17:1). This glorification is achieved through the agency of the Spirit. Into this union between Father and Son the faithful are to be incorporated through the instrumentality of the Holy Spirit (John 14:15–24). God is not to be understood as an isolated and solitary unipersonal being who would suffer from his own completeness. Kasper argues that there must be a communion of love within the divine nature. The Father is a giver and a sender, while the Son receives life, glory, and power from the Father. The Father's love is poured out in the Son. In the Spirit this love exists in the joy of pure receiving. The Son receives himself wholly from the Father, while the Spirit receives its being from the mutual love between Father and Son.[31]

The three persons of the Trinity are subsistent relations in which the one nature of God exists. Person and relation have a clear priority in our understanding of the Divinity. Kasper proposes that the doctrine of the Trinity should be considered the informing principle of all the other dogmatic treatises. After the example of the Eastern theologians, we must begin with the Father as the source and demonstrate that he possesses the one divine substance in such a way that he gives it to the Son and the Holy Spirit.[32] The primary emphasis in our preaching should always be the economic Trinity with the emphasis on soteriology—which evolves naturally into doxology.

John O'Donnell

In his early study *Trinity and Temporality,* written during a four-year residency at Christ Church, Oxford, John O'Donnell (b. 1944) addressed the question of the relationship between God and the temporality of the world.[33] Classical philosophical theism has always asserted that God is unchanging and atemporal, and that the world is related to God but God is not related to the world. This standpoint tends to create the impression that God is rather indifferent to our world. Our doctrine of God must therefore be restructured so that "God-talk" can be more meaningful. It must be reset in the context of the God of Israel and of Jesus Christ who act in history. Christians especially are compelled to rethink their notion of God based on their experience of Jesus. The Logos theology of the second century was capable of a number of interpretations until Nicaea (325), which defined Christ as consubstantial with the Father. When Constantinople I (381) declared that the Holy Spirit is worthy of divine adoration, the three divine persons were identified in the conciliar tradition.

The three suppositions of the Greek mind regarding the Deity focused on God's immutability, atemporality, and impassibility. The quality of immutability makes it extremely difficult for us to comprehend God's interventions in history. The divine eternity made it rather easy to view God as uninvolved with the world, and when the quality of impassibility was applied to Christ by the church fathers, Christ's suffering was limited to the pains he experienced solely in the flesh. Emphasizing the need to situate the gospel in a new conceptual milieu, O'Donnell examines the tools available in process thought and compares them with the theology of the cross set forth by Jürgen Moltmann.

He then selects Schubert Ogden (b. 1928) as the most representative of the process thinkers and concentrates on Ogden's early work, *The Reality of God*.[34] For Ogden the ground of his theological endeavors is the apostolic witness prior to the New Testament. It is the Jesus-kerygma that is normative. The event of Jesus is not strictly necessary for human salvation, because every person has a radical confidence in the value of life. However, we do require symbols to fortify our original confidence. Thus, Christ is the decisive religious symbol for Christian believers. Ogden therefore reasons that Jesus is not absolutely but relatively necessary for Christians. He follows Alfred North Whitehead (1861–1947) in asserting that God has two poles, that is, his primordial nature (the total realm of possibilities) and his consequent nature (God's concreteness as he is related to the world). The primordial nature is abstract, while the consequent nature is fully actual. Whitehead's disciple Charles Hartshorne (1897–2000) reformulates somewhat Whitehead's notion of the dipolarity of God, maintaining that the absolute pole is God's eternal and unchanging nature, while the relative pole is the changing and temporal nature of the Divinity. He also accepts Anselm's argument, affirming that the unsurpassably perfect one necessarily exists.[35]

Ogden's view of the Trinity is fundamentally modalistic. The divine essence can be called Father, while the objectivity of God is the divine Logos, and the divine subjectivity is the Holy Spirit. Since the Father is the original unity from which the divine objectivity and the divine subjectivity flow, Ogden reasons that the Holy Spirit proceeds from both the Father and the Son.[36] He believes it is necessary that the doctrine of God be articulated in trinitarian terms because the logic of our Christian experience requires it. He affirms that the doctrine of the

Trinity is a truth of secular reason as well as of Christian revelation.[37] God is the supreme reality who draws the ever-changing world into his own life. There was never a period when God was not related to a world of some sort. There was no creation out of nothing, and there will never be an end to the temporal process. There is in effect no ultimate future.[38]

Christian faith in Ogden's view does not assure us of subjective immortality, which is enjoyed by God alone. Nonetheless, our lives are important as they affect the one divine life that is eternal. Humankind's undying search for subjective immortality is for Ogden simply a refusal to be at peace and live in the warmth of God's pure and limitless love. He further teaches that God is disclosed always and everywhere through his primordial revelation. Moreover, Jesus is really an example or illustration of the generally accessible truths about God, rather than a unique revelation of God who otherwise could not be known at all.[39] In O'Donnell's judgment, Ogden shows little interest in the historical Jesus, but rather centers his concern on the Christ of the kerygma. The Christ event is not the full and final revelation of God's love, but rather a representative event that is reflective of this love.

O'Donnell then proceeds to evaluate the issue of the Trinity and time in the writings of Jürgen Moltmann, who employs the sufferings of the world as his backdrop.[40] If God is all-powerful, the pain of the world demonstrates that he is either not good or not omnipotent. Thus, a specifically Christian portrait of God—with its foundation in the event of the cross—must be drawn. He insists that the only sure place where God can be recognized is in the event of the cross.[41] The Son who is crucified is differentiated from the one whom he calls Father, while the bond of unity in this self-differentiation is the Spirit. Moltmann grounds this differentiation of subjects in the Deity on the principle that the divine life cannot be fully realized in only one subject or person.

The union of will between the Father and the Son, articulated at the point of their deepest separation, affirms for Moltmann the suffering of the Father, who agonized over the death of his Son. The Spirit's role then is to create occasions for the fullness of God's power in the universe. The work of the Son will not be complete until he hands over the kingdom to the Father, and it is the Spirit who continues the earthly work of Jesus. The fulfillment of the mission of the Trinity in the world constitutes the completion of the persons of the Trinity. Christ's free association with tax collectors and sinners, and his death as a political revolutionary, rendered obsolete the master-slave model of human relationships and establishes the model of friendship as the prototype.

O'Donnell pictures Moltmann's God as capable of change and suffering. The passion of the Son is answered by the copassion of the Father. The actual history of the Father, Son, and Spirit is the beginning of the doctrine of the Trinity. The Deity of Greek metaphysics must give way to a God who is involved in process and history.[42] Both the process thinkers and the eschatological theologians are forging a closer relationship between God and the historical process. Moltmann, however, firmly rejects the notion that human reason can arrive at the truths of faith. God is revealed in a very privileged way in the Christ event, and especially in the event of the cross. On the other hand, Ogden is convinced that God reveals himself in every event and that the Christ event is only important as a representation of God's love that is manifested everywhere.

While Ogden teaches that there is never an end to the temporal process, Moltmann is convinced that there will be an eschatological occurrence wherein history attains its goal. That will be the moment when Jesus hands over the kingdom to the Father. For process thinkers such as Whitehead, God is the aboriginal instance of creativity, whereas for Moltmann God is the very source of all creativity. Creativity for Whitehead is something of a first principle for which no one—not even God—is ultimately responsible. Creativity is rooted in the very élan of reality. It is to be assumed as a controlling force even with regard to God, for the Deity is dependent on the world. God is God precisely by being in relation to the world. Moltmann, on the other hand, teaches that God does not relate to the world out of necessity. Rather, his love for creation is the result of his overflowing abundance of love.

According to O'Donnell, Ogden does not adequately establish a trinitarian foundation for Christian theology because his modalism is inadequate. He also feels that Moltmann's thesis of the suffering God has to be more carefully nuanced, for it seems to be incompatible with divine infinity and immutability.[43] However, both approaches have indeed come to grips with the pressing need to relate God more closely to the world and to temporality.

In 1989 while teaching at Rome's Gregorian University, John O'Donnell published *The Mystery of the Triune God*.[44] In this later work he asserts that both the Hebrews and the early Christians associated God with historical events. He insists that the classical notion of divine immutability must be changed so that God's real relation to the world can be affirmed. Although the position of many process theologians that God could not exist apart from the world seems overdrawn, the idea that God has no real relation to the world is also no longer as popular as it once was. This makes the Deity out to be remote and indifferent to all that transpires in creation. The assertion that God is unable to suffer with humankind runs counter to our experience of the God who is revealed in the Old and New Testaments.

O'Donnell agrees with Moltmann in insisting that the Christian message can only be understood when God is viewed in trinitarian terms.[45] He disagrees with Barth, however, that the divine processions cannot be clarified in terms of analogies relating to the operation of the intellect and will. The work of the Incarnation, according to O'Donnell, remains incomplete until human beings are brought into the love relationship between the Father and the Son through the work of the Holy Spirit. Following Rahner, O'Donnell identifies Jesus as the absolute symbol of God in the sense that God expresses himself fully and uniquely in Christ. He asks if this amounts to a weakening of classical ontological Christology, and he responds that this is rather a contemporary interpretation of Chalcedon.[46] Since God the Father reveals himself in the incarnation of the Son and in the uncreated grace who is the Holy Spirit, God in his own life must exist in these three modes of being. That is, in his infinite being God must be trinitarian. Through Jesus and the Spirit, God has a new mode of being in the world. This phenomenon cannot be reduced in such a way that nothing really happens to God.

The Fourth Gospel and Paul attest to Jesus' divine sonship (e.g., John 3:16; Gal 4:4–5). O'Donnell then asks to what extent this notion can be traced back to Jesus himself. He does not want to affirm that Jesus already claimed to be the Son of God in an absolute sense.[47] However, this later doctrinal development can be traced back to Christ's own singular experience as Son (e.g., his use of the term "Abba"). He believes that Jesus' sense of mission, placing himself above the law of Moses and citing no other authority for his claims than his own word, is grounded in his unique experience of God as Father (Mark 14:36; Rom 8:15; Gal 4:6). Christ's relationship to the Father was profoundly personal (Matt 11:27) and reveals unparalleled intimacy with the Father.

Jesus is revealed as the bearer of the Spirit throughout his entire life, from his conception (Luke 1:35), baptism (Mark 1:10), and beginning of his public life (Luke 4:18) to his resurrection, in which he became a life-giving spirit (1 Cor 15:45). He portrayed himself in Isaian terms as a messenger of mercy and the servant endowed with

God's Spirit (Matt 11: 2–6). His healings and exorcisms were seen by the early church as a sign that he possessed the Holy Spirit in a unique fashion. The "Son of Man" title from Daniel 7:13–14 is seen by O'Donnell as an expression of his vocation to be loyal in his mission, even unto death. He concludes that there is good reason to believe that Jesus thought of himself as Son of God and bearer of the Spirit.[48]

The event of the cross involved the revelation of the whole Trinity. The Son was abandoned and the Father suffered the loss of his Son, while the separation between the two was bridged by the Holy Spirit. Following Moltmann, O'Donnell insists that it would be impossible to maintain that the Father's heart was unaffected by the death of his Son. Out of the event of the cross, the Holy Spirit is poured out on the world. Because the Spirit deifies, she (O'Donnell's preference) is worthy of a divine title.[49] It is the Spirit who forms Christ in the depths of the believer. Spirit Christology, which ties Jesus to the Spirit of Yahweh's activity in history, was overtaken in the church by an incarnational Christology that focused on the ontological identity of Jesus as a divine person. In O'Donnell's judgment, this resulted in a Christology that was more abstract and metaphysical. The relationship between Jesus and the Spirit so pronounced in the New Testament was lost somewhat. In the era of the church, the Spirit is a critical force, continuing and completing the work of Christ. The institutional elements of the church have become so central that the function of the Spirit who moves and unifies the whole body (Vatican II—*The Dogmatic Constitution on the Church,* para. 7) is not sufficiently appreciated. This is especially true in the Western church, whereas in the East a more charismatic view of the church has been cultivated. O'Donnell suggests that the *filioque* in the creed of Nicaea and Constantinople, since it was added unilaterally by Pope Benedict VIII (1012–1024) to the credo professed in Rome, could well be dropped. Also, it might perhaps be preferable to say that the Spirit proceeds from the Father through the Son, because this could further clarify the function of the Son in the procession of the Holy Spirit.

The concept "person" was not easily received within the history of trinitarian thought. Augustine, for example, feared that the term would lead to tritheism. It was Aquinas who identified the three divine persons as subsistent relations, each of whom is identified with the divine essence. Each divine person can be defined in terms of his relationship to the other two.[50] O'Donnell follows Moltmann in favoring a social model of the Trinity wherein being a person means being in relation. The Trinity then is the divine community of persons in relation. There are three subjects but not three consciousnesses in the Deity. Each of the three subjects possesses the same consciousness in a unique way.

Although Karl Barth objects to the idea that the human memory, intellect, and will mirror the triune God, O'Donnell insists that there is a place for the analogy of being in our effort to throw some light on the Trinity. Augustine's attempt to see in the human mind a reflection of the mystery of the triune life has conditioned the treatment of the Trinity ever since. Lateran IV (1215), however, warns that although there are similarities between the Creator and creation, it must be noted that the dissimilarities are greater than the similarities.[51] Thomas Aquinas pointed to similarities between God and created reality because of the necessary similarity between cause and effect. He asserted that it must be possible to predicate finite perfections of God after these qualities have been purified of their finite limitations.[52] O'Donnell compares the analogy of being, which points to God beyond the world, with the analogy of faith, which brings God into the range of human language. God's identification with the crucifixion of Jesus allows us to comprehend the reality of God as love. The paschal mystery radically transforms our notions about the Deity, inasmuch as God the Father did not prevent Jesus' death on the cross. But by the same token, Christ's resurrection transforms our understanding of God, assuring us that God did not abandon him and that Jesus' mission was ratified. Through the power of the Spirit, the work of the risen Lord continues in history. These signs and deeds point to the coming of the kingdom. The awesome question remains, however. How can human history be advancing toward the final eschaton when the world is steeped in suffering?

In 1 Corinthians 15:20–28, the order of God's saving actions is outlined. In the first place, Christ has been raised from the dead. Next, we are to await the general resurrection, and finally, Jesus will hand over the kingdom to the Father. This concluding event will fulfill Christ's mission. The role of the Holy Spirit is in the forefront during the time between the resurrection of Jesus and the eschaton. Thus, there is a constant involvement of the three divine figures in world history. The Deity and time are joined together. God's coming in history through the Son and the Spirit is an open-ended event. John O'Donnell summarizes: "The world does make a difference to God, but not in the sense that it adds something to God's being or increases his value (Hartshorne), but in the sense that out of the infinite possibilities of his freedom, God lets himself be participated in by some finite possibility. . . . As God lets himself be participated in by these created realities, he lets himself be enriched by them."[53]

Catherine Mowry LaCugna

One of the more notable recent studies on the Trinity was produced by Catherine LaCugna (1952–97), who taught at the University of Notre Dame during the last sixteen years of her life. Her work *God for Us* represents a major contribution to the field.[54] A more abbreviated treatment of the subject by LaCugna can be found in the first volume of *Systematic Theology*, edited by Francis Schüssler Fiorenza and John P. Galvin.[55] LaCugna's thesis is that for too long the theology of the Trinity has been separated from the mystery of salvation. She insists throughout that all of theology must be informed by a trinitarian dimension. Through the influence of Athanasius and the Cappadocians in the fourth century, the soteriological basis for the doctrine of the triune Deity was deemphasized in favor of the metaphysical aspects of the mystery. God is not self-contained, says LaCugna, but overflowing love—eager for union with all of creation (Eph 1:3–14).[56]

LaCugna reminds us that the ontological dimensions of the relationship of Father, Son, and Holy Spirit were not pursued until the second half of the fourth century. Before that time most were willing to accept some form of subordinationism that was nonetheless clearly distinct from Arianism. Justin, Irenaeus, and Tertullian reveal subordinationist tendencies, as does Origen. In the era before Arius (ca. 250–336), the economy of salvation was emphasized by most Christian writers. After Nicaea (325) and the affirmation of the full divinity of the Son *(homooúsios),* theologians such as Athanasius asserted that the divine Son, the Logos, could not be said to experience suffering. Christ's sufferings were experienced in the flesh and not in his soul.

It was the Council of Constantinople I (381) that affirmed the divinity of the Holy Spirit. The council fathers declared that there are three *hypostases* (persons) and one *ousia* (nature) in the Deity. The three divine persons were seen as differentiations within God's eternal being.[57] However, the relationships among the divine figures were studied in their ontological rather than their economic dimensions. Both Gregory of Nazianzus (330–89) and Gregory of Nyssa (ca. 335–94) elaborated a theology of divine relations. We can only identify the divine persons as they stand in relation to one another, for the divine essence remains incomprehensible. The Cappadocians are the ones who forged a clear distinction between person and nature and who affirmed that the three persons disclose the unknowable essence of God.[58]

LaCugna contends that it is impossible to conceive of the divine persons apart from their presence and activity in salvation history. Indeed, only through the Son and the Spirit is the Father disclosed to us. In the West it was Augustine (354–430) who decisively shaped subsequent trinitarian thought. His *De Trinitate* placed great emphasis on the unity of the divine essence rather than on the monarchy of the Father. This emphasis virtually eliminated ontological subordinationism, which remained a challenge in the East. For the bishop of Hippo, the contemplation of the image of the Trinity in the human soul is the most effective way to clarify our understanding of the inner life of the Deity. His task was to discover how the three divine figures are related to each other.

Augustine does not really define what constitutes a divine person. He does not employ the term "relation," but rather anticipates somewhat the medieval theologians who speak of three subsistent relations. He argues that the human faculties of memory, understanding, and will—which dwell in each human soul—are reflections of the three persons in the one divine nature. LaCugna suggests, however, that in his tendency to focus on the individual soul, his trinitarian approach rather ignores the larger issue of the economy of salvation so important in the early theology of the Trinity.

Christian prayer and worship in the first few centuries were directed to God the Father through Christ in the Holy Spirit.[59] Although an apparent subordinationism can be observed in certain Eastern doxologies after the fourth century, this simply reflects the order of salvation history and does not imply any ontological subordination of the Son to the Father. The New Testament contains one-clause creeds (e.g., 1 Cor 12:3), bipartite creeds (e.g., 1 Cor 8:6), and occasionally tripartite expressions of faith (e.g., Matt 28:19; 2 Cor 13:13). Hence, one can conclude that traces of the trinitarian pattern are evident from the first century. After Constantinople I (381) certain professions of faith such as the fifth-century Pseudo-Athanasian Creed set out the correct understanding of the inner life of God, although the activity of the divine persons in the economy of salvation was not so clearly articulated.

Thomas Aquinas (1225–74) made little of the operations of the divine persons in the salvific economy. He divided his treatment of the Divinity into two tracts, *De Deo Uno* and *De Deo Trino*. In the latter, the divine saving mission was not a significant issue. Aquinas denied that God has any real relation to the created universe. Creation has a real relation to God, but God has no real relation to creatures. He begins his work on the Trinity by explaining the processions in God. The divine persons are distinguished by the two processions. The four relations of opposition (fatherhood, sonship, spiration, and procession) give rise to the three divine persons. The Father knows himself and speaks himself in the Word, and the Spirit proceeds from both as from a single principle. The processions of the Son and the Holy Spirit are what bring about the divine missions and ground the origin of created reality outside of God. For Aquinas the Deity creates by a free act of the will, whereas Bonaventure (1221–74) teaches that God as the perfect Good necessarily communicates his love in the act of creation.[60] Because Aquinas affirms that the act of creation is common to the whole Trinity—showing forth the unity of the divine nature and not the distinction of persons—the act of creation is severed from any direct connection with the divine missions.

Catherine LaCugna maintains that in scholastic theology, *De Deo Uno* has become essentially a philosophical tract, whereas *De Deo Trino* has been reduced to a treatise outlining the divine processions, the distinction of persons, and the relations. She feels that the differences between the trinitarian theology of the East and the West are almost irreconcilable. From the early Middle Ages, the link between the theology of God and the economy of salvation had been notably weakened in the West. On the other hand, Greek theology has always been essentially economy oriented. In the West, *De Deo Trino* has been identified as the study of God's inner relatedness, having little to do with Christian life and praxis.[61] For the Greeks, "person" rather than "substance" is the ultimate metaphysical category, for it is the person of the Father, and not the divine nature, who is the source of all that exists.[62]

LaCugna then deals at some length with the question of personhood, which has evolved considerably since the days of Descartes and Locke. The understanding of God as the supreme substance gradually gave way to the notion of God as absolute subject. She asserts that Barth's replacement of the term "person" by "modes of being," and Rahner's suggestion of "distinct modes of subsisting" as a superior way of designating the divine figures, are not satisfactory. Both proposals, she argues, seem to lead to a species of modalism in the one divine subject.[63] She has recourse, for example, to the modern Scottish philosopher John Macmurray and the contemporary Orthodox theologian

John Zizioulas to assist her in crafting a more adequate definition of personhood that focuses on relationships with others as the essential ingredient in the formation of persons. She completes her approach to personhood with the help of several insights from liberation and feminist theologians. Macmurray, for example, defines a person as a heterocentric, inclusive, free relational agent, and God as a universal personal Other.[64] "I" exists only in a "you and I" frame of reference. For Zizioulas the actualization of personhood occurs in the movement of freedom toward communion with other persons.[65] Self-affirmation, the acceptance by another in love, and a uniqueness are the basic elements of personhood. The liberation theologians emphasize the social dimension of personal development, while the feminists criticize the structural domination of females by males. In fact, many feminist theologians point to the doctrine of the Trinity as the true agent behind the development of patriarchal religion.

LaCugna insists that the notion of *perichoresis,* that is, the mutual indwelling of the three divine persons, can be seen as the justification for the establishment of an egalitarian human community. The perfect trinitarian communion is diametrically opposed to the domination and hierarchicalism in the church. She affirms that persons, both divine and human, are essentially relational. With each new relationship we exist in a new way. Living as persons in communion is the essence of salvation.[66] To discover the true identity of Jesus, we must study the character and quality of his relationships. LaCugna calls him a "catholic" person because of his unflagging compassion and his consistent commitment to the poor and the disenfranchised in society. She portrays the Holy Spirit as God's outreach to creation, joining us to Christ. She reminds her readers that wherever there is genuine communion among persons, the Holy Spirit is present and active.[67]

The heart of Christian life consists in the encounter with a personal God who makes possible our union with the three divine persons and with each other.[68] LaCugna repeatedly affirms that the doctrine of the Trinity must never be separated from the economy of salvation. The basic reason for teaching that God is incomprehensible mystery is that God is supremely person. What is indeed mysterious is that God is so intent on union with others. The frame of reference for what LaCugna calls a relational ontology is the idea that God as the originating being, by virtue of his love for others, brings about all that exists. She adds that the worship of God necessarily involves identifying ourselves with those who are downtrodden and neglected. The

Christian teaching of Richard of St. Victor and Bonaventure identifies perfection as goodness that is self-diffusive.[69] It is of the very nature of the triune God to exist as persons in communion with others.

> The fecundity of God, which originates with the Unoriginate Origin, gives rise to the Son and is completed in the Spirit. . . . The images of "begetting" and "spirating" express the fruitfulness or fecundity of God who is alive from all eternity as a dynamic interchange of persons united in love. . . . The centrifugal movement of divine love does not terminate "within" God but explodes outward. . . . To be the Creator, that is, to be in relation to creation as the Creator is not a relation added on to the divine essence, ancillary to God's being. To be God is to be the Creator of the world. . . . The reason lies entirely in the unfathomable mystery of God.[70]

LaCugna argues in closing that soteriological and doxological considerations change the view of the Trinity as a speculative conundrum and shift the focus to the consideration of God's self-expression in history and in personhood.[71]

Observations

More than any other Catholic theologian, Karl Rahner prompted the renewal of trinitarian theology in the 1950s and '60s. He insists that only the Logos, as the Father's self-revelation, could assume a human nature. Rahner contends that the concept of person is troublesome because it has come to imply a distinct center of consciousness that would involve us in tritheism if applied to the Trinity. He prefers to refer to the three divine persons as three distinct manners of subsisting. Again and again Rahner affirms that our understanding of the immanent Trinity comes from the economic Trinity. It is through the Incarnation and the historical activity of the Holy Spirit that the mystery of the triune God is made available to us. Augustine's psychological explanation of the triune life is not viewed by Rahner as especially helpful because it sidesteps the work of the Trinity in the economy of salvation. It is through the missions of the Son and the Holy Spirit that the immanent Trinity is revealed to us. Rahner sensed the need for a thorough revision of the tract on the Trinity that would feature a much closer identification between the presentation of the immanent and the economic Trinity.

In the New Testament, "Father" virtually becomes the name for God, while Jesus, through his words and deeds, asserts his unique power over the Mosaic law. At Nicaea the Son is declared to be of the same substance as the Father. Walter Kasper attests that the emphasis on the theology of the cross was promoted to a notable extent by Martin Luther, and this allowed Christians to appreciate more deeply the sufferings of the divine Son. The presence of the Spirit during the entire life of Jesus is emphasized by Kasper, who is a strong proponent of Spirit Christology. The *filioque* issue still divides East and West, for the East believes that this represents an unacceptable insertion of philosophical thought into the divine mystery. The idea of one Divinity in three persons, described as the singular insight of Christianity, affirms a community of love within the Deity, who cannot be understood as a solitary figure, for this would bring about a necessary rather than a free relationship between God and the world. Kasper maintains that were it not for the divine persons actually being disclosed in the course of history, the real differences among the divine figures might be seen as nothing more than modal distinctions.

Our doctrine of God is to be more firmly situated within the context of the actions of God and Jesus in history. After reviewing the work of Schubert Ogden, John O'Donnell affirms that the process theologian's modalism is not acceptable as a credible analysis of the Trinity. He also concludes that Moltmann's thesis of the suffering God still seems to be incompatible with divine infinity and immutability. Following Rahner, O'Donnell identifies Jesus as the absolute symbol of God. Further, since God the Father reveals himself in the incarnation of the Son and in the uncreated grace who is the Holy Spirit, the Deity in its own immanent life must exist as these three distinct subsistent relations. Jesus throughout his entire life is revealed as the bearer of the Holy Spirit. In the event of the cross, there is a unique and unsurpassed revelation of the whole Trinity. The Father's heart must have been deeply affected by the death of his Son, and from the event of the cross, the Spirit is poured out on the world. Each divine person can be defined in terms of his relationship to the other two. Each possesses the one divine consciousness in a singular fashion. The order of God's saving actions, which began with Jesus' resurrection and continues through time with the intervention of the Holy Spirit, will be concluded when Jesus hands over the kingdom to the Father.

For too long the theology of the Trinity has been separated from the mystery of salvation. Catherine LaCugna contends that before Arius the economy of salvation, rather than the ontological dimensions of the Trinity, was emphasized by most Christian writers. She maintains that it is impossible to conceive of the divine persons apart from their presence and activity in salvation history. Augustine in his *De Trinitate* largely ignored the issue of the economy of salvation. Also, Aquinas in his *De Deo Trino* did not treat the triune saving missions. Since he taught that the act of creation is common to the whole Trinity, this divine activity is severed from any connection with the missions of the Son and the Holy Spirit. With the aid of certain contemporary scholars, LaCugna attempts to craft a definition of personhood that focuses on relationships and communion with others as the principal ingredients. She teaches that the notion of *perichoresis,* the mutual indwelling of the three divine persons, serves as the justification for the establishment of an egalitarian human community—for living as persons in communion is the essence of salvation. LaCugna reaffirms that the doctrine of the Trinity must never again be separated from the unfolding mystery of salvation.

Notes

1. For example, Hans Urs von Balthasar, Yves Congar, William Hill, Gerald O'Collins, and David Coffey. See the bibliography for details.

2. Karl Rahner, "Theos in the New Testament," *Theological Investigations* (vol. 1; trans. Cornelius Ernst; London: Darton, Longman & Todd, 1961), 79–148. This volume was originally published in German in 1954.

3. Ibid., 135–37. They are John 1:1, 18; 20:28; Romans 9:5; Titus 2:13; 1 John 5:20.

4. Ibid., 143.

5. Karl Rahner, *The Trinity* (trans. Joseph Donceel; Tunbridge Wells: Burns & Oates, 1970). The original German edition was published in 1967.

6. H. Denzinger and A. Schönmetzer, *Enchiridion Symbolorum,* 32d ed. (Freiburg: Herder, 1963), no. 1330.

7. Rahner, *Trinity,* 103.

8. David Tracy, *The Analogical Imagination* (New York: Crossroad, 1986), 184.

9. Denzinger and Schönmetzer, *Enchiridion,* no. 3004.

10. Karl Rahner, *Foundations of Christian Faith* (trans. William V. Dych; New York: Crossroad, 1986), 64.

11. Ibid., 177.

12. Denzinger and Schönmetzer, *Enchiridion,* no. 301.

13. Rahner, *Foundations,* 215.

14. Ibid., 116–37.

15. Ibid., 132.

16. Ibid., 133.

17. Ibid., 135.

18. Ibid., 136.

19. Walter Kasper, *The God of Jesus Christ* (trans. M. J. O'Connell; New York: Crossroad, 1988).

20. Ibid., 140.

21. Denzinger and Schönmetzer, *Enchiridion*, no. 150.

22. Ibid., nos. 805, 853.

23. Kasper, *The God of Jesus Christ,* 250.

24. Ibid., 259.

25. Ibid., 273.

26. Ibid., 275.

27. Ibid., 280.

28. Ibid., 288.

29. Ibid., 299.

30. Ibid., 303.

31. Ibid., 308–9.

32. Ibid., 314.

33. John O'Donnell, *Trinity and Temporality* (Oxford: Oxford University Press, 1983).

34. Schubert Ogden, *The Reality of God* (New York: Harper & Row, 1966).

35. O'Donnell, *Trinity and Temporality,* 75–76.

36. Ibid., 82.

37. Ibid., 86.

38. Ibid., 90.

39. Ibid., 166.

40. Jürgen Moltmann, *The Trinity and the Kingdom* (trans. Margaret Kohl; San Francisco: Harper & Row, 1981). The original German edition was published in 1980.

41. Ibid., 114.

42. Ibid., 162.

43. Ibid., 196–97.

44. John O'Donnell, *The Mystery of the Triune God* (New York: Paulist Press, 1989).

45. Ibid., 18.

46. Ibid., 31–32.

47. Ibid., 41.

48. Ibid., 55-56.

49. Ibid., 75.

50. Ibid., 102.

51. Denzinger and Schönmetzer, *Enchiridion*, no. 806.

52. O'Donnell, *The Mystery of the Triune God*, 118.

53. Ibid., 172.

54. Catherine Mowry LaCugna, *God for Us: The Trinity and Christian Life* (San Francisco: Harper Collins, 1991).

55. Catherine Mowry LaCugna, "The Trinitarian Mystery of God," *Systematic Theology: Roman Catholic Perspectives* (vol. 1; ed. Francis Schüssler Fiorenza and John P. Galvin; Minneapolis: Fortress Press, 1991), 151–92.

56. LaCugna, *God for Us,* 15.

57. Ibid., 53.

58. Ibid., 68.

59. Ibid., 126.

60. Ibid., 164.

61. Ibid., 210.

62. Ibid., 249.

63. Ibid., 254.

64. Ibid., 259.

65. Ibid., 260. John D. Zizioulas outlines his rather novel approach to personal identity in *Being as Communion* (Crestwood, N.Y.: St. Vladimir's Seminary Press, 1997), 27–65.

66. Ibid., 292.

67. Ibid., 299.

68. Ibid., 319.

69. Ibid., 353.

70. Ibid., 354–55.

71. Ibid., 367.

9
RECENT PROTESTANT CONTRIBUTIONS TO TRINITARIAN THEOLOGY

Among recent Protestant scholars there have been some quite significant refinements in trinitarian thought. Karl Barth stands out as perhaps the most important contributor to the theology of the Trinity in the mid-twentieth century. The other theologians treated in this chapter reacted to Barth either positively or negatively, but he did represent a point of departure for each of them. This chapter also covers two outstanding German theologians, Wolfhart Pannenberg and Jürgen Moltmann, as well as the American thinker Robert Jenson. These four academics can be considered a representative crosscut of Protestant trinitarian thought in the past one hundred years.

Karl Barth

Born in Basel into a predominantly ecclesiastical family, Karl Barth (1886–1968) studied in Berlin under Harnack and at Marburg under Hermann. After serving for about ten years as pastor in the small Swiss town of Safenwil, he taught theology at Göttingen, Münster, and Bonn in Germany. In 1935 Barth was banned from teaching in Germany because of his anti-Nazi views, so he returned to Switzerland and the University of Basel, where he taught until his retirement in 1962. In 1927 he published the first volume of his projected *Christian Dogmatics,* and five years later he thoroughly revised the project, taking something of a new direction that would permit him to expand the biblical, theological, and historical underpinnings of his presentation. The first half-volume entitled *The Doctrine of the Word of God,* published in 1932, represented the beginning of his celebrated *Church Dogmatics*, which eventually ran to thirteen formidable volumes, extending to more than eight thousand pages. In chapter 2 of the first volume, he sets out his formal treatment of the Trinity.[1]

Barth approaches the doctrine of the Trinity at the very outset as he deals with the question of revelation. For him the Trinity is what distinguishes the Christian doctrine of God and constitutes the kernel of Christian faith and the ground of all other dogmas.[2] Revelation need not be demonstrated or corroborated on the basis of anything else. It is its own demonstration. One who receives biblical revelation is confronted with its awesome power and simply accepts it. The lordship of God shines through the revelation and need not be legitimated in any other way. This "lordship" is what Barth calls the very root of the doctrine of the Trinity. The trinitarian doctrine is the work of the church and represents a careful analysis of the revelation. He argues, however, that it is incumbent upon us to continue age after age to develop and refine our presentation of the mystery.

According to Barth, it is impossible to speak of the nature and attributes of God without assuming that we are dealing with God the Father, the Son, and the Holy Spirit. Although we cannot expect to find an explicit rendering of the notion of the Trinity in either the Old or the New Testament, many passages serve as ground for the elaboration of the doctrine.[3] That the Scriptures disclose God's freedom to distinguish himself from himself is evident from the fact that he is not only God the Father, but also God the Son. Furthermore, God's revelation to humankind is effected in historical events occurring between God and certain specific men and women. This historical revelation comes to us vertically from heaven.

Barth takes up the ancient Augustinian question of the vestiges of the Trinity *(vestigia Trinitatis)*, which are creaturely realities that remind one of the trinitarian God. He asks whether the origin of this doctrine can be discovered somehow in the traces of the Trinity that seem to appear in creation. That is not the case, according to Barth. Those who have put forward this suggestion did not really intend to imply that there is a natural access to the Trinity that complements revelation. It seems nonetheless that this might have been what was understood. He unquestionably rejects the thesis of the *vestigia Trinitatis* inasmuch as it is divine revelation that provides the only access to the doctrine.

The so-called three "persons" in God have really nothing to do with personality in the modern sense. We are not dealing with three divine egos, but three modes of the one divine "I."[4] The oneness of God is not such that he can be considered isolated or alone. The Divine Being does not need the world, because there is perfect communion among the three persons. Barth attests, however, that the modern concept of personality has created considerable confusion. In fact, many scholars ask whether the word "person" should still be used in connection with the trinitarian tract, since the term "mode of being" seems to disclose the triune Divinity more accurately. God is one in three distinct and absolutely essential modes of being, that is, Father, Son, and Holy Spirit. Karl Barth assures us, however, that he does not wish to eliminate the concept "person," because it is a reminder of the historical continuity of the problem.[5]

In the Divine Being the first divine mode is pure origin, the second divine mode is attributed solely to the origin, and the third divine mode proceeds from the first and the second. The Father possesses himself as pure giver, the Son as receiver and giver, and the Spirit as pure receiver.[6] Karl Barth insists that each divine mode of existence participates in the other divine modes, because these three modes of existence are identical with the original relations. This *perichoresis*, that is, the passing of one into another, has been noted in church tradition from patristic times. Although the dogma of the Trinity was not fully articulated until the fourth century, the Roman and Orthodox churches, as well as the Reformers of the sixteenth century, have consistently affirmed it. The declaration that the Father, Son, and Holy Spirit are equally God has been traditionally affirmed by the Christian churches as the doctrine of the Trinity.

God the Father is fully made known as the Father and creator of all through Jesus. The name "Father" discloses God's mode of existence as the originator of the eternal Son and the Holy Spirit. Furthermore, along with the Son and the Spirit, the Father is the reconciling God and the redeeming God. These three modes of divine existence are in perpetual communion with one another. Barth contends that because Jesus reveals the Father as God, he must himself be divine. If Christ were only a creature, he would not be able to reveal God, for who can reveal God but God himself? In the process of revealing God as Father, Jesus discloses himself as the divine Son. Christ as the Word reveals the pattern of our reconciliation and radically restores our communion with God that has been destroyed by our sinfulness. This represents the second great work of God.[7] The work of reconciliation follows the initial divine activity, the creation.

The Reformers never attacked the doctrine of Christ's divinity, and they attributed great significance to the creed of Nicaea and Constantinople I. This creed encapsulates the mature faith of the early church. The Son is professed as the eternal Son, light of light, true God of true God. Both the Father and the Son exist in two distinct ways in the same divine essence. The divine Word was spoken by the Father before all time. The declaration that the Word is of one substance with the Father affirms that he is not a lesser God or a demigod, and it rejects the possibility of polytheism, because the Father and the Son are of one essence. The Son also shares in the work of creation, for he is the one through whom all things were made. The Word is the one who proclaims to us judgment and grace.

In addition to the unfolding of revelation through the action of the Father and the Son, the subjective side of the event is the work of the Holy Spirit. After Jesus' death and resurrection, Barth believes the objective revelation had been concluded and that the action of the Spirit now prepares attentive hearers to embrace the saving message. Thus, God not only comes to us from without, but also from within as an illumination and an urging. The Spirit bears witness to our spirit that we are the sons and daughters of God (Rom 8:16). We become sons and daughters of God by receiving the Holy Spirit. Although distinct from the Father and the Son, he is not less than they. The New Testament indicates that the activity of the Spirit implies his full divinity (John 4:24; 2 Cor 3:17). The Holy Spirit can be called the subjective element in the event of revelation, and this work can only be ascribed to God himself.[8]

According to Barth, the doctrine of the Holy Spirit represents the final stage in the articulation of our belief in the Trinity. It was a rather slow process to reach the faith consensus that the Spirit is fully divine and equal in divinity to the Father and the Son. With the Father and Son, the Spirit is identified as the one sovereign divine subject. The Spirit is the "common factor" between the Father and Son and is the act of "communityness" between Father and Son.[9] Their love for each other brings about someone equal to them, who with the Son is also the reconciler and an active agent in the work of creation. Barth continually reminds us that the activity of the Trinity outside of the Divine Being is shared by all three.

The Spirit comes forth from the unique procession termed spiration, although we cannot discern the "how" of the divine processions. According to Barth, it would have been perfectly logical for *filioque* to have been included in the original creed.[10] He agrees completely with the Western tradition concerning the *filioque*. He asserts that it is not fair to emphasize a passage such as John 15:26, which speaks of the procession of the Spirit from the Father, over the many pericopes that identify him as the Spirit of the Son. The denial of the immanent *filioque* destroys for Barth the idea of the complete substantial communion between the Father and Son that constitutes the essence of the Holy Spirit.

> How then should the breathing of the Spirit belong less essentially, less really and originally to the Son than to the Father? . . . Should not this Spirit be directly the Spirit of the Son as well? Is the Son here just mediately and derivatively the Giver of the Spirit, the Revealer of Love? But if he is so here immediately and directly, how can he be so, if he is not so in reality, in the reality of God, antecedently in himself?[11]

The *filioque* therefore bespeaks the common origin of the Spirit from the Father and the Son. Thus, the Father and the Son are the origin of the Spirit, who is a distinct and equal mode of God's existence, who is to be worshiped and glorified exactly as the Father and the Son. Justification and sanctification have traditionally been attributed to this third divine subject.

Some fourteen years later, after the publication of the first half of volume 1 of *Christian Dogmatics*, Barth delivered a series of lectures on the Apostles' Creed at the University of Bonn.[12] He affirms that God in the sense of the Christian confession is the one who has come to us and become ours. He is to be found in the Old Testament and New Testament, and no attempt is ever made in the Scriptures to prove God. Indeed, he is identified as the one who needs no proof. The works of creation, the covenant, and redemption are the events in which God makes himself known. The creed sets out in three articles the activity of God the creator, the work of Jesus Christ, and the operation of the Holy Spirit, one God in three "ways of being."[13] When Christians profess God as Father, we mean that he is Father himself by nature and in eternity, and also that he is Father for us as well. The Father is described first and foremost as the Almighty, the foundation of all reality, and the measure of everything that is. The Old Testament relates the creation story in the two accounts found in Genesis, chapters 1 and 2, and both of these are deeply connected with the history of the Jewish people. God is portrayed as having no need of the world. His creative activity is seen as the sheer outpouring of fatherly kindness and compassion. He continues to hold all of creation in existence solely by the work of his hand.

Barth's *The Doctrine of the Word of God*, volume 1, part 2, was published in English more than twenty years after the first half of volume 1.[14] Jesus is identified as the objective reality of revelation. The first message of the New Testament is contained in the very name of Jesus Christ, which discloses the truth of his God-manhood. The second truth revealed about Jesus is that he is the Son of God. The existence of Christ affirms that God can traverse the boundary between himself and humankind. In the mode of existence as the Son, the one nature of God entered the human condition, and thus God, as the Word or the Son, is made manifest to us. From the reality of Jesus we have come to understand that revelation is possible from God's side.[15] And this knowledge is validated through the saving words and actions of Christ's life, especially through the resurrection. The Incarnation was necessary so that God might become manifest to us, that he might be free for us.[16]

Barth then points to the Holy Spirit as the subjective reality of revelation. Through the doctrine of the Trinity we have come to know how the state of revealedness is achieved for us in the person of the Holy Spirit.[17] The Holy Spirit acting in us is also revelation, for he transforms us into recipients of divine revelation. This transforming action takes place in the church, which is the ambience of God's revelation for us. The objective signs bringing the revelation to us—for example, Scripture, preaching, baptism, the Lord's Supper—put us into contact with the saving power of God. This sign giving must be regarded as a divine activity whereby the objective revelation is addressed to us now just as it has been from apostolic times. These signs must always be reshaped and adapted so that they will speak with freshness, clarity, and vigor in every age. The subjective side of this transforming activity is supplied by the witness of the Holy Spirit who discloses the divine revelation to us. We are convinced of the truth of revelation—made available to us in and through these signs—and this is the work of the Holy Spirit.

Individuals become aware that they are children of God. Our eyes and hearts are opened and we are sealed by the objective revelation, which takes life within us. Barth affirms that this is all we can say about the transforming experience of the Holy Spirit that draws us into the reality of revelation. He calls it a miracle and points to Romans 5:5, which explains how "God has poured out his love into our hearts through the Holy Spirit whom he has given to us." Our interior acceptance of the Word of God is the result of a freedom that God has given to us. What is given to us by the outpouring of the Holy Spirit is the possibility of a singular intimacy with God, but we do not really know how this occurs. Christians are convinced that they are accepted by God, but they are also aware that they remain sinners.

We sense that we can no longer withdraw from the Word of God, because he becomes our master. We have been captured by God's supreme authority, yet we still remain independent. The purpose of the Word and the Spirit is to make the believer conformable to God.[18]

Thus, Barth expands and deepens his presentation of the immanent Trinity by emphasizing the roles of the three persons in creation, redemption, and sanctification. It is in his exposition of the economic Trinity that he completes his portrait of these three distinct modes of being—Father, Son, and Holy Spirit—in the one divine essence.

Wolfhart Pannenberg

In the earlier writings of Wolfhart Pannenberg (b. 1928), there were few references to the doctrine of the Trinity as such. Even his first studies regarding the concept of God did not make much use of trinitarian terminology.[19] He felt that the discussion of the three divine persons should take place at the end rather than at the outset of systematic theology. However, a 1981 study revealed a change of heart for Pannenberg.

> In recent years the doctrine of God has taken more and more definitive shape in my thought. Whereas in earlier years God to me was the unknown God who came close only in Jesus Christ and could be approached only in him "from below," . . . today I feel much more confident to develop a doctrine of God and to treat the subjects of dogmatics in that perspective. That doctrine will be more thoroughly trinitiarian than any example I know of.[20]

In the first volume of his *Systematic Theology,* (1991) Pannenberg presents his mature thought on the subject of the Trinity.[21] He identifies as the very heart of Jesus' message the announcement of the proximity of the divine reign. Moreover, it is in Christ that God manifests himself definitively as Father. The Old Testament only infrequently refers to the God of Israel as Father. In 2 Samuel 7:14 God declares himself to be the Father of David, the king of Israel. Much later in 3 Isaiah 63:16, common prayer is directed to God as Father because the whole people are then seen as sons and daughters of God. For Jesus, "Father" is the proper name for God. He clearly differentiates himself from the Father, whom he identifies as greater than himself (John 14:28). This differentiation is likewise reflected in the Lord's Prayer. Paul declares that by Jesus' resurrection from the dead he was confirmed as the divine Son (Rom 1:3–4) whose full stature will be disclosed only in the last days. For Pannenberg it was a short distance from this point to the affirmation of his preexistence (Gal 4:4). The term *kurios*—a proper name for God—was predicated of the risen Christ and carries the notion of his full deity (John 20:28).

The Holy Spirit is seen as the medium of communication between Jesus and the Father and the agent who shares the life of the exalted Christ with believers (Rom 8:11). By receiving the Spirit, believers share in the divine sonship of Jesus. According to Pannenberg, the fellowship of Jesus with the Father implies the person of the Spirit in the relationship. In fact, the Spirit is the medium of God's presence in Jesus, much as the Deity was present through the Spirit in the Old Testament prophets. The involvement of the Holy Spirit in the work of Christ and in the union between Jesus and the Father indicates that the Christian understanding of God reached its mature configuration in the doctrine of the Trinity.[22] The very early appearance of the baptismal formula (Matt 28:19) contributed significantly to the theology of the Trinity, particularly in the Western church.

Although the New Testament statements do not clarify the relationships among the three divine figures, they do attest to the fact that they are interrelated. Paul distinguishes between the *pneuma* and the *kurios,* but not as clearly as does John, who identifies the Holy Spirit as "another Advocate" (John 14:16). The second Advocate who will come when Jesus leaves (John 16:7) is truly distinct from the Son. This distinction between Christ and the Spirit was not clearly seen by all the Fathers in the second and third centuries (e.g., Irenaeus), but in Tertullian and Origen the Son was portrayed as distinct from both the Father and the Holy Spirit. This is what grounded the notion that there are three persons in the Trinity. The challenge, of course, was to reconcile this notion with the heavy monotheistic emphasis in the traditional biblical portrait of God. The monarchians protested against the threefold divine persons, while the subordinationists affirmed the essential supremacy of the Father. It was largely Athanasius (ca. 295–373) who dealt the fatal blow to subordinationism prior to the Council of Constantinople I (381), which professed the full divinity of both the Son and the Spirit. The Cappadocians taught that the unity of the three divine persons is rooted in their common activity, but the divine activity did not provide any real foundation for a distinction of persons.[23]

The Cappadocians also emphasized that the Father is the source of the Deity, such that the Divine Being was understood as proper to the Father alone, with the Son and the Spirit viewed as the recipients of the divinity from the Father. In the age of high scholasticism, the existence, nature, and attributes of God were consistently addressed before the consideration of the three divine persons. Anselm (1033–1109) was convinced that he could deduce the Trinity from the divine unity by distinguishing the thinker, the thought, and the love that connects them in the one essence. Richard of St. Victor (d. 1173), by focusing on God as love, insisted that this calls forth a plurality of persons, for God's love requires a fully divine person as a suitable beloved. Further, the love of Father and Son is totally expressed in the Holy Spirit, for those joined together in love should have a third to share it.[24] Thomas Aquinas (1225–74) adopted Augustine's approach and refined it. For the bishop of Hippo, the distinctions among the persons are conditioned by their mutual relations, which in the divine essence are not mutable, nor are they accidents. For Aquinas the intradivine processions establish the doctrine of the persons as subsistent relations. Pannenberg affirms that Aquinas more than anyone else formulated the classical doctrine of the Trinity.

The Reformers also treated the existence and nature of God before considering the Trinity. They insisted on the development of the doctrine from scriptural sources. By the nineteenth century, according to Pannenberg, Protestant thinkers felt the need to reestablish belief in the concept of Spirit. In the philosophy of G. W. F. Hegel (1770–1831), the doctrine of the triune God in terms of the self-conscious Spirit achieved its classical form.[25] He arrived at a plurality of persons through the notion of love but was unable to reconcile this with his idea of the self-consciousness of the absolute Spirit. Karl Barth placed the immanent Trinity as the centerpiece of his systematics, but for him there is no plurality of persons, but rather three distinct modes of being in the one divine subjectivity. In Pannenberg's judgment, the notion of love allows for a distinction among the divine persons more readily than the concept of spirit. There remains, however, the danger that the equal status of the Son and the Holy Spirit with the Father is compromised to the extent that God is first and foremost identified as Father. The most effective way to approach the doctrine of the Trinity is to reflect on how the Father, Son, and Holy Spirit manifest themselves and relate to one another in history.

Pannenberg argues that it is difficult to find clear trinitarian statements in the New Testament. Even the baptismal formula in Matthew 28:19 fails to provide an adequate base for trinitarian theology because it does not answer the question concerning the relations among the persons.[26] The New Testament affirms the divinity of the

Son (e.g., John 20:28) and of the Spirit (John 15:26; 1 Cor 2:10), but the trinitarian formulas do not clearly disclose the triune pattern of the Divinity. It is critical that we begin with the relationship between Jesus and the Father and recall that the New Testament declarations identify Christ as the divine Son. The Holy Spirit is seen as a distinct figure as we come to understand Jesus as the preexistent Son and begin to appreciate the Spirit's separate and indispensable role in salvation history.

Jesus distinguishes himself from the Father (John 14:28), and in the act of self-distinction he identifies himself as God the Son. Christ is seen as the one who fulfills the role assigned to him by the Father. This sharing of power between Father and Son reveals the radical relationship between the two. In this transfer of power, the Father's kingdom and his divinity are made dependent on the Son. In the passion and death of Jesus, the Father also is deeply affected, for he is identified as love. The distinction of the Holy Spirit from the Father and Son is dramatically disclosed in John 14:16. Pannenberg observes that the church fathers used this as a basis for their observations concerning the Spirit as a distinct person. As the Son glorifies the Father (John 17:4), so the Spirit will glorify the Son (John 16:14).[27] John's declarations concerning the coming of the Paraclete (e.g., 15:26) provide the rationale for the Spirit's role in carrying forward the mission of Christ.

Pannenberg attests that we cannot hold with Augustine that the Spirit proceeds from both the Father and the Son. He teaches that the Spirit proceeds from the Father and is received by the Son. The Son shares with the Father in the sending of the Spirit into the world. Because of this, the Spirit can rightly be called the Spirit of Christ. "But this does not alter the fact that the Spirit originates and proceeds from the Father."[28] Pannenberg recommends, therefore, that the *filioque* in the creed of Constantinople I be eliminated because it does not reflect the teaching of the New Testament and is a Western addition that has never been agreed to by the East.

For Pannenberg the divine persons are not three modes of being in the one divine subject. They are rather three separate and dynamic centers of action. They can be considered three separate centers of consciousness, whereas Karl Rahner insists that the one divine consciousness exists in a threefold mode. Pannenberg asserts that the divine subsistent relations are not merely the result of their differences of origin. In addition to generating the Son, the Father has handed over his kingdom to him and will receive it back from him in the final days. The Son is not just begotten of the Father, he is also lovingly obedient to him throughout his life on earth. Thus, he glorifies the Father as the ever faithful Son. Similarly, the Holy Spirit is not just spirated. He fills the Son and glorifies him. Each of the divine persons is related in many ways to the other two. The trinitarian relations of origin do not express the full range of the intricate relatedness among the three.

The view of the Cappadocians that the Father is the font and source of the Deity actually seems to threaten the equality of the three. The Son is equal to the Father ontologically, but he subjects himself to the Father as the divine Son, as well as in the fulfillment of his mission. As Pannenberg says, "The unity of the trinitarian God cannot be seen in detachment from his revelation and his related work in the economy of salvation."[29] The monarchy of the Father is realized through the work of the Son and the Holy Spirit, who are the divine agents in creation and in salvation history. Thus, the Father makes himself dependent on the actions of the Son and the Spirit in history. The divine persons' dependence on one another is reflected in the crucifixion, when even the deity of the Father can be questioned. The personal subjectivity of the Holy Spirit is confirmed and expressed in his glorification of the Father and the Son.

Pannenberg stresses that the full revelation of the triune God will be completed only in the eschaton. He affirms that the divine unity cannot be adequately addressed until we have set forth our best faith understanding of the triune persons. This approach reverses the treatment of the Deity that, from the Middle Ages, began with the nature and attributes of the one God and then concentrated on the Trinity of persons. Pannenberg insists that the divine persons are separate centers of action, rather than mere modes of being of the one divine subject. However, they are never to be considered as three species of a common genus, namely God. The church fathers from the earliest days insisted that we can know the existence of the Deity, even though the divine essence is beyond our grasp. Aquinas taught that God's perfection, goodness, infinity, and eternity could be deduced from the idea that he is the first cause of all things. Luther affirmed that we have an intuitive knowledge of God's existence, although God's identity and nature remain veiled in mystery. According to Pannenberg, it is imperative that we conceive of the Deity as an active and abiding presence in the world, rather than a merely transcendent reality. "The essence of the one God is revealed by both Father and Son and by their communion in a third, the Spirit, who proceeds from the Father and is received by the Son and given to his people."[30] The three persons thus constitute "a single constellation."

The qualities that we predicate of God reflect his relations to creation. His infinity and eternity remove spatial and temporal limits, while omniscience, omnipotence, and omnipresence are his positive qualities. Since there is no composition in the Deity, the triunity of God can be known to us only through supernatural faith. Hegel felt that if the concept of essence were defined in a more relational manner, this would make the three subsistent relations in the Trinity somewhat more credible to us. In Pannenberg's view, the trinitarian figures can be distinctively described as persons on the basis of their unique self-relations that are mediated through their relationships with each other.[31] He reiterates that the essence of the Deity is not to be considered a separate subject in addition to the three persons, who cannot simply be reduced to aspects of the one divine subject. Rather, the three persons and they alone are the immediate subjects of the divine activity. The Deity as such is not to be conceived as an agent distinct from the activity of the Father, Son, and Holy Spirit.

The early Christians understood that the final events of salvation history would be made known only in the last days when the saving plan of the Father, Son, and Spirit will be fully revealed. Although the Deity is not in any way completed by the divine activity in the world, God does become dependent on the fulfillment of his salvific plan in history. The statement in John that "God is Spirit" (4:24) provides a reflection of the divine essence, as does another observation in John that "God is Love" (1 John 4:18). All the other attributes of the Deity flow out of the notions of divine infinity, God as Spirit, and God as Love.

Pannenberg then proceeds to analyze the more significant of the divine attributes. Infinity, for example, is implied in a good number of the biblical descriptions of God and is related to the divine holiness. Separation from everything profane or secular is the definition of holiness, which implies the need to protect worship from defilement. By the same token, the profane world must be protected from the holy, for contact with the holy can on occasion cause death (Exod 19:12). The holiness of God is expressed first and foremost in his acts of judgment. The divine eternity stands in stark contrast to the frailty and corruptibility of all creation, and this leads to the notion that God is open to all reality—the past, the present, and the future. The divine omnipotence can be considered as a consequence of his eternity. Because all things are present to him, he has power over all of reality.[32]

Both John (3:16) and Paul (Rom 5:5) declare that the most important message revealed throughout the life of Jesus is that in him God's love is manifested in a unique and privileged manner in the world. From the history of Jesus, we discover that the three divine figures have their personal distinctiveness through their mutual relations. The Father is Father only in relation to the Son, and the Son is Son in perfect obedience to the Father. The Spirit is Spirit as he glorifies the Father and the Son and unites them. Each divine figure is distinct in the working out of his personal existence.[33] In God's disclosure to Moses of his divine name, "I will be who I will be," (Exod 3:14), God is identified through his presence and activity in history. He will be with his creation and his elect, who will never be forgotten or abandoned. The Father's transcendence is complemented in salvation history by the immanence of the Son and the Spirit who effect the reconciliation of the world. The divine omnipotence is completed through the activity of the Son and the Spirit. The triune God hovers over the world and moves it forward to its final consummation.

Pannenberg suggests that we can envision the trinitarian life as a progressive revelation and unfolding of the divine love. The manifold functions of the divine persons in the cosmos and in human history are further enunciated in dogmatic theology through the treatment of creation, reconciliation, and redemption. Only with the consummation of the world does the doctrine of God reach its final phase. At the end of history, the unique characteristics of the three divine persons will be revealed more clearly.

Jürgen Moltmann

A professor of systematic theology at Tübingen for twenty-seven years and presently a professor emeritus, Jürgen Moltmann (b. 1926) was not interested in setting out a system of dogmatics, for he believed that such systems do not readily present themselves for open discussion. His work *The Trinity and the Kingdom*, published in German in 1980 and translated into English in 1981, was dedicated to healing the schism between the Eastern and Western churches in the area of trinitarian thought. For Moltmann a critical question is whether or not the Trinity is a practical truth. He points out that Immanuel Kant insisted that the number of persons in the Deity is unimportant because one cannot derive from this difference any directives for everyday living. Because Kant was convinced that truth must be practical and concrete, he felt that a single divine person was adequate to provide a basis for responsible human behavior.

With the rise of modern subjectivity promoted by Descartes (1596–1650) and others, the proof of God's existence came to be drawn from the experience of human self-consciousness rather than from the existence and properties of the cosmos. The Divinity came to be seen as the absolutely perfect subject. However, to understand the data provided by the New Testament, theologians from the earliest times have had to devise a trinitarian concept of God. The notions from Greek philosophy of the Divine Being as immovable and impassible placed restrictions on the information disclosed in the Scriptures. Especially in the West, the unity of the absolute divine subject was emphasized to such a degree that the trinitarian persons often came to be identified as three aspects or modes of the one divine subject.

Moltmann desires to develop a historical doctrine of the Trinity from the history of the divine Son, Jesus. He begins with the trinity of persons and then focuses on the divine unity.[34] One of Moltmann's principal contributions is his abiding emphasis on God's involvement in the passion of Christ. Christian faith must be able to see God in the passion and death of Jesus, for otherwise the cross would be nothing more than a human tragedy. Moltmann insists that if God were incapable of suffering, he would also be incapable of love. A being who is able to love another opens himself up to the suffering that love for another brings him.[35] Origen (ca. 185–253), who first wrote about the suffering of God, believed that the Father is capable of suffering and is able to feel our pain. He alludes to a divine passion (i.e., the suffering of love) that exists between the Father and the Son.

Moltmann notes that Abraham Heschel, the renowned Jewish biblical scholar, opposed the notion of the apathetic God. In Israel's life God frequently manifested himself as capable of suffering. He endured persecution, defeat, and even exile with his people. This self-sacrifice of love reveals God's inner nature. The experience of Calvary dramatically discloses that self-sacrifice is at the very heart of God's being. God shows to us a deep dimension of his life through his suffering. He thus interpenetrates all living things. Moltmann concurs with Russian religious philosopher Nicolai Berdyaev that it is impossible to witness the Son's tragic end on Calvary and not acknowledge movement in the very life of God.[36]

In Moltmann's view, human suffering constitutes the very bedrock of atheism. It raises persistent doubts about the divine justice. Suffering, especially of the innocent, finds no adequate answer in the claim that pain is a punishment for sin. How do we reconcile the God who suffers in his love with the idea of a God who lives in unassailable glory? Somehow the divine happiness must be conditioned by the fulfillment of his kingdom and on the completion of the final perfection of creation. He has shaped a created universe that pleases him, and he awaits its final realization. With the creation of the world, Moltmann asserts that God's self-humiliation and self-limitation begin.[37] In a true sense, creation does subject God to the sufferings that flow from it.

The revelation of God reaches its full term in the history of Jesus, the Son. The Son reveals the Father as the Father reveals the Son (Matt 11:27). Moltmann begins his treatment with the story of Jesus, who discloses the Trinity. His messianic call took place at his baptism. Different from the somewhat threatening message of John the Baptist, Christ's announcement was a gospel, a proclamation of hope and joy. The Abba prayer of Jesus reflects the singularity of his relationship with the Father and serves as a harbinger of the uniqueness of his message. His proclamation centers around the kingdom of God his Father, and he specifies the true character of the kingdom by attending to the poor and the marginalized, giving them hope. His compassion is fatherly and motherly, as foretold by Isaiah (49:15). The call and ministry of Jesus are animated by the Spirit (Luke 4:18). God discloses himself as Father of this Son, and believers become heirs of God in Christ. The Father sends the Son in the power of the Spirit, who leads believers into the fellowship of the Son with the Father.

Gethsemane and Golgotha constitute the backdrop for the passion story between the Father and the Son. The abandonment by the Father was indeed the cup that could not pass for Jesus. The cry recorded in Mark 15:34, "My God, my God, why have you forsaken me?" expresses the utter and complete desolation experienced by Christ on the cross. Moltmann asserts that theologians and biblicists are simply incorrect when they strive to portray Jesus in his final hour as animated by an overriding inward faith and conviction without any semblance of despair. This poignant prayer from the depths of his being went unanswered, for he remained forsaken by the Father in his final hours. At this time the Father and the Son were separated. The Son was deprived of his Father and the Father was deprived of his Son in their moment of absolute surrender. The bond between them, however, was the Holy Spirit. In this manner the configuration of the Trinity was disclosed on Calvary. The sacrifice of both the Father and the Son is bonded in the Spirit.

The resurrection of Christ was realized through the Holy Spirit (Rom 1:4). The trinitarian dimension is expressed again in the resurrection in that the Father effects the raising of the Son through the Spirit. Although the Holy Spirit proceeds from the Father, he is also sent by the Son (John 15:26). It is through the Spirit that believers become participants in the triune history into which they are inducted at baptism. The eschatological future is portrayed by Paul in such a way that the Father subjects everything to the risen Christ who, when every other sovereignty and power are destroyed, will hand back the kingdom to the Father (1 Cor 15:24). It is in this manner that the lordship of the Son will come to an end.[38] The future consummation of all things is thus portrayed as a trinitarian event. The unity of the Trinity consists in the fellowship of the three persons rather than in the identity of a single subject.[39]

The relationship between God and humankind is a living relationship wherein each is affected by the other. The future of the human race is by no means a matter of indifference to God, who wills that we respond to him and love him in return. He desires to be with us and to dwell among us in the world of his creation. The divine plan anticipates the fulfillment of all creation in the messianic future when God becomes all in all (1 Cor 15:28). Moltmann views creation as the result of God's yearning for rapport with "another" and the other's free response to the divine. He attests that inner trinitarian love is the love of like for like, but it is not a created love, and it is not possible to conceive of a Divinity who is not creative.[40] It is in accord with God's nature that he communicates himself. The Deity did not wish to communicate himself only to himself. Rather, he desires to communicate Godself to the "other" as well. In Moltmann's judgment, this explains why the idea of the created universe is contained in the Father's love for his divine Son.[41]

God in some fashion limits himself to make room for created reality. He makes space in his own omnipresence for creation. The Father effects this creative activity through his love for the Son in the power and energy of the Holy Spirit, and the goal of this activity is to realize a response to his love in time.[42] Moltmann considers why God became man and concludes that the divine Son became Son first and foremost to serve as the foundation of a new creation. If the purpose of the

Incarnation is primarily to repair the damage of humankind's sin, Christ's role would have been essentially complete after his redemptive intervention. As the ground of the new creation, he becomes the ideal self-communication of God to the world. Through Christ the Divine Being strives to gather humankind into his family as sons and daughters. By means of the Incarnation, the triune Deity is conjoined to humanity and awaits a free response from men and women. In this manner the Trinity limits and empties itself.[43] Moltmann affirms that God is never nobler than in his willingness to submit to this humiliation. The triune God thus opens Godself to creation to become the Father of a free and responsive humankind.

With the release of the Holy Spirit at Pentecost, the prophecy of Joel is wonderfully fulfilled (3:1–2), and the risen Christ becomes the life-giving Spirit (1 Cor 15:45). In fact, it can now be said that "the Lord is the Spirit" (2 Cor 3:17). With the outpouring of the Spirit, God extends his dwelling in the world. Moltmann asks whether the Holy Spirit is to be understood as a divine energy or as a divine person. The Gospel of John suggests that the Spirit is a person, whereas for Paul the personhood of the Spirit is not quite as explicit.[44] The Spirit is described as the subject who unites and glorifies the Father and the Son, and hence the Spirit is a person. The Holy Spirit proceeds from the Father, and the Son shapes the Spirit into the spirit of sonship. The Spirit communicates the divine life to humankind and then returns the graced world to the Father.

For Moltmann the dogma of the Trinity developed out of Christology. The gradual acceptance of the monotheistic notion of God in the Roman Empire and its embellishment through the teaching on the Trinity was one of the greatest theological developments of the early church.[45] The initial tendency to subordinationism reached its climax with Arius, who insisted that Christ was a creature, pure and simple, while modalism reached its greatest acceptance in the century before Nicaea (325). Traces of modalism, however, have continued to crop up through the centuries. Schleiermacher, for example, was tempted to modalism in the nineteenth century, while several twentieth-century theologians preferred to identify the three divine figures as modes of being of the one divine subject rather than as three persons. The temptation here, as was the case, for example, for Karl Barth, is to transfer the acting subject to a Deity situated behind the three persons.[46] This creates the danger of reducing the three persons to modes of being of the one divine subject. Barth's tendency to identify the Holy Spirit as essentially the common bond uniting Father and Son seems to make the Spirit appear to be an energy rather than a person.[47] The theological tradition runs counter to this, identifying the Spirit as a third person rather than merely the bond of unity between Father and Son. Moltmann contends that roughly the same criticism regarding modalism can be offered concerning the trinitarian position of Karl Rahner.

Moltmann feels that for Rahner there is in God one subject who is the Father. The Son is portrayed as the divine instrument in history, and the Holy Spirit is the agent of God's self-communication.[48] If we begin by emphasizing the unity of the absolute subject as Rahner seems to do, we are tending toward a modalist position, because the one subject is in the foreground, and the three persons are relegated to a secondary importance. On the other hand, if the three persons are given primary consideration, the divine substance is no longer central, and then there is danger of succumbing to tritheism. Moltmann holds that it seems more appropriate to begin with the divine persons as they are reflected in the history of Jesus, since this is the approach that we find in the biblical testimony. This leaves us with the challenge of explaining the unity of the divine persons who present themselves in the New Testament. This unity is to be realized in the *perichoresis* (i.e., the mutual indwelling) of the three persons.

For Moltmann the economic and the immanent Trinity blend together. He insists that the God who loves and shows himself to the world really cannot in any way correspond to a God who lives unto himself and is fully sufficient in himself. Moltmann advocates a social doctrine of the Trinity in contrast to a psychological doctrine (e.g., Augustine's triad of memory, understanding, and will reflecting the triune life of God). The social doctrine is based on salvation history and emphasizes God's open trinitarian fellowship. The at-oneness is grounded in the *perichoresis* of the Father, Son, and Holy Spirit as they open themselves to receive the whole of creation into the triune life.[49] The cross of Christ conditions not only the economic Trinity, but also the immanent Trinity. The salvation achieved on Calvary does not just affect the whole of creation; rather, the pain of the cross has a deep resonance in the very inner life of God. It can be said that when all of creation resides in God and the Deity is all in all, then the economic Trinity and the immanent Trinity effectively merge.

In union with Christ we believe that his Father is our Father too. In fellowship with Jesus, there is no longer Jew or Greek, male or female, but all are one (Gal 3:28). The Holy Spirit is not just a divine energy but a divine subject as well. The Spirit is identified as the one who is responsible for the task of sanctification. Like the Son, the Holy Spirit issues eternally from the Father's being. He proceeds from the Father but is also sent by the Son (John 15:26). Father, Son, and Spirit are noninterchangeable subjects of the one common divine substance that is endowed with consciousness and will. They have the divine nature in common, but the inner identity of the persons is determined by their mutual relationships. They are dependent on one another and, in a true sense, exist in one another in light of their mutual love.

> In their perichoresis and because of it, the trinitarian persons are not to be understood as three individuals who only subsequently enter into relationship with one another (which is the customary reproach, under the name of "tritheism"). But they are not, either, three modes of being or three repetitions of the one God, as the modalistic interpretation suggests. . . . The unity of the triunity lies in the eternal perichoresis of the trinitarian persons. . . . The trinitarian persons form their own unity by themselves in the circulation of the divine life.[50]

For Moltmann the *filioque* problem is what still keeps the East and the West divided. This schism of one thousand years can be healed only when a consensus is reached regarding the relationship between the Son and the Holy Spirit. He attests that the Spirit proceeds from the Father (John 15:26) and does not proceed from the Son. Because the two divine processions are simultaneous, however, it must be affirmed that the Spirit proceeds from the Father in the presence of the Son, and hence the Son has "some kind of involvement" in the Spirit's procession. Although the Holy Spirit receives from the Father his "perfect divine existence," he receives his "relational form" from both the Father and the Son.[51] These constitute two rather distinct developments, the first from the Father alone, and the latter from both the Father and the Son. Since the Middle Ages the emphasis on the one divine substance has taken center stage in the West and has resulted in an abiding Western tendency toward modalism.

In the concluding chapter of *The Trinity and the Kingdom*, "The Kingdom of Freedom," Moltmann deals with a number of political issues that over the centuries have been affected by the continuing emphasis on the divine monarchy in Western thought. A form of political monotheism developed early on with the second-century apologists and certainly emerged as a dominant theme after Christianity became the state church during the reigns of Constantine and his first successors. The one empire and the one church were representative of the one God. Moltmann insists that the doctrine of the Trinity can overturn this image of the absolute monarch because it exemplifies a community wherein persons are defined by their relations with one another.[52] In the church the monarchical episcopate created unity at the cost of the elimination of many of the charismatic elements that were evident from apostolic times. The presbyteral and synodal forms of government that more directly reflect the doctrine of the social Trinity gave way to a more monarchical configuration represented by the one bishop and the one pope. Perhaps one day Joachim of Fiore's (1132–1202) "kingdom of the Spirit" will prevail, wherein lordship will fade away in favor of communality, and we will come to see ourselves no longer as masters and servants, but rather as friends who are gathered together as equals.

In 1991 Jürgen Moltmann published a second study on the Trinity, *History and the Triune God*, that appeared in English the following year.[53] It brings together a series of articles written during the ten years after the appearance of *The Trinity and the Kingdom* that reemphasize the social doctrine of the Trinity. He stresses again that the notion of the impassibility of the Divinity must be replaced by "the passion of the eternal love of God." It is his intention to search out a nonpatriarchal way of talking about God the Father, especially for our age when we are evolving into what he calls a fatherless society. He observes that even political patriarchalism faded after the Enlightenment and the French Revolution. The intimacy and informality of the Abba address employed by Jesus struck a blow against patriarchy. Christ and his followers, both men and women, sensed that they were living very close to God and were forming a community beyond patriarchy.

The New Testament (e.g., Matt 11:27; John 10:30) sketched out a new portrait of the Father, who gives birth to his Son in a motherly and fatherly way.[54] Moltmann points out that the Eleventh Council of Toledo in 675 taught that the Son came forth from the Father's womb (*"de utero Patris . . . genitus"*).[55] This has to be considered an early repudiation of patriarchal theism. Also, the Pauline insistence that the Father gave up his own Son (Rom 8:32) leads us to the conviction that with the surrender of the divine Son, the boundless pain of the Father begins. This allows us to affirm that the Father identifies with us in our anxiety and grief.

It is through the living out of his Abba rapport with the Father that Jesus grows into the relationship of Son of God.[56] His bond with humankind is dramatically articulated in Romans 8:29, where he is declared to be the firstborn among many brothers and sisters. Indeed, the Holy Spirit bears witness that we are the children of God (Rom 8:16). As brothers and sisters we are drawn into the Son's mission to free the poor, reconcile sinners, and cure the sick. Through the Son the Father reaches out into the world of creation with his contagious love. Christ the brother brings about a social communion of profound fellowship among those who strive to bear one another's burdens.[57] Jesus is continually portrayed in the Gospels as standing with the underprivileged, with the poor against the powerful, with the victims against the aggressors. It is clear that God's preferential option is for the poor (Matt 25). Moltmann complains that a world order has taken over in which the poor become poorer and the rich become richer. He identifies as evidence of structural sin the fact that the deserts are expanding, the forests are contracting, the greenhouse effect is worsening, and the hole in the ozone layer is enlarging.[58] Thus, all of us, rich and poor, are becoming victims as a result of the exploitation of the planet by the industrial first world.

Moltmann contends that it is critical never to subordinate the Holy Spirit to the Father and the Son. The introduction of the *filioque* in the West resulted in a subordination of this sort. He complains that since the *filioque* tends to depersonalize and diminish the Holy Spirit, it should be dropped, and we should simply affirm that the Spirit issues from the Father. The description of the Trinity as one divine subject with three different modes of being unduly emphasizes the unity of God over the three divine persons. The triune unity really consists in the unique communion among the three persons, the *perichoresis* of the three existing for each other and in each other.[59] The social image of God is evident in a number of the Greek fathers, particularly in Gregory of Nazianzus, who taught that an ideal image of the triunity is to be found in the primal cell of the human community, that is, in the family unit comprised of husband, wife, and child.[60]

In the West from the second century on, there has been an extremely heavy emphasis on the authority of the ministry in the church, to the considerable disadvantage of the church's inherent charismatic structure. This must be overcome through the return to the New Testament stress on the charismatic community of believers, all of whom share unique and irreplaceable gifts of the Spirit. Without the recognition and activation of all the charisms inherent in the community, the church will never possess the direction, inspiration, and vitality infused into it by the divine Spirit. Moltmann suggests that the ancient Syrian notion of the motherhood of the Spirit will help to soften and relativize the heavy emphasis on patriarchalism and male domination in the church.[61]

The Word and the Spirit are intended to complement each other in the unfolding of creation and in human history. The Word differentiates, while the Spirit unites and brings things together. Moltmann attests that there is still much to do regarding the development of the theology of the Trinity. Neither Barth nor Rahner, with their emphasis on the one divine substance, has adequately uncovered the precious elements of salvation history that have been revealed in the interplay among Jesus, Abba, and the Spirit in the Scriptures.[62] The biblical history of the Father, Son, and Holy Spirit has to be the point of departure for the doctrine of the Trinity. The unique collaboration of these three subjects in the history of salvation constitutes the primary source of our faith approach to trinitarian theology. The Son in the Father, the Father in the Son, the Holy Spirit in the Father and the Son—this perfect interpenetration of the persons in and with one another is what has been termed *perichoresis*. This notion rises above the problems of modalism and tritheism, and the preferred term for this idea is triunity. This interpenetration of the three divine subjects is an open, inviting unity that brings humankind into an intimate relationship with the Father, Son, and Spirit. This kind of vision is what Moltmann proposes to us as the most appropriate, the truest, and the most inspiring representation of the triune life of God.

Robert W. Jenson

After teaching for some years at the Gettysburg Lutheran Seminary in Pennsylvania and at St. Olaf's College in Minnesota, Robert W. Jenson was appointed senior scholar for research at the Center for Theological Inquiry at Princeton University in 1999. With Carl Braaten he edited a popular two-volume text on Christian dogmatics in 1984. Jenson wrote the section on the Trinity.[63]

Israel's God is identified historically in this 1984 work simply as the one who led the Jewish people out of Egypt (Exod 20:2). In fact, the exodus event became the focal element of Israel's creed (cf. Deut 29:5–9). In the New Testament God is typically designated as the one who raised Jesus from the dead. The privileged place occupied by Yahweh in the old law gives way to the Father, the Son, and the Holy Spirit in the New Testament. Although there are several references to the Trinity in the New Testament (e.g., 2 Cor 13:13; Eph 2:17–18), the true home of the new triune designation is in the primitive liturgy, especially in connection with the celebration of baptism and the eucharist. Jenson affirms that the most important and concise trinitarian formula is found in Matthew 28:19.

The task of theology is to examine and discover what is truly intended in the declaration that God is the one who raised Israel's Jesus from the dead.[64] Jenson insists that we are unable to talk about God other than in the manner in which he has revealed himself historically. Jesus has given us the opportunity to call his God our Father, while Christ's resurrection has lifted up the Son into the range of eternity. The Spirit is God as the power to transform the now into the fulfillment that is yet to come. The Father is the one who comes to us through Jesus, while Jesus is the present possibility of God's reality for us. Finally, the Spirit can be described as the power of the future. The portrayal of God in the New Testament, according to Jenson, follows these three arrows of time and keeps the three divine persons in perspective.[65] All of the metaphysical dialectics surrounding the discussion of the Trinity came later as reflections on the historical appearances of the three in the New Testament narrative.

The attempts to translate the successive New Testament revelations of the Trinity into the thought patterns of Greek philosophy generated a number of complicated problems that still remain enigmatic today. God's eternity in the Jewish tradition is not defined metaphysically but is translated in terms of his fidelity to his chosen people. His promises are fulfilled as the history of this people unfolds. This constancy dramatically reflects his personal character. God the Father and the Spirit are bound together in the unfolding of the divine activity in the world, while Christ and the Spirit are specifically identified in the work of salvation. Jesus is the power and wisdom of God (1 Cor 1:24) who reveals the divine attributes of abiding love, mercy, and forgiveness most clearly to humankind. After Jesus' resurrection the early church professed that believers in the new dispensation now have access through Christ in one Spirit to the Father (Eph 2:18).

Jenson points to Romans chapter 8 as a most valuable revelation of the Trinity. God the Father appears as the agent of the salvation that was accomplished in Christ through the sending of the Spirit. Jesus and the Spirit are designated as divine because their functions are clearly divine activities that are inseparable from the Father. Early Christians spoke of God in an orderly pattern, addressing the Father with the Son, in the Spirit.[66] With the rise of Greek theology, the narrative quality of the Christian message (1 Cor 15:3–7) gave way to emphasis on the divine qualities of immortality and impassibility. God came to be portrayed as intangible and essentially unaffected by external happenings. The Deity in effect became distant.[67] Both forms of discourse about God, the biblical and the Hellenic, were placed next to each other so that the divine attributes predicated by the Greeks were simply added to the biblical ones.

In the writings of the early fathers like Ignatius and Justin, the God who led Israel out of the desert and into the Promised Land was pictured as changeless and impassible, yet compassionate and responsive. The apologists, according to Jenson, were kept on track in terms of their trinitarian thought through their participation in the ongoing liturgical life of the church and the increasingly popular three-part creedal structure grounded in the ancient baptismal profession.[68] Both modalism and subordinationism had their adherents in the second and third centuries, although with Tertullian in the West and Origen in the East, subordinationist systems proved to be more popular in the two or three generations before Nicaea (325). Origen's understanding of the Trinity featured the Logos and the Spirit as descending mediations from God the Father, who was seen as the Hellenic Deity in its most perfect representation.[69] It was the stark subordinationism of Arius that precipitated the dogmatic declarations of Nicaea wherein Christ is affirmed to be of the very same substance as the Father and equal to him as God. Although the term *homooúsios* was not uniformly understood by all the delegates at Nicaea and at Constantinople I (381), it did eventually become the accepted term to express the truth that the Father and the Son share the same divine substance and are equal in Deity. At Constantinople I the Holy Spirit was also acknowledged as a divine subject who is to be glorified and adored in precisely the same manner as the Father and the Son. Thus, the trinitarian dogma was essentially articulated.

The Cappadocians just before and after Constantinople I are the ones who affirmed that the three subjects who share the Godhead are to be individually identified by virtue of the relations they have to one another. These relations constitute the distinct manner in which the three subjects form together the one triune Deity. These theologians set out the individual divine subjects horizontally in time so that they appear to us as the divine persons who have worked and continue to work among us. The three identities in the Godhead possess three distinct names and descriptions, yet they point to the same divine reality.[70] Gregory of Nyssa especially emphasized the one being of God.

According to Jenson, the term "God" refers to the divine activity that is directed toward us, beginning from the Father, operative through the Son, and brought to fulfillment in the Spirit. "It is precisely Deity as infinity which the Father gives, the Son receives, and the Spirit communicates; by their relations, the action of each is temporally unlimited, to be God's action. But it is the work, the creative event, done through Jesus' life, death, resurrection, and future advent, done by his Father for their Spirit, that is the one God."[71]

In the West the blending together of Eastern thought with Western theology on the Trinity was largely the work of Augustine, who was adamantly opposed to the notion that God's relation to time involved any suggestion that God experienced change. Jenson considers it a grave error that the Son's eternal procession from the Father and his temporal mission to redeem humankind came to be thought of as two discreet events. This kind of theologizing gave rise to the distinction between the immanent Trinity (the Deity in itself) and the economic Trinity (God's actions in the universe). This separation (immanent and economic) is unfortunate, according to Jenson, because in light of this twofold structure, the divine activity in the world has traditionally been considered the work of the undifferentiated Trinity. This would seem to eliminate the essential connection between the divine persons and their critical roles in the unfolding of salvation history. Augustine's discussion of the Trinity grew not out of the revelation of the three divine persons in history, but out of his evaluation of the workings of the human soul (memory, knowledge, will) to explain the relations in the triune Deity. Further, Jenson does not at all agree with Aquinas that the three persons are to be defined as subsistent relations, for this seems to be an explanation that applies specifically to the idea of the immanent Trinity. For him there is but one Trinity, which is revealed historically in the Scriptures as Father, Son, and Holy Spirit.

After discussing the trinitarian positions of Schleiermacher and Hegel, Jenson praises Karl Barth for his outstanding approach to the Trinity because it is grounded in the historic revelation of the triune Deity. The Father is revealed, Christ the Son reveals him, and the Spirit appears as the agent for the fulfillment of the divine plan in history. Jenson freely admits that Barth's influence is evident in every phase of his own thought on the Trinity.[72] Rather than viewing Christ's divinity as a separate identity that always existed, we should view Jesus' historical life in terms of its final, transcending outcome, and therefore as eternal. Jesus' historical life grew out of his mission from the Father that occurred in time. After his triumphal resurrection, Christ shares an eternal destiny, and the Spirit is the very breath of this future. These saving events are God's final transcendence of time, God's eternity.[73] Thus, for Jenson it is unnecessary to posit the eternally existing Logos and the eternally existing Spirit to affirm the eternity of the Son and Holy Spirit as they triumph in history. The scriptural understanding of eternity is nothing other than faithfulness to the final future. "Truly, the Trinity is simply the Father and the man Jesus and their Spirit as the Spirit of the believing community. The 'economic' Trinity is eschatologically God 'himself,' an immanent Trinity."[74]

Jenson urges that we must not focus on the being of God first and then turn to his triune character later, for this distorts the picture reflected in the New Testament. Like Barth, Jenson insists that the Divinity must be considered first of all as an event rather than as a substance. The process thinkers see all of reality as a continuous chain of events, one following after the other. God himself can be viewed as a series of events, and the events that God is comprise all the events that make up the history of the world.[75] The subject of this series of God-events is the Father, the Son, and the Holy Spirit who contribute to the collective action that is God. Jenson adds that the scriptural accounts clearly reveal that God is a personal Deity. The "person" and "event" dimensions are simply alternative aspects of the one divine reality. In Jenson's view, God is what he terms "an enduring entity" by virtue of his triune identity, and the privileged reflection of this is Jesus, especially in his abiding concern for others. The reality that allows us to come to grips with the Divinity is the human Jesus who lived and died in Palestine and who was raised from the dead into eternal life.

The discourse between God and humankind began with communication from the Deity, and this constitutes God's Word to us. He addresses us and thus approaches us. Then there is the Spirit who opens us to the future and leads us into the full range of the truth imparted by the Word. "God is a conversation. Or choosing a more dignified word: God is discourse."[76] At this stage of history, the gospel is embodied in the objective life of the church—the sights, the sounds, and the rituals. This is the risen body of Jesus and, in a sense, the body of God. This God is infinite (i.e., limited by no temporal conditions), he is faithful to his promises, and he is present to every creature. At the same time, we can suggest that God is mortal because he dies and suffers with Jesus. Jenson affirms that Jesus' death is constitutive for his relation to the Father and indeed both for his divinity and the Father's as well. "God is the universally transforming event between Jesus the Israelite, and the transcendence he called to as 'Father,' and their Spirit among us."[77]

In the first volume of a two-volume study entitled *Systematic Theology* published in 1997, Robert Jenson returns to the subject of the Trinity.[78] He again identifies the God who reveals himself in the Old Testament as the one who delivered the Jews out of Egypt (Deut 26:8–9). In the New Testament the Deity is once more recognized as the one who raised Jesus from the dead (Rom 4:24). He is the one whom Jesus addressed as Father, and on this basis, Jesus is properly called the Son. The Spirit, the third person in the Christian drama, is referred to by Jenson as "the enabling future." This triune God is identified with temporal happenings in the real world. He was introduced to Israel as the God of all the nations who has taken up his abode among this particular people. He wants to be known as one who in a special manner dwells among the Israelites, caring for them and providing them with a unique destiny. We must follow the biblical narrative to discover the God of the Scriptures. The Deity is truly identified with the events of the exodus and Jesus' resurrection. Jenson ever reminds us that this God is a triune God.

God's history is interwoven with the story of humankind such that, for Jenson, he has no identity except the one that is revealed in his dealings with humankind.[79] His relationships with the Jews always led them forward to new challenges, new promises, and new hopes. From the time of Abraham, the Israelites lived out of the promises made by Yahweh. The Jews are designated as his children (Deut 14:1), and he is a vital actor in every stage of their history. With Jesus, on the other hand, God is disclosed more explicitly as the Father, and Jesus as the divine Son. In Isaiah 40–55, the Servant did not directly foretell the Incarnation of the Son, but after Jesus' coming, we can see the gathering of Israel's hopes around this one messianic figure. All of Israel's history seems to be directed toward a single, culminating, eschatological event that is foreshadowed in the resurrection of Christ.

The third person in what Jenson terms "the drama of God" is the Holy Spirit. Jenson describes the Holy Spirit as God's life as he transcends himself to enliven and enrich beings other than himself. The Spirit is also the agent of prophecy who in the last days (Acts 2:17) will be poured out on all humankind (Joel 3:1–2).[80] Jenson brings together the three divine persons in this way: "Not only the Son and the Spirit appear as *dramatis dei personae*; also the God whose Son and

Spirit these are is identified as himself one *persona* of God, as the Father of the Son and sender of the Spirit. The God of Israel appears as himself one of the *personae dramatis* of the very God he is."[81]

Jesus' priestly prayer in John 17 can be considered his personal revelation concerning the relationship between the Father and the Son, as well as the nature of the mission the Father gave the Son to complete. In chapters 14 and 16 of John's Gospel, the role of the Advocate and his relation to the Father and the Son are dramatically delineated. The Spirit is to be sent by the Father (14:26) and by the Son (16:17) to lead believers into the full range of truth and to make known the things that are to come. Jesus affirms, "He [the Spirit] will take from what is mine and will declare it to you" (John 16:14).

Jenson then addresses the question of the nature of the divinity of Christ and the Spirit. He contends that what kept the early fathers on track regarding the Trinity was the church's liturgical life. At Nicaea the Word was defined not as an image of the Father's divinity, but as sharing the very same divine nature. Constantinople I made a similar declaration concerning the divinity of the Holy Spirit. It was to a great extent the liturgical tradition that moved the council to extend its arguments from the Son to the Holy Spirit.[82] The Son was given the fullness of power and authority that could belong only to the Father (Matt 11:27), and the Spirit is identified as "another," the Spirit of Truth (John 16:13) who, along with the Son, is a personal identity like the Son. Thus, Father, Son, and Holy Spirit are mutually consubstantial.

Jenson points out that his concept of person is somewhat different from the explanation he offers in his 1984 *Christian Dogmatics* considered above. He prefers the term "identity," because for him it seems to include the idea of extension along the horizon of time, which the concept "person" does not.[83] The distinction of roles among the three divine persons is quite unambiguous in the biblical narrative. Because of their distinct roles, Father, Son, and Holy Spirit are not personal in exactly the same way. Each can be addressed in a unique manner. Jenson refers to Karl Barth, who asks three questions that reveal the three distinct divine identities: (1) Who reveals himself? (2) What happens to reveal him? (3) What is the outcome of this revelation? Barth's answer to question one is the Father. His answer to question two is the Son, while his response to question three is the Holy Spirit.

After the Council of Chalcedon (451), it became necessary to consider how God the Son ontologically preceded Jesus the Son. Jenson asks what kind of preexistence this could be. He responds by citing John 8:58, "Before Abraham was, I am." Putting his antecedence to

Abraham in the present tense does not allow us to conceive of the Son's existence as an entity that has not yet become the human person of the Gospels.[84] Jenson reasons that since God *is* his act of choice, in deciding to become the man Jesus, he in fact *is* the man Jesus. The Incarnation that happens in eternity is the ground of its occurrence in time. "There must be in God's eternity . . . a way in which the one Jesus Christ as God precedes himself as man, in the very triune life which he lives eternally as the God-man."[85] Jenson asks, "What if God had not created the universe or humankind, would there have been an incarnate Logos?" His reply is that we can know nothing as to how God could have been other than the one we have come to know in the Scriptures, that is, Jesus the Son, his Father, and their Spirit. He adds that as a creature Christ has an origin, but as Son of God he has not an origin but a *determination* through God's eternal decision.[86]

As one of the triune identities, the Holy Spirit who appears in John's Gospel as another Advocate (14:16) is distinguished by his relations to the Father and the Son inasmuch as he is sent by both the Father and the Son to perform the personal tasks of teaching and inspiring Christ's followers (John 16:13–14). Like Barth, Jenson defines the perfect fellowship between the Father and the Son as the very being of the Holy Spirit.[87] In the freely given love between Father and Son, a third party intervenes, constituting a distinct divine entity. The Spirit is the power of the divine future that is still not fully disclosed. The Father alone, for Jenson, is the source of the Spirit's being, but his energy or agency in the divine life can be said to proceed from the Father and the Son.

Jenson then discusses what we mean when we speak of the *being* of God. Although some have affirmed that the Deity is without being, this is a dangerous position.[88] For Aquinas, "He who is" is the most accurate designation for God. Barth teaches that nothing escapes God by fading into the past, and future events are equally present to him. In like fashion, for Jenson nothing recedes into the past or approaches from the future.[89] The Father is the "whence" of God's life, the Spirit is the "whither," and the Son is life's crucial present. God is in fact what occurs between Jesus, his Father, and their Spirit. God is in the final analysis a conversation, and because he addresses us, we possess a future.[90]

Observations

In Karl Barth's judgment, the doctrine of the Trinity has been distilled out of a careful analysis of many Old and New Testament passages by the church. The one God exists in three distinct modes of being. We are not dealing with three divine egos, but three modes of the one divine "I." Although the designation of the three divine figures as persons is problematic, the traditional use of the word "person" compels us to retain it. God the Father is the originator, while the Son through his human existence is the revealer of the divinity of the Father. This establishes the Son as divine, because who can reveal God but God himself? The Holy Spirit is the one who prepares hearers to embrace the Word, and this implies his full divinity. The love between the Father and the Son brings forth someone equal to them, the Holy Spirit. Barth agrees with the orthodoxy of the *filioque*, because for him both the Father and the Son are involved in the procession of the Spirit. Barth deepens and enriches his presentation of the immanent Trinity by emphasizing the roles of the three in creation, redemption, and sanctification.

In his three-volume masterwork, *Systematic Theology*, Wolfhart Pannenberg attests that it is with Christ that God fully identifies himself as Father. Through his resurrection Jesus was confirmed as the divine Son, the *kurios*. The Holy Spirit is portrayed as the medium of communication between Father and Son, the second Advocate, distinct from the Son. The way in which the three manifest themselves and relate to one another in history is really the most valid approach to our appreciation of the Trinity. Pannenberg insists that the Spirit proceeds from the Father alone, but the Son shares with the Father in the sending of the Spirit into the world. Thus, the *filioque* should be eliminated from the creed, for it is merely a Western addition. The three divine persons are three separate and dynamic centers of action, three separate centers of consciousness. Although the Father is the font of the Deity, he makes himself dependent on the actions of the Son and the Holy Spirit in salvation history. Although the Deity is not in any way completed by the divine activity in the world, God does become dependent on the fulfillment of his saving plan in history. The transcendence of the Father is complemented in the drama of salvation by the immanence of the Son and the Spirit who effect the reconciliation of the world. Only at the end of history will the unique characteristics of the divine persons be revealed more fully.

Emphasis on the absolute divine subject in the West has, according to Jürgen Moltmann, been stressed to such a degree that the trinitarian persons tend to be identified as three aspects or modes of the one divine subject. Moltmann begins his treatment with the trinity of persons and then focuses on the divine unity. The experience of Calvary is what reveals the divine self-sacrifice at the very heart of God's inner nature. Indeed, with the creation of the world, God's self-limitation begins. Jesus' life discloses the triune Deity's deep concern for the poor and the marginalized. With Jesus' resurrection the Trinity is very much in evidence, because the Father effects the raising of the Son through the Spirit. Moltmann views creation as the result of God's yearning for rapport with someone outside himself and the other's response to God's love. The purpose of the Incarnation is to serve as the ground of the new creation in which the Deity is conjoined with a free and responsive humankind. The tendency toward modalism in Barth and Rahner needs to be countered by an approach that begins with the divine persons as they are individually reflected in the history of Jesus, while the unity of the three is to be found in their mutual *perichoresis*. The *filioque* problem is still to be addressed by the formulation of a consensus involving the whole of Christendom. For Moltmann the Spirit proceeds from the Father and not from the Son, but the Son has something to do with the Spirit's procession.

Robert Jenson prefers to identify Israel's God simply as the one who led the Jewish people out of exile, and the New Testament God as the one who raised Jesus from the dead. He insists that we are unable to talk about God other than in the manner in which he has revealed himself in history. The Father is the one who comes to us through Jesus, while Jesus is the present possibility of God's reality. We can describe the Spirit as the divine power of the future. The separate treatment of the immanent and the economic Trinity is unfortunate, because there is but one Trinity, which is revealed historically in the Scriptures as Father, Son, and Holy Spirit. For Jenson it is unnecessary to posit the eternally existing Logos and the eternally existing Spirit in order to affirm the eternity of the Son and the Holy Spirit as they move through history. The Trinity is simply the Father, the man Jesus, and the Spirit as the Spirit of the believing community. All of Israel's history seems to be directed toward a single, culminating, eschatological event that is foreshadowed in the resurrection of Jesus. As they appear in the New Testament narrative, the three divine figures are distinct yet mutually consubstantial identities. For Jenson the Father alone is the source of the Spirit's being, but the Spirit's energy or agency in the divine life can be said to proceed from both the Father and the Son.

NOTES

1. Karl Barth, *The Doctrine of the Word of God* (vol. 1, pt. 1 of *Church Dogmatics;* trans. G. T. Thomson; New York: Scribner's, 1936). References will be made to this edition.

2. Ibid., 346.

3. For example, Isa 61:1; Matt 28:19; Rom 1:1–4; 1 Pet 1:2.

4. Barth, *Doctrine of the Word,* 403.

5. Ibid., 412.

6. Ibid., 418.

7. Ibid., 469.

8. Ibid., 533–34.

9. Ibid., 536–37.

10. Ibid., 547.

11. Ibid., 554.

12. These lectures were published in English in 1959: Karl Barth, *Dogmatics in Outline* (trans. G. T. Thomson; New York: Harper Torchbooks, 1959). In the foreword to the Harper Torchbooks edition, Barth identifies this work as an outline of the multivolume *Church Dogmatics.*

13. Ibid., 42.

14. Karl Barth, *The Doctrine of the Word of God* (vol. 1, pt. 2 of *Church Dogmatics;* trans. G. T. Thomson and H. Knight; New York: Scribner's, 1956).

15. Ibid., 37.

16. Ibid., 43.

17. Ibid., 203–4.

18. Ibid., 277.

19. Herbert Burhenn, "Pannenberg's Doctrine of God," *The Scottish Journal of Theology* 28 (1975): 535.

20. Wolfhart Pannenberg, "God's Presence in History," *The Christian Century* 98 (11 March 1981): 263.

21. Wolfhart Pannenberg, *Systematic Theology* (vol. 1; trans. G. W. Bromiley; Grand Rapids: Eerdmans, 1991).

22. Ibid., 268.

23. Ibid., 278.

24. Ibid., 287.

25. Ibid., 292.

26. Ibid., 301.

27. Ibid., 315.

28. Ibid., 317.

29. Ibid., 327.

30. Ibid., 358–59.

31. Ibid., 384.

32. Ibid., 415.

33. Ibid., 428.

34. Jürgen Moltmann, *The Trinity and the Kingdom* (trans. Margaret Kohl; San Francisco: Harper & Row, 1981).

35. Ibid., 23.

36. Ibid., 45.

37. Ibid., 59.

38. Ibid., 92.

39. Ibid., 95.

40. Ibid., 106.

41. Ibid., 108.

42. Ibid., 113.

43. Ibid., 119.

44. Ibid., 125.

45. Ibid., 131.

46. Ibid., 139.

47. Ibid., 142.

48. Ibid., 147.

49. Ibid., 157.

50. Ibid., 175.

51. Ibid., 186.

52. Ibid., 198.

53. Jürgen Moltmann, *History and the Triune God* (trans. John Bowden; New York: Crossroad, 1992).

54. Ibid., 22.

55. H. Denzinger and A. Schönmetzer, *Enchiridion Symbolorum*, 32d ed. (Freiburg: Herder, 1963), no. 526.

56. Moltmann, *History and the Triune God,* 35.

57. Ibid., 41.

58. Ibid., 54.

59. Ibid., 59.

60. Ibid., 60.

61. Ibid., 65.

62. Ibid., 82.

63. Robert W. Jenson, "The Triune God," in *Christian Dogmatics* (vol. 2; ed. Carl E. Braaten and Robert W. Jenson; Philadelphia: Fortress Press, 1984), 83–191.

64. Ibid., 99.

65. Ibid., 101.

66. Ibid., 109.

67. Ibid., 117.

68. Ibid., 122.

69. Ibid., 124.

70. Ibid., 137–38.

71. Ibid., 140.

72. Ibid., 154.

73. Ibid., 155.

74. Ibid.

75. Ibid., 167.

76. Ibid., 176.

77. Ibid., 190.

78. Robert W. Jenson, *Systematic Theology* (vol. 1; New York: Oxford University Press, 1997).

79. Ibid., 65.

80. Ibid., 86.

81. Ibid., 89.

82. Ibid., 106.

83. Ibid., 118.

84. Ibid., 138.

85. Ibid., 140–41. This approach to Christ's preexistence is new for Jenson, compared with his treatment of the subject in *Triune Identity*, published in 1982.

86. Ibid., 141.

87. Ibid., 155.

88. Ibid., 211.

89. Ibid., 218.

90. Ibid., 223.

10

OTHER IMPORTANT VOICES

In addition to the Catholic and Protestant scholars already considered, several other directions in trinitarian thought merit our attention because they focus new light on the mystery and expand the dialogue significantly. The work of Vladimir Lossky, for example, opens up the rich field of Orthodox thought and its emphasis on the incomprehensibility of the Deity. In the theology of Leonardo Boff, we discover the importance of trinitarian *koinonia* and shared trinitarian life *(perichoresis)*, which should be the model of egalitarian existence in the church and in society. Elizabeth A. Johnson leads us convincingly to the realization that putting an exclusively masculine face on the Deity amounts to idolatry, because God transcends gender. The process theologians Joseph A. Bracken and Marjorie Hewitt Suchocki show us a dynamic view of God that brings God and world together in an exciting synergy of expanding life. Finally, Kathryn Tanner and Peter C. Hodgson chart out fresh approaches to the divine Triad, thus expanding further the contemporary trinitarian dialogue.

An Orthodox Trinitarian Position: Vladimir Lossky

The Orthodox theologian Vladimir Lossky (1903–58) was exiled from Russia in 1922 and worked in Paris among the Russian émigré community until his death. Although he published only one full volume *(The Mystical Theology of the Eastern Church)* during his lifetime, a number of his other shorter studies were issued posthumously. Lossky is widely considered to be one of the more notable Orthodox theologians of the twentieth century.

For Eastern scholars, God's nature remains essentially unknowable. The Incarnation, however, stands as the source and foundation of authentic Christian theologizing. Furthermore, it carries us to the very heart of the mystery of the Trinity.[1] The first divine manifestation was in the creation, and this was the era of the Father. Following this era was the era of the Son, which ended with the ascension, and since that time we have been living in the epoch of the Holy Spirit.

The Son and the Spirit are the two divine persons sent into the world. The Son's role is to quicken and expand our personal liberty, while the work of the Spirit is to enter into our nature and reinvigorate it.[2] These two divine persons have between them a relationship of reciprocity. The Spirit was with Jesus all during his public life, and after the ascension Jesus sent the Spirit from the Father to inspire and instruct the disciples. The three persons or hypostases constitute the divine nature. They share that nature without limitation or restriction. The distinction among the divine persons must be precisely defined through their relationships with one another. The Father is the Unoriginate One, the Son is generated by the Father, and the Holy Spirit proceeds from the Father alone. The relationships among them are relationships not of opposition, but rather of diversity.

Unlike Western theologians, the majority of Eastern scholars believe the Holy Spirit proceeds from the Father as from a single principle. The *filioque,* that is, the procession of the Holy Spirit from the Father and the Son as affirmed by the West, is radically rejected by Lossky and noted as the principal point of difference between the Eastern and Western positions. He defines the Father as the source, the Son as the manifestation, and the Spirit as the force of that manifestation. Lossky makes no effort to set out a relationship of origin for the Spirit that would have him proceed also from the Son. Inasmuch as the Spirit originates from the Father alone, there is no relation of opposition between the Son and the Spirit. The Father generates the Son, and the Holy Spirit proceeds from the Father. Both of these modes of origin from the Father are different, so that there are mutual relations of diversity rather than of opposition among the three.[3] The difference here between East and West is critical for Lossky, and this difference is what determines the whole thrust and direction of Eastern and Western theology.

The monarchy of the Father creates the perfect equilibrium between the divine nature and the persons. For Lossky and for many of the Orthodox thinkers, causality within the Trinity is attributed to the Father alone, and thus the monarchy of the Father is the principle of unity within the Triad. The Western thesis of the procession from the divine intellect generating the Son and the procession from the will spirating the Holy Spirit is termed by Lossky "an inadmissible error" that is grounded in a philosophical anthropomorphism that leads us away from the divine reality.[4] The different relations of origin ground the true diversity of the three divine figures, while the unity among the three is rooted in the monarchy of the Father.

Orthodox theology draws a distinction between the divine essence and the divine energies that reveal the incommunicable divine essence. Every energy comes from the Father and is expressed in the Son. The Holy Spirit is the one who sends forth these energies into the world. The Father reveals his nature through the Son, and the divinity of the Son is shown forth in the Holy Spirit. In the order of these natural manifestations, the Spirit proceeds from the Father and the Son, although in his hypostatic existence, the Spirit proceeds from the Father alone.[5] Lossky notes that the early church fathers often used expressions referring to the hypostatic existence of the Spirit and his manifestations in creation interchangeably. Nonetheless, it is clear that these Fathers distinguished between the Spirit's hypostatic existence that proceeds from the Father alone and his natural manifestations that proceed from both the Father and the Son. The Spirit is linked to the Son as the source of energies showered upon created beings, but the very being of the Spirit proceeds only from the Father.

In Lossky's judgment, the failures to distinguish between the hypostatic existence of the Holy Spirit and the divine manifestations from the Son and the Spirit in creation were due to the uneducated minds of Western Christians during the Carolingian period. He believes this confusion is the cause of the insertion of the *filioque* formula into the creed in Spain and Gaul prior to the tenth century.

The publication of *The Mystical Theology of the Eastern Church* in 1944 established Vladimir Lossky as one of the truly outstanding Orthodox theologians.[6] He distinguishes between mysticism and theology, observing that the former is essentially a personal experience of the divine mysteries, while the latter is the study of the dogmas affirmed by the church. Mystical theology can be described as a personal "working out" or assimilation of the content of faith.[7] Lossky again insists that the dogmatic dissimilarity between East and West is due largely to their differing views on the procession of the Holy Spirit. Another of the unique features of the Orthodox approach is the distinction between positive and negative theology, popularized by Dionysius the Areopagite (fifth century) but already observable in most of the earlier Eastern church fathers. Apophatic or negative theology proceeds by a series of negations. Lossky writes: "It is by unknowing that we may know him who is above every possible object of knowledge. Proceeding by negations one ascends from the inferior degrees of being to the highest, by progressively setting aside all that is known, in order to draw near to the Unknown in the darkness of absolute ignorance."[8]

According to Aquinas and scholastic theologians, we can attribute certain finite perfections to God, but we can only predicate them of the Deity in a most sublime manner, because he infinitely exceeds those finite perfections in richness.

The three divine persons share a single nature, a single will, and a single operation. Each of the three possesses the one divine nature according to the manner proper to each. Lossky cites John of Damascus (675–749), who taught that although there is a difference between the generation of the Son and the procession of the Spirit, we do not in any way understand this difference.[9] The fact that the one is begotten and the other proceeds points to their distinctive modes of origin. This is all we need to know in order to distinguish them. Gregory of Nazianzus (ca. 330–89), often called the minstrel of the Trinity, warns that we must not busy ourselves about the precise manner in which the processions of the Son and the Spirit are different. They are indeed different, and that should be enough for us. For Lossky the Western doctrine of the generation of the Son and the spiration of the Spirit confuses somewhat the personhood of the Father vis-à-vis the personhood of the Son. Moreover, asserting that the Holy Spirit is the bond of union between Father and Son tends to weaken the distinctiveness of the three divine figures.

The Eastern fathers never tired of expounding the unknowable and inaccessible character of the Deity. They regularly emphasized the divine energies whereby God communicates himself outside of himself. The energies are forces proper to and inseparable from the divine essence. Through the energies God goes forth from himself and gives himself to the world.[10] Lossky affirms that it is this distinction between the divine essence and his energies that constitutes the dogmatic basis for our union with God. The energies, which are common operations of the Trinity, show forth in creation those qualities and attributes that can be known of God, while the divine essence remains inaccessible. These uncreated divine energies flow eternally from the divine nature. They penetrate all of created reality. Furthermore, even if the created universe did not exist, God would still somehow manifest himself beyond his essence.[11] The eternal energies are what cause the greatness and majesty of God to be reflected everywhere.

Lossky emphasizes that the eternal processions of the persons in the Trinity are the proper objects of theology, while their manifestation in the world of creation reflects the temporal missions of the Son and the Spirit. These latter missions constitute the work of the economic Trinity, which originates from the Father and is communicated by the Son in the Holy Spirit.[12] The Son makes known the Father, and the Holy Spirit gives testimony to the Son. The Spirit "remains unmanifested," having no image in another person; however, the Spirit will manifest himself at the end of days in the persons whom he deifies. The multitude of the blessed will be his lasting image.[13] We in the West would use the term "grace" to describe the deifying energies that the Spirit communicates to us. When the deifying energies are received by the just, these believers become the recipients of the indwelling of the Holy Spirit. According to the Gospel of John, the Spirit, the Comforter, is sent into the world by the Son. "He is the Spirit of truth who proceeds from the Father and he will bear witness to me" (15:26). Lossky quotes Gregory of Nazianzus in this connection: "The Old Testament manifested the Father plainly, the Son obscurely. The New Testament revealed the Son and hinted at the divinity of the Holy Spirit. Today the Spirit dwells among us and makes himself known more clearly."[14] On the eternal level of the divine persons, Lossky assumes that the Son and the Spirit proceed from the Father alone. On the level of the temporal missions, however, the Son is sent by the Father and is rendered incarnate by the Holy Spirit.[15]

Finally, one of the principal tenets of Orthodox theologians, including Vladimir Lossky, is the utter inaccessibility and unknowability of the divine essence. This controlling notion is captured poetically by Dionyius the Areopagite in the opening verses of his work, *The Mystical Theology:*

> Trinity!! Higher than any being,
>   any divinity, any goodness!
> Guide of Christians
>   in the wisdom of heaven!
> Leads us up beyond unknowing and light,
>   up to the farthest, highest peak
>   of mystic scripture,
>   where the mysteries of God's Word
>   lie simple, absolute and unchangeable
>   in the brilliant darkness of a hidden silence.
>   Amid the deepest shadow
>   they pour overwhelming light
>   on what is most manifest.

Amid the wholly unsensed and unseen
they completely fill our sightless minds
with treasures beyond all beauty.[16]

Liberation Theology and the Trinity: Leonardo Boff

Along with his brother, Clodovis, Leonardo Boff (b. 1938) lived and worked among the poor of Petropolis, Brazil, for a large part of his life. These oppressed people constitute the base ecclesial communities that served as the inspiration for the development of liberation theology. Leonardo also taught for many years at the Franciscan Institute in Petropolis. His excellent study on the triune God, *Trinity and Society*, was issued in Portuguese in 1986 and translated into English in 1988.

Boff asserts that while the Orthodox stress the Father as the sole source and origin of both the Son and the Spirit, Western Christians have emphasized the one divine spiritual nature that embraces Father, Son, and Holy Spirit. Modern theologians are inclined to emphasize the interpenetration and eternal corelatedness of the three divine figures. The term for this concept, *perichoresis,* was popularized by the Greek theologian John of Damascus (675–749). Boff employs this concept as the controlling notion for his analysis of the Trinity. The eternal community of Father, Son, and Spirit is portrayed as the prototype of all human societies and associations, from the family to the church to the nation, that are aspiring toward the perfectly fulfilled life. The role of theology is to deepen our understanding of the God of revelation and then to inspire us to build the type of society that most adequately reflects that understanding.[17] The heavy and consistent emphasis over the years on the monarchy of the Father has left us with a somewhat oppressive image of God that has tended to verticalize the relational climate in families, in civil society, and also in the church. The pyramidal vision of society and the church should be replaced by a more communal model based on the openness and interpenetration of the perichoretic Trinity.

According to Boff, the early liturgies of baptism and eucharist were the first settings in which the Trinity was expressed. Theological reflection on the mystery followed sometime thereafter. Parables like the prodigal son (Luke 15:11–32) forcefully portray the tender and abiding character of the Father's love for humankind. Passages such as Luke 10:21–22 reveal the unique and intimate relationship between the Father and Son. Jesus shows who God is by demonstrating how God relates to the poor, the oppressed, and those who approach him

in simplicity and without deceit. The revelation of the Holy Spirit at
Mary's conception of Jesus (Luke 1:35), at Jesus' baptism (Luke
3:21–22), and in connection with the miracles of Jesus' public life
(Matt 12:28), tells us a great deal about the Spirit's role and mission.[18]
He comes from the Father (John 15:26) at the request of the Son
(John 14:16), and he speaks no other truth but the truth of the Son
(John 16:14).

The doctrine of the Trinity experienced a very gradual development.
Key New Testament passages such as Matthew 28:19, 1 Corinthians
12:4–6, and 2 Corinthians 13:13 were read and appreciated but did
not generate much in the way of doctrinal development. It was in the
disputes against the modalists and subordinationists that the doctrine
began to take shape in the third century. At Nicaea (325) the consubstantiality of the Father and Son was defined, while Constantinople I
(381) did the same for the Holy Spirit. The Third Provincial Council
of Toledo in Spain (589) affirmed the procession of the Spirit from the
Father and the Son, which eventually became commonplace in the
West and served as the dogmatic ground for the separation of the
Eastern and Western churches in the eleventh century. The Council of
Florence, in the decree for the Greeks (1439), affirmed that the Holy
Spirit proceeds from the Father and the Son as from a single principle,
and in the decree for the Jacobites (1442), articulated the notion of
perichoresis. Although the idea of *perichoresis* did not become popular
among theologians until the last century, it carries special importance
for the promotion of greater participation, communion, and egalitarian relationships in the church and in society at large.

Boff concedes that his views on the communal dimension of the
Trinity were largely inspired by Jürgen Moltmann.[19] He also insists
that it is crucial to replace the domination model with the communion model in society and in the church and to promote the idea of the
maternal as well as paternal characteristics of the Deity. Boff cites the
Eleventh Council of Toledo (675), which taught that the Son came
forth from the womb of the Father, to indicate that feminine symbolism is as apt as masculine symbolism to describe the triune God. The
notion of communion seems to be the most effective way of expressing the revelation of the Trinity in the Scriptures. God can be understood as a dynamism of eternal communion and interpenetration
(*perichoresis*).[20] The three divine persons are always and eternally in
intimate relationship with one another. Moreover, both Paul (Gal
3:27–28; 1 Cor 15:28) and John (17:21) teach that all people are to
be included in the communal unity of the Trinity.

This triune community is to serve as the inspiration for the continual improvement of human society. For Boff the capitalist regimes have created the deepest rifts between the rich and the poor, the haves and the have-nots. In fact, the thriving capitalist countries of the first world have significantly contributed to the impoverishment and enslavement of the poor nations, snatching up their natural and even their human resources before they themselves have an opportunity to develop them. He points out that socialist societies, although founded on the right principle that natural resources are to be held in common, almost always fail to provide sufficient protection for human rights and adequate opportunities for education and cultural development for the majority. Since equality is therefore denied under both capitalism and socialism for the great numbers of citizens, the process of liberation must start from the oppressed themselves.[21]

Boff observes that in the church there is such a heavy concentration of power in the hands of the few that it is difficult to speak truthfully about an ecclesial community of all the faithful. There should be more participation and less hierarchy, more mutual respect and less bending of the knee before authority. He insists that the Trinity is present on earth wherever there is mutual rapport and genuine communion among believers. It is in these situations of authentic communality that the glory of the triune God truly shines forth.

Boff designates God the Father as the origin of all liberation. Because he is invisible, our only access to the Father is through the Son (Matt 11:27). God's fatherhood is the foundation for universal fellowship among all men and women. All beings are invited to share in the sonship of the Son (1 John 3:11–17). The perichoretic life of God expands ever outward. In the Old Testament we observe that the Father first forms his people and then frees them from their oppressors. This maternal Father and paternal Mother is revealed again and again as protector and defender of the poor and the helpless.[22] The New Testament image of the father in the parable of the prodigal son stunningly reflects the Father's maternal and paternal tenderness (Luke 15:11–32).

The Son, who is designated as the mediator of divine liberation, always acts in the power of the Spirit. Jesus too reveals the feminine dimension of humanity through his sensitivity, his mercy, and his kindness.[23] Boff writes that one can take two directions in describing the purpose of the Incarnation. One emphasizes the goal of healing human sinfulness and infirmity, while the other fixes on the creation of companions in love for the glory of God. Creation, according to this second approach, grew out of the wish of the divine figures to include others in their life of communion. This latter view, which was taught by the Franciscan John Duns Scotus (ca. 1266–1308), is preferred by Boff and many others because it is not based on the hypothesis of the sinful deficiencies of humankind, which contends that without human sin the Incarnation would seem to lack a purpose.

The Holy Spirit is portrayed as the driving force of liberation.[24] The Spirit is viewed as the power of renewal in all things (Mark 1:9–11; Rom 1:4) who keeps believers mindful of Jesus' words and teaching (John 15:26). Boff affirms that the Spirit is the one who creates differences among believers by distributing various gifts and who then establishes community among them (1 Cor 12:4–11). He also reminds us that Gregory of Nazianzus taught that God is neither masculine nor feminine.[25] The transforming mission of the Holy Spirit consists in respecting and fostering diversity and at the same time creating communion (Acts 2:11). The Spirit is especially operative when the poor become aware of their oppression, gather their forces together, and protest against those who have kept them in bondage.[26] Although the church possesses necessary institutional gifts, "it also contains the eruption of gifts and charisms (cf. 1 Cor 12; Rom 12), of charismatic figures who shake the rigid body of the institution, . . . who usher in new ways of attending to the needs of the community."[27]

In his discussion of the economic Trinity, Boff insists that the triune Deity creates in order to communicate itself with reality outside of itself. He views created reality as the very body of the Trinity. Although creation is not necessary, it is conatural to the divine essence because the divine persons wish to include others in their perichoretic communion. Boff speaks of the age of the Father, who watches over the human family; the age of the Son, who reveals the filial nature of all beings and promotes the movement of liberation especially among the helpless; and finally, the age of the Spirit, who interiorizes in individuals and in social movements the new and vibrant life proclaimed by the Son.

Our God is a triune God whom we first praise and then contemplate. The Trinity is revealed in the life of Jesus and in the outpourings of the Holy Spirit. For Boff the most effective way to understand the Deity is to view the three "Unique Ones" in an everlasting *perichoresis;* this approach serves well as a pattern for the revitalization of humankind's social relationships. The perichoretic Trinity with its eternal communion and interpenetration radiates especially forceful impulses for the liberation and reorganization of society and the church.

In 1988 Boff published *Holy Trinity, Perfect Community* in Portuguese, with the English edition released in 2000.[28] This brief work offers roughly the same message as *Trinity and Society*, but in a more comprehensible language aimed at those he describes as ordinary people. The study brings his recurring theme of the perichoretic Trinity to a wider audience in order to lead believers to a richer and more credible appreciation of the triune God. As a result of his 1981 study, *The Church: Charism and Power*, Leonardo Boff was silenced by the Vatican in 1985 for one year because his notions of the Catholic Church were seen as a danger to sound doctrine. He submitted to the restriction but left the Catholic ministry in 1992.

Feminist Trinitarian Thought: Elizabeth A. Johnson

A distinguished professor of theology at Fordham University where she has taught since 1991, Elizabeth A. Johnson (b. 1941) published several important monographs on the mystery of God prior to her 1993 study, *She Who Is*.[29] In this work she identifies the idea of God as the primary symbol of the entire religious system. The first part of her work focuses on the approach of feminist theologians who criticize the unequal status of women in the church. The prevailing structure of patriarchy in the church effectively excludes women from the processes of decision-making and deprives them of the right to hold jurisdictional offices in the organization. Johnson takes her stand within the liberation stream of Catholic feminist theology.

Feminists strongly endorse the reform of patriarchal church structures and the ideology that supports them so that all church members can enjoy full status within the organization. Johnson's aim is to bring together the treasures of the classical tradition with the expanding resources of feminist Christian wisdom. Feminists are confronting the oppressive and sometimes idolatrous forces at work in the church that portray God almost exclusively from the male point of view, as if this were the only approach to speaking about the Deity. The feminist premise is that both society and the church are pervaded by sexism, patriarchy, and androcentrism. Patriarchy is characterized by sexist social structures prejudicial to women, while androcentrism assumes that the characteristics of ruling men must be normative for all of humankind. Johnson asserts that this radical antifeminist bias is deeply ingrained in the traditional religious institutional patterns. She insists that women are virtually excluded from full participation in the church's official life. Perhaps the greatest danger inherent in this situation is that women have come to believe in and accept their marginal position within the church.[30]

These unfair organizational patterns and symbol systems, Johnson affirms, must be changed so that a new community can be created wherein women are able to be genuine partners in what she terms "communities of mutuality." Changing a rigid and uncompromising patriarchy into a benevolent one is hardly the answer. Speech about God framed in exclusively male terminology does not bring about equal participation of men and women in the religious life of the church. As long as the Deity is referred to in exclusively patriarchal terms, men will continue to understand themselves as superior to women. Portraying God as a being more like men than women borders on idolatry. Female symbols must be inserted when speaking of God in order to expand the language patterns. Yet adding feminine characteristics to the Deity, who is seen to be predominantly male, simply exaggerates the subordination of women. Johnson advocates positing the existence of the feminine in God. She points out that Yves Congar and Leonardo Boff speak of the Holy Spirit in feminine terms; however, this will not liberate or empower women, because God-language would still be largely androcentric, and the feminine could easily be subordinated. Only when women and men enter into the symbolism of God as equals will the problem be fully addressed. To ground this awareness, Johnson chooses to employ principally feminine symbolism for God.

The first of the female symbols for God is that of spirit, or *ruah* (Gen 1:2). *Ruah's* activities are primarily directed toward the creation of new life and the renovation of what has been injured or damaged. The Spirit descended upon Jesus at his baptism (Luke 3:22) and was with him from the outset of his public life (Luke 4:18). In John's Gospel the Spirit is identified as the Paraclete or Comforter (16:13) who will guide the disciples into the full range of truth, "taking from what is mine and proclaiming it to you" (16:13–14). The most thoroughly developed personification of God's presence in the Old Testament is that of Wisdom or Sophia, the dispenser of life and knowledge. In the Wisdom of Solomon (first century B.C.), omnipotence is attributed to Sophia, who protected the patriarchs with her saving power. While the interpretation of the Old Testament personification of Wisdom is still widely debated, Johnson seems to prefer Wisdom "as a female personification of God's own being in creative and saving involvement with the world."[31]

In the Christian context, Spirit and Sophia are practically identified as one and the same, which makes it quite appropriate to refer to the Holy Spirit in female symbols. Moreover, the activities of Sophia have also been associated with Jesus. Referring to him as the image of the invisible God and the firstborn of all creation (Col 1:15) is suggestive of a Wisdom theme. Johnson asserts that Christ appears as the embodiment of Wisdom, especially in the Gospel of John. In fact, John's prologue can almost be considered the story of Sophia. According to the trend of Wisdom Christology, Jesus can be seen as the human being whom Sophia became. A third biblical image that portrays the Deity is that of a mother who watches over her children and protects them from danger (Isa 42:14). The fact that God has many names makes it easier for feminists to enrich and expand speech about God.

Johnson begins her presentation of the triune God from the experience of the Spirit who is actively present in the world, although the full dimensions of the Spirit's activity have largely been lost. The Spirit is the agent who brought Jesus into the world and who instructed the disciples after the resurrection. Today, the efforts of the Spirit renew lives and confront social injustices (Isa 61:1–2). The Spirit is the source of individuation for creatures and the source of the growth of community.[32] The Spirit dwells in the heart of every creature and holds all things together. Indeed, the Spirit is the one who pours the love of God into our hearts (Rom 5:5). Since Spirit-Sophia can justly be called friend, the experience of women can certainly contribute to the enrichment of the image of friend. The activity of the Spirit, when viewed as the work of a female subject, allows us to expand considerably our notions about the Deity and lessens the overriding impact of the patriarchal picture of God.

The second Sophia figure in the Trinity is Jesus, who is Wisdom or Sophia made flesh. Johnson maintains that over the years Christology gradually adopted the worldview of patriarchy. Jesus' maleness as set forth in androcentric theology and church life has lifted up maleness as an indispensable characteristic of the Deity.

> While there [i.e., at Chalcedon] it is confessed that between the human nature and the divine nature of Jesus Christ there is no mixing, no confusion, so that each nature keeps its own properties, still the androcentric imagination occasions a certain leakage of Jesus' human maleness into the divine nature, so that maleness appears to be of the essence of the God made known in Christ.[33]

Johnson describes Jesus as Wisdom's child, Sophia incarnate. She stresses that it is not Jesus' maleness that is significant from a dogmatic point of view, but rather his humanity in solidarity with the whole human race. Neither the divinity nor the humanity of Christ calls for maleness as an essential prerequisite. His overriding preference for the poor and the marginalized, not his sex, is what constitutes his most distinguishing characteristic. With Jesus-Sophia, women and men are equally capable of fully representing Christ and participating in his mission. Sophia is present and active in Jesus, who is designated as "the power and wisdom of God" (1 Cor 1:24).

The third divine figure described in the Sophia context is Mother-Sophia, the unoriginate source who is appropriately called God as Mother. The maternal identification reflects a rather different and complementary vision. Holy Wisdom, the unoriginate source of all creation, continually looks after all living beings and gives new birth to those who accept her word of life. Her intense maternal involvement in creation and her abiding concern for justice and liberation supply some of the deficiencies of classical theism and add further credibility to the Deity's overriding solicitude for the world.

While the exclusive use of male symbols creates the impression that maleness is an essential dimension of the Trinity, the feminine approach to the divine reality opens up a variety of options that underline the radical equality of persons within the Trinity. Emphasis on the processions of the Son and the Spirit suggests a hierarchical pattern that brings to mind a subtle subordination within the Deity. Johnson notes that even though the equality of the divine persons is continually affirmed, the origination of the Son and the Holy Spirit from the Father reveals a pattern that seems to be consonant with patriarchal organizational structures within the church.

Our religious heritage discloses a threefold dimension in the Divine Being, for three distinct ranges of experience come to us from the one God. Johnson reminds us that it is not always necessary to refer to the Deity in the metaphors of Father, Son, and Holy Spirit. Actually, the use of female images is needed so that we can move beyond the "unconscious emphasis" that the prevailing male symbols have forced on us.[34] God as Spirit-Sophia reaches into every corner of reality as an uplifting, vivifying power. God as Jesus Christ, Sophia's child, reveals the pattern of Wisdom's contagious and saving love for all humankind. And God as Mother Wisdom, or Holy Wisdom, is the unoriginate source who is unknown and unknowable. The three are all in all and all in one. In this context the Trinity is revealed as a unique and unspeakable relatedness of total mutuality among the three figures, whose relationships to one another constitute their distinctiveness. These relationships are not hierarchical but are mutually enhancing, with no hint of subordination. Spirit-Sophia can be readily identified in terms of friendship, and the same is true of Jesus-Sophia (John 15:15). In fact, the same can be said of Mother Wisdom with her maternal concern for all of creation. "In this living friendliness the hypostases are not determined by their point of origin or rank in the order of processions, but exist in each other in genuine mutuality."[35] These patterns of differentiation—mutuality, friendship, maternal concern—clearly reveal the distinctive ways of women's activity in the world. Johnson describes *perichoresis* as "the idea of all three persons existing in each other in an exuberant movement of mutual relations."[36] Their unsurpassed communion of love stands as the ideal model of mutuality for all people in the world.

Contrary to the position of classical theism, Johnson insists that God does have a real relationship to the world. The traditional thesis is that creation has a real relation to God but not vice versa, for this would imply dependence in the Deity. The Sophia-God creates not out of necessity, but rather out of superabundant graciousness. While Spirit-Sophia dwells in the world and animates it with her liberating breath, Jesus-Sophia reveals the nearness of God, especially to the poor and the downtrodden. Moreover, Holy Wisdom continues to be disclosed as the unoriginate Mother of all creation.

For Johnson the more congenial model for relating created reality to God is the panentheistic paradigm that views the Deity as penetrating the entire universe but in no way being exhausted by it.[37] This model of the world dwelling in God opens up the possibility of poignant maternal imagery. Portraying God in this kind of intimate relationship, with each dwelling in the other, calls forth a striking reflection of the maternal experience of women. Johnson concludes that there is every reason for feminists to speak of God as "She Who Is."

From the unforgivable betrayal of the Levite's concubine as recorded in Judges 19:22–26, to the wanton execution of women by the Inquisition and other persecutions, to the frequent and flagrant abuse of women through the centuries, Sophia-God enters into the pain and agony of these souls profaned by humanity even to our day. God assuredly can be found on the side of all those who are oppressed in society and in the church. Feminist theologians continue to search for language to articulate that silent power rising out of the experience of women in suffering who want a full voice and who desire an equal place at the table in the familial gathering of the "friends of God and the prophets" (Wis 7:27).

In a 1997 study Johnson repeats many of her themes from *She Who Is*.[38] She emphasizes that the Trinity can best be viewed as a communion in relationship that invites all of us into its circle. The incomprehensible threefold *koinonia* opens out to create a community of sisters and brothers. This vision had largely been lost for a thousand years or more in favor of the image of a solitary God. Recently, she observes, there has been a dramatic return to the idea of the Deity as a community in relation. Since relationships constitute persons, these mutual relationships are at the heart of the Divine Being. Furthermore, the divine relationships of mutuality call for the church to reshape itself as a community of equals. Johnson writes: "Only a community of equals related in profound mutuality, only a community pouring itself out for justice, peace, and the integrity of creation, corresponds to the triune symbol. For too long, this symbol has been imprisoned in misunderstandings. It is time to set it free to sing again."[39]

Process Theology and Trinity: Joseph A. Bracken and Marjorie Hewitt Suchocki

A professor of theology for many years at Xavier University in Cincinnati, Joseph A. Bracken insists that the time is ripe for the development of a new systematic theology. He notes that David Tracy of the University of Chicago has shown interest in the categories of process philosophy for the reinterpretation of the central concepts of theology.[40] Bracken teaches that the notion of substance as the primary category of being should be replaced by the concept of process as the controlling category. Paraphrasing Alfred North Whitehead (1861–1947), the father of process thought, Bracken affirms: "[The world] is never the same from moment to moment. Our senses, to be sure, give us the picture of the world as an unchanging material reality. But this is illusory; all that really endures are the orderly patterns created by successive generations of momentary occasions [i.e., the final things of which the world is temporarily composed]."[41] The world as such continues, although its individual components are constantly changing. It is a totality whose individual parts are never the same from one moment to the next.

Bracken states that because everything depends on the notion of God, it is appropriate to initiate one's theologizing with the Trinity. He teaches that Father, Son, and Holy Spirit constitute a divine community. For him a community implies a higher type of existence and activity than the existence of the individual members acting on their own. Inasmuch as all of reality is in process, communities are also in continuous interaction with one another, and they are thereby greater than the sum of their parts. They arise out of the fusion of what Bracken terms "the many processes of interpretation occurring among the individual members of the community."[42] The members are involved in various types of cooperative activities within the communities. These collective activities can be considered ongoing processes of interpretation. The community develops a shared mentality and a shared will or purpose and also exercises a common agency.

Within this context Bracken concentrates on the Trinity, which he terms "the divine community." He predicates total unanimity of mind and will of the divine persons and hence identifies the Trinity as the perfect community. The divine figures do not possess their own minds and wills, but share the one divine mind and will. Although each possesses a distinct consciousness, together they constitute a single, shared consciousness and relate to created reality as a single divine agent. For Bracken the relationships among the three divine persons are developing continually. These developments are enhancements and thus are to be evaluated positively. He follows Charles Hartshorne (1897–2000), who holds that God's goodness, although constantly increasing in depth and richness, is unsurpassable by anyone other than the Divine Being itself. The individuation of the Father, the Son, and the Holy Spirit is brought about entirely through their relationships with one another.

Bracken views the nature of God as an interpersonal process. The divine figures exist by reason of their common participation in the process.[43] Within the divine community the process of self-giving love is what binds the three together and constitutes them as the one God.[44] For Bracken a "democratically organized structured society" is the model for the Trinity. Such a society possesses a unity and exercises an agency proper to itself, and in some sense the activity of such a community transcends the existence and activity of its individual members.[45] The three divine persons, then, are one God because of their common participation in an ongoing process of interpretation that is their life in community. The Father, the Son, and the Holy Spirit are distinct persons only because they are concomitantly members of the interpersonal process that is their common nature.[46]

Bracken considers the Father the primal cause, the principle by which everything exists. The Son is the primal effect who transforms possibility into actuality for all three persons. The Spirit is the vivifying principle who prompts the Father to offer ever new possibilities of existence for the divine persons and who prompts the Son to accept the Father's proposals.⁴⁷ Bracken views the Father as principally associated with what he calls the primordial nature of God, that is, God's grasp of all possibilities for the Divine Being, for this world, and for all possible worlds. The Son is chiefly associated with the divine consequent nature, because he converts possibilities into actualities and integrates them with all that has been taken up into the divine nature. Finally, the Spirit is particularly associated with the superjective nature of God, that is, the influence that God exercises over the finite processes in the world. This makes the Spirit in a singular fashion responsible for the constantly evolving God-world relationship. Whereas the Father is primarily responsible for the conceptual origination of the universe, the Son is principally focused on the perfected actuation of finite reality. The Spirit, then, is the animating force of the entire creative process.

The Father communicates himself entirely to the Son, the Son responds completely to the initiatives of the Father, and the Spirit facilitates the exchange of life and love among the three equal persons. The world process is only a small part of the infinite reality of the triune persons, who comprise the ultimate society, the divine community.⁴⁸ Whereas for Whitehead creativity seems to be the ultimate principle on which even God depends, Bracken views all creativity as grounded in God and especially predicated of the Father. The triune persons renew the act of creating from moment to moment and thus transmit existence to one another and to all creatures. He judges that panentheism is the most appropriate way to describe the God-world relationship. In the panentheistic view the world is included in God's being, but the world in no way exhausts God's being or creativity.

In a study published in 1991, *Society and Spirit: A Trinitarian Cosmology,* Joseph Bracken states that "only a trinitarian understanding of God as a community of three divine persons who share a common field of activity with all their creatures, allows for a genuinely panentheistic understanding of the God-world relationship."⁴⁹ In this study he leans heavily on his 1985 work, *The Triune Symbol.* He describes the created universe as a cosmic society under the headship of the Son, with the Spirit as the creative and vivifying principle.⁵⁰ Bracken insists that creativity is an essential dimension of the nature of God. Along with creation, the Divinity posits its existence at every moment in virtue of the principle of creativity. All three persons pervade the entire field of what Bracken calls the extensive continuum (i.e., the widest society conceivable in our current state of knowledge). The world as distinct from God survives as a totality, although its components are never the same from moment to moment.

According to Bracken, one purpose of the world is to provide for the continual expansion of the actuality of God.[51] The individual finite entities are incorporated into God as soon as they acquire actual existence in the created order, but creation as a totality endures. Ultimate reality is the society in which the divine persons share their common life with all their creatures.[52] The field of activity proper to creation is identified as a semiautonomous reality governed by its own empirical laws of development. In this manner the three divine persons can be at work in the cosmos, achieving their own purposes without interfering with the freedom of rational creatures or with the laws controlling the evolution of the universe.[53] Thus, Bracken reconciles his view of the triune Deity with the existence of the created universe.

~

Marjorie Hewitt Suchocki (b. 1933) is the Ingraham Professor of Theology at the Claremont Graduate School of Theology in California. Like John B. Cobb Jr. and David Ray Griffin, she considers herself a disciple of Alfred North Whitehead. Her important work, *God, Christ, Church*, published in 1982 and revised in 1989, presents an overall view of the major themes of Christian faith. In her exposition of the Deity, she places considerable emphasis on the divine attributes: God as Presence, God as Wisdom, and God as Power. After the fashion of Friedrich Schleiermacher, she treats the Trinity at the end of her study.

Suchocki deals with the pervasive experience of loneliness and the inadequacy of daily human relationships. These moments provide an opportunity for God's entrance into our lives, although his coming is usually hidden. We often fail to appreciate it, but in the midst of our loneliness, we are continually confronted by the Deity as our Alpha and Omega. In this context she defines objective immortality as the passage of a finite entity from the temporal scene to its entrance into the being of God. Subjective immortality, on the other hand, is enjoyed only by God, for all finite entities, after their brief moment of actualization, are taken up into the Divine Being. As we contemplate the divine *presence,* we come to an appreciation of the faithfulness of God and are drawn to accept the life of Jesus as the most intensive presence of the divine in history.

The second attribute emphasized by Suchocki is the divine *wisdom* that results in the perfect integration of the Deity's primordial and consequent nature. Whereas we finite creatures find ourselves in a state of perennial ambiguity and frustration in regard to the inexorable movement of time, God views all possibilities and contingencies by virtue of the divine primordial nature, while the divine consequent nature embraces and contains every actual entity that ever existed. The perfect integration of the primordial nature and the consequent nature constitutes the wisdom of God, who apprehends the universe as it is and as it might be. The Divinity lures the becoming world toward its optimal realization; however, since creatures in varying degrees assume their own directions regarding the pursuit of the future, God is also subjected to some element of contingency inasmuch as he has to wait on the world's decisions. Nonetheless, the divine wisdom is the ideal response to the ambiguity and uncertainty of time.

As God provides a response to our individual problems of loneliness and insecurity, his *power* addresses the societal need for justice, which Suchocki describes as the inclusive well-being of society. The oppressed and the marginal within our borders and beyond cannot be ignored. Oppressed groups, women, and peoples of third world countries deserve our constant attention. She reminds us that in a process universe everything affects everything else. The power of God is what makes justice possible, and the effort of concerned men and women is what makes justice real.[54]

Suchocki speaks of the life and activity of Jesus and the Old Testament narrative of the history of the Jewish people as special privileged revelation. She points to the incarnation of Jesus Christ as the full communication of God's nature among humankind. She reminds us that in process thought the challenge is not to explain how Jesus can be both human and divine, but rather to clarify how and to what extent he is the unique manifestation of God among us.[55] His most precious revelation is the reversal of the social order, concentrating on sinners rather than the righteous, addressing women as well as men, and focusing on the outcasts of society rather than the prominent and the noteworthy. Jesus loves in the same manner that God loves, transcending boundaries and offering superabundant forgiveness and salvation. He reveals the nature of God through his selfless life and death. Further, he opens up new possibilities for a resurrected life. God as power expresses the triumph of God over evil.

Suchocki concludes her work *God, Christ, Church* with a brief chapter on the Trinity. She asks whether there are adequate grounds for transposing the discussion of the three divine attributes into a presentation of the Trinity. In this manner we would be evolving a doctrine of the Trinity grounded in our human experience of God. She replies that the doctrine of Trinity preserves the Deity's infinite complexity and prevents us from thinking that God is "but humanity writ large upon some cosmic screen."[56] For Suchocki, then, the notion of Trinity is a symbol of God's complexity. "If we thus retain the term trinity to indicate the infinite complexity in unity of the divine nature, we push the word far beyond its traditional meaning of threeness."[57] She further explains her position: "God is the supremely complex one. If trinity can be expanded beyond its traditional use to indicate this mighty complexity in unity, then it retains a symbolic appropriateness in its designation of the inner nature of God."[58]

Suchocki contends that what she has explained as divine *presence, wisdom*, and *power* have traditionally been expressed as Father, Son, and Holy Spirit. While her Christology evolves out of God's singular presence in Jesus, her ecclesiology is grounded in our understanding of God's wisdom in providing and sustaining the church through the agency of the Holy Spirit. Finally, her approach to eschatology rests on our belief in the divine agency centered in the depths of God as power. For Suchocki the designations of Father, Son, and Holy Spirit are terms that have a particular rather than a universal significance and hence must be translated consistently in the light of changing times if one is to be faithful to the root meanings. She insists that "we cannot take the designation of trinity as Father, Son, and Holy Spirit in an absolute sense." Furthermore, there "are serious considerations for moving today toward emphasizing this trinity as power, wisdom, and presence rather than as Father, Son, and Spirit."[59] Suchocki concludes her thought:

> We advocate, then, that the triune nature of God be expressed directly through the understanding of God's *presence* with us and for us through Jesus of Nazareth, through the *wisdom* of God whereby God brings the church to birth in each generation, guiding it through divine providence in its manifestation of apostolicity, unity, and holiness, and through the *power* of God, bringing the world to justice within the transformation of the divine nature and guiding the finite world toward societal forms of justice.[60] (Italics added.)

In a 1997 monograph written for the book *Trinity in Process*, entitled "Spirit in and through the World," Suchocki affirms that in the seventeenth century the word "person" began to take on the notion of individual self-consciousness, rendering the traditional understanding of the divine persons as but three expressions of the single, intelligent nature of God much more problematic. Since then, many attempts have been made to refine the notion of person as it applies to the Deity. She stresses again the profound complexity of the Divine Being. Although the economic Trinity is revealed in three modes, the Trinity in the life of God remains symbolic of the everlastingly deep complexity that surpasses all number.[61]

Also in 1997 Suchocki published a study, "The Contextualization of God," in which she questions whether there are adequate reasons for talking about a triune God beyond the historical constructions of doctrine.[62] She emphasizes that theology must energetically embrace an open epistemology and the findings of all the sciences to give a full account of humankind's religious experience. Suchocki proposes that when this is achieved, the trinitarian doctrine may cease to be valid inasmuch as it was "formulated in a non-contextually conscious age."[63] It is Suchocki's feeling that this might very well occur.

New Triune Configurations: Kathryn Tanner and Peter C. Hodgson

Kathryn Tanner did her theological studies at Yale University and taught at Yale before taking an appointment at the University of Chicago Divinity School. In her *God and Creation in Christian Theology*, published in 1988, she affirms a more traditional view of the divine transcendence, insisting that "God is not one agent among others in the world but operates on a completely different plane of agency, so that events can be both the results of creatures' activities and the acts of God."[64] She defended her position in an essay included in the volume *The God Who Acts*, published in 1994.[65] The discussions of this rather ponderous subject are vaguely reminiscent of the acrimonious debates between the Jesuits and the Dominicans in the sixteenth and early seventeenth centuries over the efficacy of divine grace versus human free will.[66]

Recently Tanner has published *Jesus, Humanity, and the Trinity*, which charts an outline of a systematic theology that she intends to write in the coming years.[67] She can accurately be categorized as a postliberal theologian who is a representative of the Yale school, which has included such prominent scholars as Hans Frei and George Lindbeck. Tanner has been influenced throughout by the work of Karl

Barth and his neo-orthodox theology. Barth was the theologian who spearheaded the movement away from the liberal theology of the nineteenth century.

Tanner's thoughts on the divine Triad are dispersed throughout *Jesus, Humanity, and the Trinity*, giving the reader a reasonably good idea of the direction to be taken in her future, fuller treatment. She affirms at the outset that there are two principles that guide her work. First, a noncompetitive relationship between the actions of God and the agency of humans must always be maintained. Second, all limitations in the concept of God's agency must be completely removed. God and creatures are on a totally different level of being and causality. This allows Tanner to cope more effectively with those situations where the divine activity and the acts of humans intersect. In fact, it is this divine transcendence that opens up the possibility for this intimate union and collaboration with humankind.

This is exemplified first and foremost in the Incarnation where God becomes incarnate to save us, and, at the same time, is different from us *in order* to save us.[68] It is God's absolute transcendence that enables the divinity to intersect with humanity in such a full and complete fashion. This exquisitely noncompetitive relationship is what brings about the convergence of the divine and the human in Christ. Tanner identifies the Father as the source of difference within the Trinity. The Father brings about what is different in the divine being—that is, the Son and the Spirit. The Son is all that the Father is without fatherhood, for he is the Son. The Spirit brings the Father and the Son to us. Thus, the Holy Spirit opens the Trinity out toward what is not God. The Son's love for the Father is returned by the Holy Spirit. The interpenetration and co-inherence of the divine persons are absolutely complete. What the Father is essentially is communicated totally to the other two, except for his fatherhood and his procession of the Spirit through the Son.

According to Tanner, there are three ways of reflecting on the unity of the Trinity. There is the unity of essence whereby the three persons are a single substance in three modes of being: "They are like three distinct appearances of the same thing from different angles."[69] Also, the three perfectly co-inhere. The divine substance appears in them in different modes of existence. The three are equal and coexist from all eternity and forever. Finally, the three are united in indivisible action outside the Triad. Each makes a distinctive contribution. The Father is the source, the Son is the shape, and the Holy Spirit is the one who effects and completes.[70]

In their functions outside the Trinity, they always act as one because of the single divine will and operation that they share: "From the Father through the Son, in the Spirit, is the world created, saved and brought to its end or consummation."[71] Tanner attests that the Father acts, the Son acts, and the Spirit acts—each in a distinct mode—and what is brought into being bears the stamp of all three operating as one. In the Incarnation all three persons are active: "Assumed by the Word, Jesus' humanity receives everything for its good directly from its source of goodness that is the Father, through the power of the Spirit. . . . Jesus in working for our salvation exhibits a perfect form of human partnership with the Father and the Spirit, a human version of the Son's action in common with the other members of the Trinity."[72] The humanity of the Son becomes the effective instrument for the distribution of benefits to the world.[73]

One can be confident that Kathryn Tanner's forthcoming systematic theology will breathe new life and direction into the postliberal rendering of the mysteries of the Trinity and the Incarnation.

After completing his doctoral studies at Yale, Peter C. Hodgson (b. 1934) began his teaching career at the Vanderbilt University Divinity School in 1965, where he remains today. He can be identified as a postmodern theologian who recognizes that the paradigm of modernity—dating from the Enlightenment—has begun to obsolesce. Hodgson feels that this is not the time for writing a systematic theology. Rather, what is needed are constructive proposals that chart new and tentative theological directions. Thus, he calls his effort a "constructive Christian theology." In his *God in History: Shapes of Freedom*, published in 1989, Hodgson worked out what could be called a Hegelian trinitarian theology, which he refines and clarifies in *Winds of the Spirit*, published in 1994.[74]

In chapter 10 of the latter work, Hodgson addresses the challenging issue of the relation between God and being. He concludes that God is being itself, or the power of being. Tillich's memorable description of God as the "ground of being" is not as acceptable as his "power of being," because the latter phrase more effectively portrays being as an event. For Tillich, God is indeed the power of being by which all things are. Hodgson views God's creative power of being as a primal energy working through all of creation.[75] He appreciates the insight of Karl Rahner, who asserts that God is the being who has being absolutely, the one who communicates being to the rest of reality. Hodgson translates Exodus 3:14 as follows: "I am the One who lets be." In Hodgson's judgment, God and God alone is the one true and perfect person. Furthermore, he portrays the Deity as infinite subjectivity.[76]

Chapter 11 of *Winds of the Spirit*, entitled "The Triune Figuration," sets out Hodgson's understanding of the three modalities of the divine life. The three figures in which God appears have been identified as persons in the Christian tradition. We have come to view these persons as three male subjects—Father, Son, and Holy Spirit—and have largely deemphasized the female imagery for God that is revealed in both the Old and the New Testaments. Hodgson is convinced it is a mistake to view God as a triad of male figures, and that it would be best to devise a new language for the three modalities who constitute the Divinity.

According to Hodgson, God is the one perfect person who subsists in three modes of being, but these modes of being are not three supernatural persons. His position does indeed sound like modalism, and he admits as much, but he hopes to counter this by outlining a social model of the Trinity.[77] The figure of the One is God's own self-relation prescinding from his relations to the created universe. The world constitutes God's otherness, and all created things can be included under the gestalt of Christ. Hodgson defines the Christ-gestalt as the definitive shape of God in history. The figure of the Spirit comes forth out of the interplay between God and the world. This trinitarian model is based on the Hegelian design of identity, difference, and mediation, or unity, separation, and synthesis. This movement for Hegel lies at the very heart of the life process. And for Hodgson it constitutes the dynamism of the divine being.

For Hodgson, the one God is unbegotten and remains an inexhaustible mystery for humankind.

> In the moment of identity God is constituted as "God" through the relation of *aseity* or *self-generation* (the inner divine "play" of self and other). In the moment of *difference* God constitutes the "world" as object, as other-than-God with its own internal complexity, through the relation of creative/ redemptive love. In the moment of *mediation*, God and world are co-conditioned and consummated as "Spirit" through the relation of freedom.[78]

Although God's aseity or unoriginate character has come to be identified as fatherhood, Hodgson insists that we must replace the patriarchal father figure, for it emits too many negative signals to women and to the underpriviledged. Like Elizabeth Johnson and Sallie McFague, he argues that the use of the image of God as Mother could restore some balance in light of the prevailing masculine images that have been employed so consistently throughout our tradition. He expresses a preference, however, for the generic name "God," for it communicates the oneness, the wholeness, the aseity, of the Divinity upon whom all things depend.

In an outpouring of love, God goes forth from Godself and creates a universe, establishing it as God's own body. The Divinity creates the whole cosmos that reveals the figure and the shape of Godself. For Christians, it is Jesus who is the focus and epicenter of God's love for the world. The shape of that divine love is most dramatically expressed for Christian believers in Jesus' life for others and his suffering death. For Hodgson this is what constitutes Jesus as the Christ.

> Precisely his no-Godness, his common identity with the world, is the bearer of divinity. What makes him Christ is not a priviledged, superhuman divine nature but utter identification with the anguish and joy of human nature. It is the intensity of his humanity that radiates divinity; it is as "son of humanity" that he is "son of God."[79]

Hodgson insists on the full humanity of Jesus, and he emphasizes that God is especially present in him. However, the divine redemptive presence in the universe is verified through what he calls the Christ-gestalt, that is, the specific shapes and patterns of activity in human society that best contribute to the development of the human community. This Christ-gestalt, whenever and wherever it is present and active, constitutes the shape or pattern of God in the world. It can be called the contour or structure of the incarnate praxis of redemptive love and reconciliatory emancipation that will transform the world.[80] Jesus, through his life and death, became identified with this praxis, and represents for Christians the definitive shape of God in history. Hodgson, however, affirms that Jesus is not the sole bearer of the Christ-gestalt, which seems to have analogues in other world religions.[81]

For Hodgson, the Spirit, the third modality in God, is the figure of mediation who reestablishes communion through the return of all things into God "that God may be all in all" (1 Cor 15:28). Hodgson is not especially happy with what he terms Karl Barth's christocentrism, because it distorts true trinitarianism. The Spirit in the Barthian scheme becomes "an appendage" to the altogether dominating relationship between Father and Son.[82] We must affirm that the Spirit who moves through the world like the wind, transforming pockets of domination into relations of accord and freedom, is the power of liberation for the created universe: "The Spirit is already present in the second moment, the moment of creation and differentiation, but it is fully recognized only in the third moment, the moment of liberation and consummation. This is because the Spirit is an *emergent* figure; it emerges out of the interaction of God and the world."[83]

According to Hodgson, the Spirit is neither a masculine nor a feminine figure. All three of the divine modalities go beyond the description of male and female. Although the doctrine of the Spirit is perhaps the most obscure of Christian doctrines, God as Spirit seems to be best identified as primal energy. The Spirit is that modality of divine activity whereby God indwells and energizes the forces of nature, human communities, and individuals, bringing them into liberating communion with the Deity.[84] For Hodgson, the Spirit does not pre-exist as a supernatural divine person. Although there is in God a vital interplay of identity, difference, and mediation, he does not believe that this complexity in God results in subsistent divine persons. The Spirit comes forth as a result of the interaction of God and the universe. It emerges as something of a personal reality in and through its exchanges with the world. For Hodgson, this portrayal of God through the Christ-gestalt giving shape to humankind and the world, and through the Spirit drawing humankind and the cosmos back to God, amounts to a social understanding of God that is neither essentially modalistic nor tritheistic.[85] When the divine Spirit resides in individuals or in communities, these people experience an unusual empowerment to pour out the Spirit into their environment.

The Spirit is the instrument of Christ's presence among believers and the means whereby the Christ-gestalt is promulgated throughout creation. Hodgson insists that it is the Spirit that remains the more inclusive symbol of divine presence within the human community: "Today we must recognize a plurality of saving shapes of divine presence, and we should be able to affirm that the Spirit proceeds from this plurality and not from Christ alone."[86]

Observations

Among recent Orthodox theologians, Vladimir Lossky stands in the first rank. For him the Father is the Unoriginate One, the Son is generated by the Father, and the Spirit proceeds from the Father alone. The different understanding of the origin of the Spirit determines the whole direction of Eastern and Western theology. Western speculation concerning the spiration of the Spirit from the Father and the Son is for Lossky an "inadmissible error" that weakens the monarchy of the Father emphasized so heavily by the Cappadocian fathers. The distinction between the eternal procession of the Spirit from the Father and the divine manifestations of the Spirit in creation coming from the Father and the Son was never understood by the West, precipitating the insertion of the *filioque* formula in the West. Lossky never tires of stressing the unknowability and inaccessibility of God, which he feels has not been properly respected in the West. The divine energies, which are proper to and inseparable from the divine essence, are what constitute the basis for our union with God. These uncreated divine energies flow eternally from the divine nature and show forth in creation those qualities that can be known of God.

Leonardo Boff has especially attempted to reconcile trinitarian thought with the directions of liberation theology. He employs the concept of *perichoresis* as the controlling notion for his analysis of the triune God. Inasmuch as repeated emphasis over the centuries on the monarchy of the Father has verticalized the relational climate in society and in the church, a perichoretic model would serve as a base for changing this. He also stresses that feminine symbolism must be utilized more frequently to describe the triune Deity. Boff insists that the Trinity is present on earth wherever there is mutual rapport and genuine communality among persons. The Holy Spirit is portrayed as the driving force of liberation who is particularly operative in alleviating the plight of the poor and the downtrodden. Boff sees creation as co-natural to the divine essence because the divine persons desire to include others in their perichoretic community.

After summarizing the work of feminist theologians who have justly criticized the unequal status of women in the church, Elizabeth A. Johnson endeavors to portray the Deity through the use of feminine symbols. The Holy Spirit is described as Spirit-Sophia, who can be considered a female subject who dwells in the hearts of creatures and holds all things together. The Spirit-Sophia is the source of individuation for creation and is the community builder. The second Sophia is Jesus, who is Wisdom's child, Sophia incarnate. Jesus' maleness is not dogmatically significant, but rather his humanity in solidarity with all of humankind is what is most critical. With Jesus-Sophia, men and women are equally capable of fully representing Christ and participating in his mission. The third divine figure she describes as Mother-Sophia, the unoriginate source who can appropriately be called God as Mother. Johnson insists that these feminine symbols reveal the total mutuality of the three divine persons. Their relationships to one another are not hierarchical but rather mutually enhancing, with no hint of subordination. These divine relationships of mutuality challenge the church to reshape itself as a community of equals.

Two rather different positions in process trinitarian thought can be seen in the work of Joseph A. Bracken and Marjorie Hewitt Suchocki. Whereas Bracken makes every effort to reconcile orthodox trinitarianism with process categories, Suchocki openly raises questions about the continuing validity of the traditional notion of Trinity as applied to the nature of God. Both consider themselves disciples of Alfred North Whitehead, but Suchocki remains closer to Whitehead's views regarding the identity of the Deity. For Bracken the Father is principally associated with the primordial nature of God, while the Son is chiefly associated with the divine consequent nature. The Spirit is related primarily to the superjective nature of God that exercises influence over all finite processes in the world. Suchocki concentrates on three attributes of God: God as Presence, God as Wisdom, and God as Power. She then questions whether these qualities can more appropriately express the complex reality of God than the traditional references to the three divine persons. She urges that the doctrine of the Trinity must be reworked in light of an open epistemology and all the related findings of science to determine whether or not it speaks to believers today.

In Kathryn Tanner's outline of trinitarian theology, she portrays the Father as the source of difference in the Godhead. The Son is equal to the Father, as is the Holy Spirit. These three modes of divine being coexist eternally, and perfectly co-inhere with one another. Outside the Trinity they act as one, for there is one divine will and operation. In their actions *ad extra* the divine activity is such that the Father is the source, the Son the shape, and the Holy Spirit the one who completes and finalizes. In the Incarnation all three are active. Jesus achieves a perfect human partnership with the Father and the Holy Spirit, mirroring the Son's activity in common with the Father and the Spirit in the trinitarian life. Tanner's voice is important for she provides new vitality and a new direction to postliberal, Barthian thought in the twenty-first century.

Peter C. Hodgson invites us to examine the trinitarian mystery from the viewpoint of his postmodern constructive theology. The three modalities that constitute the divinity should no longer be looked upon as three male figures, for they are beyond gender. The first divine figure is seen as the Unoriginate One, upon whom all things depend. God goes forth and creates a universe that is God's own body, revealing the figure and shape of the Godhead. For Christians, it is Jesus who is the focal point of God's love for the world. It is not a superhuman divine nature, but the intensity of Jesus' humanity that radiates divinity. The Spirit, the third modality in God, brings about the return of all things into God. The Spirit indwells and energizes the forces of nature and humankind, drawing them into liberating communion with the Deity.

NOTES

1. Vladimir Lossky, *Orthodox Theology: An Introduction* (trans. Jan and Ihita Kesarcodi-Watson; Crestwood, N.Y.: St. Vladimir's Seminary Press, 1989).
2. Ibid., 39.
3. Vladimir Lossky, "The Procession of the Holy Spirit in Trinitarian Theology," in *Eastern Orthodox Theology* (ed. D. B. Clendenin; Grand Rapids: Baker, 1995), 170.
4. Ibid., 175.
5. Ibid., 180.
6. Vladimir Lossky, *The Mystical Theology of the Eastern Church* (1st French ed., 1944; English trans., 1957; repr., Crestwood, N.Y.: St. Vladimir's Seminary Press, 1998).
7. Ibid., 9.
8. Ibid., 25.
9. Ibid., 55.
10. Ibid., 70.
11. Ibid., 74.
12. Ibid., 82.
13. Ibid., 172–73.
14. Ibid., 161.
15. Ibid., 158.
16. Pseudo-Dionysius, "The Mystical Theology," *The Complete Works* (trans. Colm Luibheid; New York: Paulist Press, 1987), 135.
17. Leonardo Boff, *Trinity and Society* (trans. Paul Burns; Maryknoll, N.Y.: Orbis, 1988), 10.
18. Ibid., 32–33.
19. Ibid., 118.

20. Ibid., 128.

21. Ibid., 152.

22. For an expanded treatment of his views on this subject, see Leonardo Boff, *The Maternal Face of God: The Feminine and Its Religious Expression* (San Francisco: Harper & Row, 1987).

23. Ibid., 182.

24. Ibid., 189.

25. Ibid., 198.

26. Ibid., 208.

27. Ibid., 209.

28. Leonardo Boff, *Holy Trinity, Perfect Community* (trans. Phillip Berryman; Maryknoll, N.Y.: Orbis, 2000).

29. Elizabeth A. Johnson, *She Who Is* (New York: Crossroad, 1993). Several of her significant articles include "The Right Way to Speak about God? Pannenberg on Analogy," *Theological Studies* 43 (December 1982): 673–692; "Christology's Impact on the Doctrine of God," *The Heythrop Journal* 26 (April l985): 143–163; "Mary and the Female Face of God," *Theological Studies* 50 (September 1989): 500–526.

30. Johnson, *She Who Is,* 26.

31. Ibid., 91.

32. Ibid., 134.

33. Ibid., 152.

34. Ibid., 212.

35. Ibid., 218.

36. Ibid., 221.

37. Ibid., 231.

38. Elizabeth A. Johnson, "Trinity: To Let the Symbol Sing Again," *Theology Today* 54 (October 1997): 299–311.

39. Ibid., 311.

40. Joseph A. Bracken, *The Triune Symbol* (Lanham, Md.: University Press of America, 1985), 2. Compare David Tracy, *The Analogical Imagination* (New York: Crossroad, 1986.), 439–40.

41. Joseph A. Bracken, *Society and Spirit* (Cranbury, N.J.: Associated University Presses, 1991), 135.

42. Bracken, *The Triune Symbol,* 21.

43. Joseph A. Bracken, "Process Philosophy and Trinitarian Theology—I," *Process Studies* 8 (winter 1978): 220.

44. Ibid., 219.

45. Ibid., 225.

46. Ibid., 226.

47. Joseph A. Bracken, "Process Philosophy and Trinitarian Theology—II," *Process Studies* 11 (summer 1981): 86–89.

48. Bracken, *The Triune Symbol*, 43.

49. Bracken, *Society and Spirit*, 15.

50. Ibid., 126.

51. Ibid., 135.

52. Ibid., 136.

53. Joseph A. Bracken, "Panentheism from a Process Perspective," in *Trinity in Process: A Relational Theology of God* (ed. Joseph A. Bracken and Marjorie Hewitt Suchocki; New York: Continuum, 1997), 109.

54. Marjorie Hewitt Suchocki, *God, Christ, Church* (New York: Crossroad, 1989), 83.

55. Ibid., 91–92, no. 1.

56. Ibid., 228.

57. Ibid., 229.

58. Ibid.

59. Ibid., 231.

60. Ibid., 234.

61. Marjorie Hewitt Suchocki, "Spirit in and through the World," *Trinity in Process: A Relational Theology of God* (ed. Joseph A. Bracken and Marjorie Hewitt Suchocki; New York: Continuum, 1997), 189.

62. Marjorie Hewitt Suchocki, "The Contextualization of God," in *Philosophy and Theological Discourse* (ed. Stephen T. Davis; New York: St. Martin's Press, 1997), 140.

63. Ibid., 142.

64. William Placher, "Postliberal Theology," in *The Modern Theologians*, 2nd ed. (ed. David Ford; Cambridge, Mass.: Blackwell Publishers, 1997), 353.

65. Kathryn Tanner, "Human Freedom, Human Sin, and God the Creator," in *The God Who Acts: Philosophical and Theological Explorations* (ed. Thomas F. Tracy; University Park, Pa.: Pennsylvania State University Press, 1994), 111–36.

66. For a brief summary of these debates, see La Due, *The Chair of Saint Peter* (Maryknoll, N.Y.: Orbis, 1999), 208–9.

67. Kathryn Tanner, *Jesus, Humanity, and the Trinity: A Brief Systematic Theology* (Minneapolis: Fortress, 2001).

68. Ibid., 10.

69. Ibid., 38.

70. Ibid., 40.

71. Ibid.

72. Ibid., 51.

73. Ibid., 48.

74. Peter Hodgson, *Winds of the Spirit: A Constructive Christian Theology* (Louisville, Ky.: Westminster John Knox, 1994).

75. Ibid., 141.

76. Ibid., 148.

77. Ibid., 152.

78. Ibid., 159, emphasis added.

79. Ibid., 168.

80. Ibid., 252–53.

81. Ibid., 255.

82. Ibid., 170.

83. Ibid., 171.

84. Ibid., 729–81.

85. Ibid., 284.

86. Ibid., 291.

AFTERWORD

In the last two centuries with the gradual but startling development of the concepts of person and personality, Christian theologians of all persuasions have gone back to restudy how this expanded notion of person affects our traditional trinitarian doctrine. We have examined the Old and New Testament disclosures of the reality of the personhood of God and summarized the early church developments, especially the enactments of the great councils, which served and continue to serve as the ground of our trinitarian belief.

The current ferment reflected in this volume is a strong indication of the collective Christian mind searching out a more convincing and satisfying appreciation of the doctrine that lies within the very matrix of our faith. The more we begin to grasp the triune nature of God and how these persons relate to one another and affect our daily lives, the greater will be our allegiance to them. A deeper awareness of the reality of the Father, the Son, and the Holy Spirit will expand and enrich our love for the God who lives in community and who prompts us to live as coequals within the human family.

BIBLIOGRAPHY

Adolf von Harnack: Liberal Theology at Its Height. Edited by Martin Rumscheidt. San Francisco: Harper & Row, 1989.

Alberigo, G., et al. *Decrees of the Ecumenical Councils.* 2 vols. Edited by Norman P. Tanner. Washington, D.C.: Georgetown University Press, 1990.

Altaner, Berthold. *Patrology.* Translated by Hilda Graef. New York: Herder & Herder, 1960.

Anderson, Bernhard W. *Understanding the Old Testament.* 4th ed. Englewood Cliffs, N.J.: Prentice-Hall, 1986.

The Ante-Nicene Fathers. Vol. 1. Edited by A. Roberts and J. Donaldson. Repr., Grand Rapids: Eerdmans, 1989.

The Ante-Nicene Fathers. Vols. 3 and 7. Edited by A. Roberts and J. Donaldson. Repr., New York: Scribner's, 1926.

The Apostolic Fathers. 2d ed. Translated by J. B. Lightfoot and J. R. Harmer. Edited and revised by Michael W. Holmes. Grand Rapids: Baker, 1989.

Aquinas, Thomas. *Summa Theologiae.* Prima Pars. Madrid: Biblioteca de Autores Cristianos, 1978.

————. *Summa Theologiae.* 7 vols. Latin text and English translation. London: Blackfriars; New York: McGraw-Hill, 1964.

Augustine of Hippo. *Augustine: Later Works.* Translated and edited by John Burnaby. Philadelphia: Westminster, 1955.

————. *The Trinity.* Edited by John Rotelle. Translated by Edmund Hill. Brooklyn, N.Y.: New City Press, 1991.

Balthasar, Hans Urs von. *Mysterium Paschale.* Translated by Aidan Nichols. Grand Rapids: Eerdmans, 1993.

————. *A Theology of History.* Repr., San Francisco: Ignatius Press, 1994.

————. *The von Balthasar Reader.* Edited by Medard Kehl and Werner Löser. Translated by Robert J. Daly and Fred Lawrence. New York: Crossroad, 1982.

Barth, Karl. *The Doctrine of the Word of God.* Vol. 1, pt. 1 of *Church Dogmatics.* Translated by G. T. Thomson. New York: Scribner's, 1936.

——. *The Doctrine of the Word of God.* Vol. 1, pt. 2 of *Church Dogmatics.* Translated by G. T. Thomson and H. Knight. New York: Scribner's, 1956.

——. *The Doctrine of God.* Vol. 2, pt. 1 of *Church Dogmatics.* Translated by T. H. L. Parker, W. B. Johnston, H. Knight, and J. L. M. Haire. Edinburgh: T&T Clark, 1957.

——. *Church Dogmatics: A Selection.* Compiled by Helmut Gollwitzer. 1st American edition. Translated and edited by G. W. Bromiley. Louisville, Ky.: Westminster John Knox, 1994.

——. *Credo.* Foreword by Robert McAfee Brown. New York: Scribner's, 1962.

——. *Dogmatics in Outline.* Translated by G. T. Thomson. New York: Harper Torchbooks, 1959.

——. *Evangelical Theology: An Introduction.* Translated by Grover Foley. Grand Rapids: Eerdmans, 1963.

Bauckham, Richard. *The Theology of Jürgen Moltmann.* Edinburgh: T&T Clark, 1995.

Baum, Gregory. "Ratzinger explains how condemnation was right then, wrong now." *National Catholic Reporter* 38 (15 January, 2002): 18.

Baus, Karl. "Part Two: The Theological Disputes in East and West to the Middle of the Fifth Century." *History of the Church.* Vol. 2. Edited by Hubert Jedin and John Dolan. London: Burns & Oates, 1980.

Beck, Hans-Georg. "Part Four: The Early Byzantine Church." *History of the Church.* Vol. 2. Edited by Hubert Jedin and John Dolan. London: Burns & Oates, 1980.

Bobrinskoy, Boris. *The Mystery of the Trinity.* Translated by Anthony P. Gythiel. Crestwood, N.Y.: St. Vladimir's Seminary Press, 1999.

Boff, Leonardo. *Holy Trinity, Perfect Community.* Translated by Phillip Berryman. Maryknoll, N.Y.: Orbis, 2000.

——. *Trinity and Society.* Translated by Paul Burns. Maryknoll, N.Y.: Orbis, 1988.

Boyer, Charles. *Synopsis Praelectionum de SS. Trinitate.* Rome: Gregorian University, 1949.

Bowden, John. *Karl Barth. Theologian.* London: SCM Press, 1983.

Bracken, Joseph A. "The Divine Pleroma." *Chicago Studies* 26 (April 1987): 25–36.

———. "Panentheism from a Process Perspective." *Trinity in Process: A Relational Theology of God.* Edited by Joseph A. Bracken and Marjorie Hewitt Suchocki. New York: Continuum, 1997: 95–113.

———. "Process Philosophy and Trinitarian Theology—I." *Process Studies* 8 (winter 1978): 217–30.

———. "Process Philosophy and Trinitarian Theology—II." *Process Studies* 11 (summer 1981): 83–96.

———. *Society and Spirit.* Cranbury, N.J.: Associated University Presses, 1991.

———. *The Triune Symbol.* Lanham, Md.: University Press of America, 1985.

Bromiley, Geoffrey W. *Introduction to the Theology of Karl Barth.* Grand Rapids: Eerdmans, 1979.

Brown, Raymond E. *An Introduction to the New Testament.* New York: Doubleday, 1997.

———. *An Introduction to New Testament Christology.* Mahwah, N.J.: Paulist Press, 1994.

———. *Jesus God and Man.* New York: Macmillan, 1967.

Brueggemann, Walter. *Theology of the Old Testament.* Minneapolis: Fortress, 1997.

Burhenn, Herbert. "Pannenberg's Doctrine of God." *The Scottish Journal of Theology* 8 (1975): 535–549.

Calvin's Institutes: A New Compend. Edited by Hugh Kerr. Louisville, Ky.: Westminster John Knox, 1989.

Cassirer, Ernst. *The Philosophy of the Enlightenment.* Translated by Fritz Koelln and J. Pettegrove. Princeton, N.J.: Princeton University Press, 1968.

The Catholic Study Bible. Edited by Donald Senior. New York: Oxford University Press, 1990.

Chadwick, Owen. *The Secularization of the European Mind in the Nineteenth Century.* Cambridge: Cambridge University Press, 1975.

Childs, Brevard S. *Biblical Theology of the Old and New Testaments.* Minneapolis: Fortress, 1993.

The Christian Faith. 5th ed. Edited by J. Neuner and J. Dupuis. London: Harper Collins Religious, 1990.

Clements, Keith. *Friedrich Schleiermacher: Pioneer of Modern Theology.* San Francisco: Collins, 1987.

Coffey, David. *Deus Trinitas: The Doctrine of the Triune God.* New York: Oxford University Press, 1999.

Congar, Yves. *I Believe in the Holy Spirit.* 3 vols. Translated by David Smith. New York: Seabury Press, 1983.

———. *The Word and the Spirit.* Translated by David Smith. San Francisco: Harper & Row, 1986.

Creeds of the Churches. 3d ed. Edited by John Leith. Louisville, Ky.: John Knox, 1982.

Crouzel, Henri. *Origen.* Translated by A.S. Worrall. San Francisco: Harper & Row, 1989.

Davies, W. D. and Dale C. Allison. *The Gospel According to Saint Matthew.* Vol. 3. Edinburgh: T&T Clark, 1997.

de Margerie, Bertrand. *The Christian Trinity in History.* Translated by E. J. Fortman. Petersham, Mass.: St. Bede's Publications, 1982.

Denzinger, H., and A. Schönmetzer. *Enchiridion Symbolorum.* 32d ed. Freiburg: Herder, 1963.

Dictionary of Biblical Theology. Translated by P. Joseph Cahill. Edited by Xavier Leon-Dufour. New York: Desclee, 1967.

Dunn, James D. G. *The Christ and the Spirit.* Vol. 1. Grand Rapids: Eerdmans, 1998.

———. *Christology in the Making.* 2d ed. Grand Rapids: Eerdmans, 1989.

———. *Jesus and the Spirit.* Grand Rapids: Eerdmans, 1975.

———. *Unity and Diversity in the New Testament.* 2d ed. Philadelphia: Trinity Press International, 1990.

Eichrodt, Walther. *Theology of the Old Testament.* 2 vols. Translated by J. A. Baker. Philadelphia: Westminster, 1961, 1967.

Gay, Peter. *The Enlightenment: An Interpretation.* 2 vols. New York: Norton, 1977.

Gelin, Albert. *The Key Concepts of the Old Testament.* New York: Sheed & Ward, 1955.

Grant, Robert M. *Irenaeus of Lyons.* New York: Routledge, 1997.

Green, Clifford. *Karl Barth. Theologian of Freedom.* San Francisco: Harper & Row, 1989.

Grenz, Stanley J. *Reason for Hope. The Systematic Theology of Wolfhart Pannenberg.* New York: Oxford University Press, 1990.

Grillmeier, Aloys. *Christ in Christian Tradition.* Vol. 1. Translated by John Bowden. Atlanta: John Knox Press, 1975.

———. *Christ in Christian Tradition.* Vol. 2, pt. 1. Translated by P. Allen and J. Cawte. Atlanta: John Knox, 1987.

Grillmeier, Aloys, with Theresia Hainthaler. *Christ in Christian Tradition.* Translated by P. Allen and J. Cawte. Louisville, Ky.: Westminster John Knox, 1995.

Harnack, Adolf von. *The History of Dogma.* 7 vols. Translated by Neil Buchanan. New York: Dover Publications, 1961.

———. *Outlines of the History of Dogma.* Translated by E. K. Mitchell. New York: Starr King Press, 1957.

———. *What Is Christianity?* Translated by T. B. Saunders. Philadelphia: Fortress, 1986.

Heschel, Abraham J. *The Prophets.* 2 vols. San Francisco: Harper & Row, 1962.

Hill, William J. "The Doctrine of God after Vatican II." *The Thomist* 51 (July 1987): 395–419.

———. *The Three-Personed God.* Washington, D.C.: Catholic University Press, 1982.

Hodgson, Peter C. *Winds of the Spirit: A Constructive Christian Theology.* Louisville, Ky.: Westminster John Knox, 1994.

Jenson, Robert W. "The Holy Spirit." *Christian Dogmatics.* Vol. 2. Edited by Carl E. Braaten and Robert W. Jenson. Philadelphia: Fortress, 1984: 103–77.

———. *Systematic Theology.* Vol. 1. *The Triune God.* New York: Oxford University Press, 1997.

———. *The Triune Identity.* Philadelphia: Fortress, 1982.

———. "The Triune God." *Christian Dogmatics.* Vol. 2. Edited by Carl E. Braaten and Robert W. Jenson. Philadelphia: Fortress, 1984: 83–191.

Johnson, Elizabeth A. "Christology's Impact on the Doctrine of God." *The Heythrop Journal* 26 (April 1985): 143–63.

———. "Mary and the Female Face of God." *Theological Studies* 50 (September 1989): 500–526.

———. "The Right Way to Speak about God? Pannenberg on Analogy." *Theological Studies* 43 (December 1982): 673–92.

———. *She Who Is.* New York: Crossroad, 1993.

———. "Trinity: To Let the Symbol Sing Again." *Theology Today* 54 (October 1997): 299–311.

Jones, A. H. M. *The Later Roman Empire 284–602.* 2 vols. 1964; Repr., Baltimore: Johns Hopkins University Press, 1990.

Jüngel, Eberhard. *Karl Barth. A Theological Legacy.* Translated by Garrett E. Paul. Philadelphia: Westminster, 1986.

Kasper, Walter. *The God of Jesus Christ.* Translated by Matthew J. O'Connell. New York: Crossroad, 1988.

Kelly, J. N. D. *Early Christian Creeds.* 3d ed. New York: Longman, 1972.

———. *Early Christian Doctrines.* San Francisco: Harper & Row, 1978.

LaCugna, Catherine Mowry. "The Baptismal Formula, Feminist Objections, and Trinitarian Theology." *Journal of Ecumenical Studies* 26 (spring 1989): 235–50.

———. *God for Us: The Trinity and Christian Life.* San Francisco: HarperCollins, 1993.

La Due, William J. *The Chair of Saint Peter.* Maryknoll, N.Y.: Orbis, 1999.

Lennerz, H. *De Deo Uno.* 5th ed. Rome: Gregorian University, 1955.

Lonergan, Bernard. *The Way to Nicaea: Dialectical Development of Trinitarian Theology.* Translated by Conn O'Donovan. London: Darton, Longman & Todd, 1976.

Lossky, Vladimir. *The Mystical Theology of the Eastern Church.* 1st French edition, 1944. English translation, 1957. Repr., Crestwood, N.Y.: St. Vladimir's Seminary Press, 1998.

———. *Orthodox Theology: An Introduction.* Translated by Ian and Ihita Kesarcodi-Watson. Crestwood, N.Y.: St. Vladimir's Seminary Press, 1978.

———. "The Procession of the Holy Spirit in Trinitarian Theology." *Eastern Orthodox Theology.* Edited by D. B. Clendenin, 163–82. Grand Rapids: Baker, 1995.

Matthew. Vol. 26 of *The Anchor Bible.* Translated and edited by W. F. Albright and C. S. Mann. New York: Doubleday, 1971.

McCool, Gerald. *The Neo-Thomists.* Milwaukee, Wis.: Marquette University Press, 1994.

———. *Nineteenth-Century Scholasticism.* New York: Fordham University Press, 1989.

Moltmann, Jürgen. *Experiences of God.* Translated by Margaret Kohl. 1st American edition. Philadelphia: Fortress, 1980.

———. *History and the Triune God.* Translated by John Bowden. New York: Crossroad, 1992.

———. *How I Have Changed.* Translated by John Bowden. Harrisburg, Pa.: Trinity International Press, 1997.

———. *The Trinity and the Kingdom.* Translated by Margaret Kohl. San Francisco: Harper & Row, 1981.

Murphy, Roland E. *The Tree of Life: An Exploration of Biblical Wisdom Literature.* New York: Doubleday, 1990.

Murphy-O'Connor, Jerome. *Paul: A Critical Life.* New York: Oxford Press, 1996.

Murray, John Courtney. *The Problem of God.* New Haven: Yale University Press, 1964.

O'Collins, Gerald. *The Tripersonal God.* Mahwah, N.J.: Paulist Press, 1999.

O'Donnell, John J. *The Mystery of the Triune God.* Mahwah, N.J.: Paulist Press, 1989.

———. *Trinity and Temporality.* New York: Oxford University Press, 1983.

Ogden, Schubert. *The Reality of God.* New York: Harper & Row, 1966.

Pannenberg, Wolfhart. *The Apostles' Creed: In the Light of Today's Questions.* Translated by Margaret Kohl. Philadelphia: Westminster, 1972.

———. "God's Presence in History." *The Christian Century* 98 (11 March 1981): 260–263.

———. *Metaphysics and the Idea of God.* Translated by Philip Clayton. Grand Rapids: Eerdmans, 1990.

———. *Systematic Theology.* Vol. 1. Translated by Geoffrey W. Bromiley. Grand Rapids: Eerdmans, 1991.

———. *Theology and the Kingdom of God.* Philadelphia: Westminster, 1969.

Patrology. Vol. 4. Translated by Placid Solari. Edited by Angelo Di Berardino. Westminster, Md.: Christian Classics, 1991.

Pauck, Wilhelm. "Adolf von Harnack." *A Handbook of Christian Theologians.* Edited by Martin E. Marty and Dean G. Peerman. Nashville: Abingdon, 1984.

Placher, William. "Postliberal Theology." Pages 343–56 in *The Modern Theologians.* 2d ed. Edited by David Ford. Cambridge, Mass.: Blackwell Publishers, 1997.

Portalié, Eugène. *A Guide to the Thought of Saint Augustine.* Translated by Ralph J. Bastian. Westport, Conn.: Greenwood Press, 1960.

Pseudo-Dionysius. *The Complete Works.* Translated by Colm Luibheid. New York: Paulist Press, 1987.

Quasten, Johannes. *Patrology.* 3 vols. Westminster, Md.: Christian Classics, 1990.

Rahner, Karl. *Foundations of Christian Faith.* Translated by William V. Dych. New York: Crossroad, 1986.

———. "Remarks on the Dogmatic Treatise *De Trinitate.*" *Theological Investigations.* Vol. 4. Translated by Kevin Smyth. London: Darton, Longman & Todd, 1966.

———. "Theos in the New Testament." *Theological Investigations.* Vol. 1. Translated by Cornelius Ernst. London: Darton, Longman & Todd, 1961.

———. *The Trinity.* Translated by Joseph Donceel. Tunbridge Wells: Burns & Oates, 1970.

Schleiermacher, Friedrich. *The Christian Faith.* Translated from the 2d German ed. Edited by H. R. MacKintosh and J. S. Stewart. Edinburgh: T&T Clark, 1986.

———. *On Religion: Speeches to Its Cultured Despisers.* Edited by Richard Crouter. Cambridge: Cambridge University Press, repr. 2000.

Schweizer, Eduard. *The Good News According to Matthew.* Translated by David Green. Atlanta: John Knox, 1975.

Smith, Huston. "Has Process Theology Dismantled Classical Theism?" *Theology Digest* 35 (winter 1988): 303–18.

Solomon, Robert C. *Continental Philosophy Since 1750: The Rise and Fall of the Self.* New York: Oxford University Press, 1988.

Studer, Basil. *Trinity and Incarnation.* Translated by M. Westerhoff. Edited by Andrew Louth. Collegeville, Minn.: Liturgical Press, 1993.

Suchocki, Marjorie Hewitt. "The Contextualization of God." *Philosophy and Theological Discourse.* Edited by Stephen T. Davis. New York: St. Martin's Press, 1997: 130–47.

———. *God, Christ, Church.* New York: Crossroad, 1982, revised 1989.

———. "The Idea of God in Feminist Philosophy." *Hypatia* 9 (fall 1994): 57–67.

———. "John Cobb's Trinity: Implications for the University." *Theology and the University.* Edited by David Ray Griffin and Joseph C. Hough Jr. Albany, N.Y.: State University of New York Press, 1991: 148–65.

———. "Radical Empiricism: Radical Enough?" *American Journal of Theology and Philosophy* 13 (September 1992): 171–81.

———. "Spirit in and through the World." *Trinity in Process: A Relational Theology of God.* Edited by Joseph A. Bracken and Marjorie Hewitt Suchocki. New York: Continuum, 1997: 173–90.

Systematic Theology: Roman Catholic Perspectives. Vol. 1. Edited by Francis Schüssler Fiorenza and John P. Galvin. Minneapolis: Fortress, 1991.

The Theology of Wolfhart Pannenberg. Edited by Carl E. Braaten and Philip Clayton. Minneapolis: Augsburg, 1988.

Things New and Old: Essays on the Theology of Elizabeth A. Johnson. Edited by Phyllis Zagano and Terrence W. Tilley. New York: Crossroad, 1999.

Tanner, Kathryn. "Eschatology without a Future?" Pages 222–37 in *The End of the World and the Ends of God*. Edited by John Polkinghorne and Michael Walker. Harrisburg, Pa.: Trinity Press International, 2000.

———. "Human Freedom, Human Sin, and God the Creator." Pages 111–36 in *The God Who Acts: Philosophical and Theological Explorations*. Edited by Thomas F. Tracy. University Park, Pa.: Pennsylvania State University Press, 1994.

———. *Jesus, Humanity and the Trinity*. Minneapolis: Fortress, 2001.

Tracy, David. *The Analogical Imagination*. New York: Crossroad, 1986.

Trinity in Process: A Relational Theology of God. Edited by Joseph A. Bracken and Marjorie Hewitt Suchocki. New York: Continuum, 1997.

von Rad, Gerhard. *Old Testament Theology*. 2 vols. Translated by D. M. G. Stalker. San Francisco: Harper & Row, 1962, 1965.

———. *Wisdom in Israel*. New York: Abingdon Press, 1972.

Weinandy, Thomas. "The Immanent and the Economic Trinity." *The Thomist* 57 (October 1993): 655–66.

Welch, Claude. *Protestant Thought in the Nineteenth Century*. 2 vols. New Haven: Yale University Press, 1972, 1985.

INDEX